ACCOUNTABILITY
IN
ATHENIAN
GOVERNMENT

WISCONSIN STUDIES IN CLASSICS
General Editors

BARBARA HUGHES FOWLER *and* WARREN G. MOON

E. A. THOMPSON
Romans and Barbarians: The Decline of the Western Empire

JENNIFER TOLBERT ROBERTS
Accountability in Athenian Government

H. I. MARROU
A History of Education in Antiquity
Histoire de l'Education dans l'Antiquité, translated by George Lamb
(originally published in English by Sheed and Ward, 1956)

ERIKA SIMON
Festivals of Attica: An Archaeological Commentary

G. MICHAEL WOLOCH
Roman Cities: Les villes romaines by Pierre Grimal, translated
and edited by G. Michael Woloch, together with
A Descriptive Catalogue of Roman Cities
by G. Michael Woloch

WARREN G. MOON, *editor*
Ancient Greek Art and Iconography

Accountability

in

Athenian

Government

Jennifer Tolbert Roberts

The University of Wisconsin Press

Published 1982

The University of Wisconsin Press
114 North Murray Street
Madison, Wisconsin 53715

The University of Wisconsin Press, Ltd.
1 Gower Street
London WC1E 6HA, England

First printing

Printed in the United States of America

For LC CIP information see the colophon

ISBN 0-299-08680-1

Publication of this book was made possible in part by grants
from the Andrew W. Mellon Foundation,
the National Endowment for the Humanities,
and Wheaton College.

For My Parents

CONTENTS

Preface   ix

Chapter I
INTRODUCTION   3

Chapter II
ATHENIAN OFFICIALS AND THE LAW: THE MACHINERY
OF CONTROL AND THE KNOWN CASES OF ITS APPLICATION   14

Chapter III
POLITICS AND POLICY   30

Chapter IV
FACTIONAL STRIFE   55

Chapter V
THE IMPEACHMENT TRIALS OF THE CORINTHIAN WAR   84

Chapter VI
GUILT AND INADEQUACY   107

Chapter VII
THUCYDIDES, PLUTARCH, AND ATHENS' GENERALS   124

Chapter VIII
THE ACCOUNTABILITY OF PRIVATE CITIZENS   142

Chapter IX
CONCLUSION: ACCOUNTABILITY AND THE ATHENIAN
DEMOCRACY   161

Abbreviations   185

Notes   189

Bibliography   235

Index   253

Index of Greek Terms   269

PREFACE

THESE words, which appear first, were, of course, written last, in the heat of a Texas summer. The Introduction delineates the nature and intent of the book; the Preface I have reserved for expressing the many debts I have amassed during the years which have witnessed the manuscript's development and completion. This, in other words, is the place eager prosopographers must look to see how many names they recognize — and to learn whether their own will appear.

This study grew out of a brief Yale doctoral dissertation (New Haven, 1976) on the impeachment of στρατηγοί; the dissertation was in part the product of several years during which I had the privilege of studying with Donald Kagan both as an undergraduate and as a graduate student. To his inspired teaching I owe more than I can say. I have profited too from many conversations which I have had about the issues raised in this book with (in alphabetical order) Jack Balcer, Edmund Bloedow, Alan Boegehold, John Buckler, W. Robert Connor, Charles Fornara, Harold Hack, Charles Hamilton, Kenneth Harl, J. H. Hexter, Konrad Kinzl, Ronald Legon, Robert Lenardon, Brook Manville, Kurt Raaflaub, Paul Rahe, Robin Seager, Raphael Sealey, Barry Strauss, Robert Tannenbaum, and Lawrence Tritle. Important encouragement in dark hours was provided by many friends and colleagues. Their names, for safety's sake, shall appear in alphabetical order also: Jeremy Adams, Robert Bennett, Hanny Billigmeier, Robert Billigmeier, Darlene Boroviak, Jay Bregman, Frederick Brenk, S. J., Barbara Clinger, Kevin Crotty, Phyllis Culham, Katherine Dennison, Elizabeth Ezer, Michael Gagarin, Edward Gallagher, Judith Godfrey, Jay Goodman, Judith Hallett, C. John Herington, Michael Jacobster, Ann Koloski-Ostrow, John Kricher, Donald Lateiner, Anthony Molho, Steven Ostrow, Elizabeth Roberts, Stanley Roberts, Robert J. Rowland, Jr. (who not only encouraged the completion of the manuscript but also advocated the use of alphabetical order here lest anyone complain of the billing), Kenneth Sacks, Paul Sapir, R. J. Schork, Jr., Sheila Shaw, Paul Sprosty, J. P. Sullivan, John Teahan, Page V. Tolbert, Donna Tuttle, Kenneth Walters, David Weber, Jocelyn Wender, Leslie Wender, Melissa Wender, Bonnie Wheeler, and R. Hal Williams. Allen Ward deserves a sentence of his own for the support and encouragement he has offered me over these last years. I am enormously indebted to Ernst Badian for the many hours he spent with me going over the problems which the evidence presents. John and L'Ana Burton kindly took care to keep me in touch with the Wisconsin Press while I was traveling during the summer of 1980. Judith Hallett (who thus attains double billing) put me in touch with Jorgen Meier, and Jorgen Meier went to great lengths to keep me in close touch with Mogens Herman Hansen, who was kind enough to take time out from an unusually busy schedule to read portions of the manuscript, making suggestions and offering corrections. Frank J. Frost, Jr., offered both advice and encouragement, and Eva Stehle cheerfully relieved me of some other duties while I checked footnotes, an enterprise in which she also offered some welcome assistance. I owe a special debt to Erich S. Gruen, who has read the manuscript in its entirety and provided much constructive criticism.

I am extremely grateful to the National Endowment for the Humanities for a grant towards the publication of this book; I must also thank Wheaton College for two grants, one to do much of the research involved in Chapter V and another towards publication costs. Kathleen Francis, Alice Peterson, Kathleen Rogers, and Nancy Shepardson typed parts of the manuscript and much correspondence pertaining to it. I would also like to thank the editors of *Classical World* and

Hermes for permission to reproduce portions of articles previously published in those journals.

Pericles Georges and Elizabeth Steinberg of the Press have worked with me closely in the final stages of preparing the manuscript for publication. Disagreements, to be sure, were so frequent that I was moved at one point to propose that we simply publish our lively correspondence and add portions of the original typescript as a rather anticlimactic appendix; but I am deeply grateful to both Mr. Georges and Mrs. Steinberg for the care they took in helping me search for the best format in which to present this large body of material. I must also thank the anonymous readers of the Press for their meticulous readings of the text and Jeffrey Pinkham for his hard work compiling the index.

This book could never have been brought to completion without the support of several special people. My son Christopher Michael Roberts has been a constant source of comfort, collation, and proof-reading. Jon-Christian Billigmeier has served as both a haven in a storm and a verifier of obscure references. (I must report with great weariness that in the absence of any alternative I verified the large body of references myself, and any errors which remain are, of course, my responsibility.) Dorothea Wender, as is her custom, has provided invaluable advice and wisdom of many kinds over the years. Last, but far from least, my parents, John and Elinor Tolbert, know better than anyone the effort that has gone into this book and must know too that it could never have been either begun or completed without their unflagging support.

Southern Methodist University
July, 1981

ACCOUNTABILITY
IN
ATHENIAN
GOVERNMENT

I INTRODUCTION

THE writing of ancient history is a dangerous business. While I was working on this book, I showed a colleague who is not an ancient historian a draft of a chapter that included a sentence beginning, "It is difficult and dangerous to generalize on the basis of so few examples, but. . . ." My colleague frowned. "Difficult, perhaps," she said skeptically, "But — dangerous?" "Oh, yes," I said solemnly. "Come now," she scoffed. "*Dangerous*? Surely it can't be as dangerous as, say, wading in a pool of alligators." I am not so certain that she was right. I am sometimes visited by terrible images of future historians seeking to reconstruct the history of the United States in the twentieth century from the kinds of evidence on which we seek to found our knowledge of the ancient world. I see a long (and sometimes vicious) scholarly debate over whether Theodore Roosevelt and Franklin Roosevelt were the same man — even the same, perhaps, as Teddy Roosevelt. I see historians reading of Eisenhower's coronary and Nixon's presidency and enshrining in the textbooks the fact that Nixon became president when Eisenhower died in office. It goes without saying, I suppose, that historians will accept the identity of John and Robert Kennedy and hold that the story of the two assassinations constitutes precisely the sort of irritating doublet for which we today censure poor Diodorus. The picture of eager

scholars sorting through fragments of videotape in hope of
finding political allusions in *Ozzie and Harriet* is not a pleasing
one. These visions are profoundly unsettling.

And indeed our ability to understand even the present is far
from adequate. "The historian of antiquity need only contem-
plate the pitfalls in the quest for truth about events contemporary with himself to feel even more deeply the pangs of doubt
and dismay": such is the comment of Robert Lenardon in the
introduction to his biography of Themistocles. Lenardon goes
on to comment on the grave uncertainties that surround the
assassination of John F. Kennedy — an event, which, after
all, was captured on the film of more than one camera. We
should be wary, Lenardon concludes,

> of being seduced by a brilliant hypothesis into believing that it
> represents anything more than a probable likelihood. I need
> only refer again to a contemporary example. If the incredible
> revelations of Watergate had never been made public, a logical
> and credible history of the Nixon administration would inevi-
> tably be not only incomplete but inaccurate. The platitude that
> truth is stranger than fiction is most disturbing to any serious
> historian.[1]

Nixon resigned because, he said, his power base had eroded
hopelessly, and he could no longer govern effectively. In a
sense, Nixon was right; his power base had eroded so far that,
had he not resigned, he would surely have been removed from
his position by the Congress. Nixon had no real choice about
leaving his office; he was forced out. Although many people
had foreseen Nixon's departure from office, when he appeared
on national television on 8 August 1974 to announce his res-
ignation, shock waves were felt throughout the United States
and the rest of the world. For it had not been the custom in the
United States for an elected official to be prevented by the will
of the people (or its representatives) from filling out his term —
certainly not for the most powerful elected official in the land
forcibly to be ejected from office.

In classical Athens the situation was very different. Indeed, the hallmark of the Athenian state was its concern for the accountability of its officials; the theme of accountability in government was particularly prominent in the proud and still slightly self-conscious democracy of the fifth century. It appears, for example, in *Prometheus Bound*, in which the author — probably Aeschylus — portrays Zeus as the prototypical tyrant, who "rules alone, is harsh and undergoes no audit for his actions."[2] The danger of unaccountability is stressed even in the case of legitimate monarchs: thus in *The Persians* Aeschylus underlines Xerxes' lack of accountability to his subjects. The king's worried mother reassures herself by dwelling on the fact that Xerxes, "should he succeed, would be admired. But should he fail, he cannot be held accountable. In either case, if he returns safely, he shall be the sovereign ruler of this land."[3] Aeschylus here paints with heavy strokes the difference which the Greeks perceived between themselves and the Persians. The theme of accountability reemerges in the debate set in Persia by Herodotus in which the comparative merits of different types of government are discussed. Otanes, who argues that the management of public affairs should be entrusted to the nation as a whole, begins his discourse by reminding his audience of the dangers of unanswerable power. What virtue is there to be found in monarchy, he asks, "when the ruler can do whatever he wants and not be held to account for it?" This sort of power, he maintains, will turn any man into a hybristic tyrant. "Give absolute power to the best man on earth," he concludes, "and his former sanity will depart; for the advantage that he holds breeds hybris."[4]

The theme was continued in the literature of the fourth century. Aeschines declared with pride that "nothing in the state is free from audit."[5] Even those political theorists who had no affection for Athenian democracy were concerned about accountability. Thus Aristotle, for example, was critical of oligarchies which did not hold their highest officials to account.[6] Plato, who dreamed of a state over which a kingly being would preside — someone whose wisdom would lift him above law — nonetheless conceded that, as such men are hard to find, "we must choose what is second best, namely ordinance and law." For, he explains,

> it really is necessary for men to make themselves laws and to live accordingly. Otherwise they will not differ from the most savage of beasts. For no man's nature is able both to perceive what is of benefit to the community and, perceiving it, to be alike able and willing to practice what is best. . . . And even if a man fully grasps this, if he attains absolute political power and is responsible to nobody . . . his mortal nature will always urge him on to grasping and self-interested action.[7]

Not even Plato could escape. For the men of Athens, to have officials held accountable was the key to responsible government: unaccountability meant lawlessness.

Accordingly a rigorous system existed at Athens for the control of all officials. In order to prevent the concentration of power, every important Athenian officer served a one-year term, nonrenewable, except for στρατηγοί, the board of ten generals who led the military forces of the state and served, during the fifth century at least, as respected political advisers. Though the generalship was renewable, the Athenians had taken care radically to dilute the power of the office — the most prestigious position in the government — by dividing it among ten men. In addition, Athenians possessed a variety of legal resources to obtain redress or simply to remove the offending official from his post. Before any man could assume the office for which he had been chosen, he had to undergo δοκιμασία, a scrutiny of his legal qualifications. Ten times during the official year he might be deposed from his office by a vote of ἀποχειροτονία; he might also be indicted by the procedure known as εἰσαγγελία, roughly translated as impeachment and usually entailing the accusation of grave wrongdoing. At the end of his term he had to undergo εὔθυναι, a scrutiny reviewing his official conduct, in which any dissatisfied citizen could bring charges. Only when the εὔθυναι (and any trials arising from them) were completed could a man lay down his office with honor and continue in possession of his civic rights.

Thus the opportunities of the Athenians for monitoring the behavior of their government were manifold. Indeed, in his study of the jurisprudence of the city-state Vinogradoff has written starkly, in a sentence that stands alone as a paragraph, "The first thing that strikes one in the study of Greek criminal law is the extraordinary development of repressive actions against officials."[8] Clearly A. H. M. Jones was correct in writing that although the Athenian democracy was founded on the principle that "all citizens could be trusted to take their part in the government of the city," nonetheless "on one point the Athenians were distrustful of human nature, on its ability to resist the temptations of irresponsible power."[9] Athenian law, as we shall see in Chapter VIII, also provided a variety of sanctions which could be used against private citizens whose actions seemed to compromise the wellbeing of the state — against those, in effect, who seemed to be abusing the post of Athenian citizen.

The combination of multiple rotating offices with a comprehensive program of scrutiny was designed to ensure that political power would remain in the hands of the people; and so it did. Even the ancient critics of democracy, such as the pamphlet writer known as pseudo-Xenophon or the "Old Oligarch," were forced to acknowledge that, whatever one might think of the premise of the democratic system, the Athenians preserved it remarkably well. This success was due in large measure to the accountability of Athenian officials before the assembly and the courts. Yet there were two overlapping groups at Athens who remained unaccountable. These were the private citizens in their capacity as voters in the assembly and in the dicasteries. These men nobody could hold to account. A man could be impeached for giving bad advice, but not for taking it. The lack of accountability of the Athenian juror is underlined in Aristophanes' play *The Wasps*, in which the life of the juror is extolled and the Athenian judicial system parodied. In Thucydides' famous report of the debate on the fate of Mytilene, the speaker Diodotus contrasts the accountability of Athens' political leaders with the assembly's freedom from any such responsibility. Diodotus complains that the

Athenians are so suspicious of their advisers that a man must proceed very carefully in addressing them, for even when someone offers the best advice, the Athenians suspect some base and reprehensible motive. But even so, he concludes, "those of us who give advice must think it our duty to look a bit farther ahead than those of you who consider matters only briefly — particularly since we are accountable advisers, while you are unaccountable listeners." [10]

To the minds of many students of government, the unaccountability of the citizen body as a whole seriously impairs the claim of Athens to have lived by the rule of law. For Plato and Aristotle, the link between tyranny and democracy went far beyond the historical fortuity which had seen the tyrants of the city-states arise in the seventh and sixth centuries as champions of the masses. Aristotle complains that in a radical democracy — one that makes no distinctions between social classes in the allotment of privileges — affairs are conducted not according to law but by the whim of the people, for they, not the law, are sovereign:

> a democracy of this order, being in the nature of an autocrat and not being governed by law, begins to attempt an autocracy. It grows despotic; flatterers come to be held in honor; it becomes analogous to the tyrannical form of one-man rule. Both show a similar temper; both behave like despots to the better class of citizens; the decrees of the one are like the edicts of the other. [11]

Many more recent scholars agree that the Athenian democracy was basically a form of mob rule. [12] According to Cavaignac, the Athenians forced their officials to live under a reign of terror, their policy decisions "boxed in on all sides" and "paralyzed by the crushing weight of the responsibility of their offices." [13] Ancient and modern thinkers alike have concentrated their censure of the Athenians' use of the machinery of control on the treatment of Athens' highest officials, the στρατηγοί. From the first the στρατηγοί had been elected for their abilities, not chosen by lot like so many other officials. The board of ten generals, at least during the fifth century, was the closest the Athenians came to an executive power. Perhaps as many as a thousand men held this office during the period from the Persian Wars to the battle of Chaeronea. Of these we know specifically of some fifty who found themselves in serious difficulties through the Athenian system of accountability; there were probably many more. These fifty men form a catalogue of leading figures in Athenian military and political history. They include Miltiades, the victor of Marathon; his son Cimon, who did more than any other general to put Athens' first naval empire on a firm military footing; Pericles, Athens' greatest statesman; and his son Pericles the younger. The historian Thucydides; the notorious Alcibiades; Anytus, famous for his prosecution of Socrates; Thrasybulus of Steiria, who led the democracy to victory over the oligarchic regime in 403; and the outstanding military leaders of the fourth century — Chabrias, Timotheus, Iphicrates — all faced impeachment in connection with their generalships. The notion that the frequency of these impeachments constituted an abuse of the system of accountability appears already in the writings of Thucydides and has continued to our own day. Thucydides explains that the Athenians' condemnation of the generals Sophocles, Pythodorus, and Eurymedon for bribery after they withdrew from Sicily was the product of emotions which made a mockery of justice: "to such an extent," he writes, "because of their current good fortune, did the Athenians expect to be frustrated in nothing, and believed that regardless of the strength of their forces they could achieve equally what was easy and what was difficult" — hence the Athenians' assumption that only bribery could have caused the failure in Sicily.[14] In recounting the fate of the later expedition to Sicily under Nicias, Thucydides portrays that general as hesitant to withdraw from Syracuse without orders from home because of the fate he thought that he could expect if he moved without them. For the Athenians, Thucydides' Nicias complains, would not accept it, and those who would judge their case would not be eyewitnesses deciding on the basis of what they had themselves seen, but rather would be persuaded by any calumnies uttered by a clever speaker. Of the soldiers in Sicily who were

crying out to return home, Nicias continued, many "as soon
as they arrived would cry out just the opposite, that their generals had been bribed to withdraw." Consequently, he preferred to remain and die, if he must, in battle, rather than return home, "knowing as he did the nature of the Athenians,"
to be put to death on a shameful charge.[15] Craterus, according to Plutarch, claimed that after the exile of Themistocles,
the Athenians spawned a mass of sycophants who subjected
the most prominent men to the malice of the multitude, which
was exalted because of its prosperity and power, and to this
Craterus attributes the end of Aristides; according to Plutarch, the cruel fate of great men at Athens made Nicias hesitant to undertake any laborious or long commands.[16] Marcus
Antonius, grandfather of the triumvir, was to remark in Cicero's *De oratore* that Thucydides' exile was an example of the
fate that "usually befell all of Athens' best men."[17]

Modern scholars have come to similar conclusions. Butcher
writes that "the people took their estimate of the generals from
the lips of the orators" and "quick to suspect guilt where there
was failure, looked to the orators to give effect to their
displeasure."[18] Morton Smith writes that "even successful
generals were not safe from the passion or stupidity of the
people."[19] Beloch maintains that the frequency of impeachment trials at Athens shattered the confidence of the troops in
their commanders, and Glotz concludes that their anxiety
about popular disapproval deprived many Athenian generals
of "the spirit of initiative and the security indispensable for
the proper discharging of their functions."[20] Henderson in
his history of the Peloponnesian War takes the occasion of
Thucydides' exile after his generalship to comment on the
"over-responsibility of the Athenian executive," which he
describes as "the utterly fatal blemish in the Athenian democracy." Henderson concludes that "if ever a democracy
deserved ruin for its treatment of its own servants, Athens
was that democracy."[21]

It is the purpose of this book to call into question these
ancient and modern strictures on the Athenian democracy by
presenting what I consider to be a more balanced view of the

motivations of the Athenians in challenging the conduct of their officials and to study the way in which accountability trials functioned as a part of Athenian political life. Chapter II will set forth the nature of the laws which the Athenians devised to insure the accountability of their officials and list the known cases of their application. Chapters III–VI will examine the motives of the Athenians in bringing accusations against their officials. The view of the Athenians' treatment of their leaders presented by Thucydides and Plutarch forms the subject of Chapter VII. In Chapter VIII, I will show in what way the Athenians held accountable even those private citizens who, without holding an official position in the government, nonetheless participated in politics. The role of accountability trials in Athenian political life will be discussed in Chapter IX.

This is a speculative book. The material set forth in Chapter II is fairly straightforward; to a lesser degree, so is that in Chapter VIII. The same cannot be said of the chapters in between — the chapters that deal with motivation — or, consequently, of the conclusion. It is the writing of these chapters which compares so unfavorably with wading in a pool of alligators. Chapter III analyzes the role of policy questions in Athenian impeachment trials. Chapter IV treats the part played by factional disputes. Chapter V discusses in depth the role played by political considerations of all kinds in one particular group of accountability trials, those which broke out during the Corinthian War. Chapter VI will examine cases in which officials seem to have given the Athenians reason to suspect that they had carried out their duties badly.

The method employed will be the study in depth of individual case histories. I have tried to analyze every instance of an accountability trial between the Persian Wars and the death of Philip of Macedon about which I think the evidence makes it possible to say anything meaningful. I have ended this book shortly after the Battle of Chaeronea with what I consider to be sound reason; the period between the death of Philip and that of his son Alexander is a special time with special problems of its own. I have also avoided the celebrated impeachments of 415 which arose from the profanation of the Mysteries and the mutilation of the Hermae, since so very much ink has been spilt on these scandals over the years, and to it I have nothing to add.

To describe this book as a collection of "case histories," however, would suggest an objectivity which is specious. For the nature both of the evidence and of the questions I have sought to answer dictates that these chapters be speculative. Some readers are bound to feel that I have analyzed a number of cases in which the evidence does not admit of responsible speculation. But it is my hope that even those who disagree with some of my interpretations will find the material I have collected useful in shedding some light on the role which political and military accountability trials played in Athenian public life during the fifth and fourth centuries B.C.

This subject in its totality has not been studied closely before. The known cases of εἰσαγγελία, probably the commonest form of impeachment, have recently been collected in M. H. Hansen's important monograph *Eisangelia* (1975), but Hansen is concerned primarily with the legalistic aspects of εἰσαγγελία and deals very little with the motivation of the Athenians in bringing this kind of accusation. The subject of the εἰσαγγελία is also treated by H. Hager in the *Journal of Philology* 4 (1871): 74–112. In addition, the impeachment of στρατηγοί has received some attention in A. Hauvette-Besnault's *Les Stratèges athéniens* (1885) and P. Cloché's survey article, "Les procès de stratèges athéniens," *REA* 27 (1925): 97–118. Other works deal with yet more specific aspects of the issue. — J. Carcopino's book *L'ostracisme athénien* (1935), for example, and most recently Hansen's study of the γραφὴ παρανόμων, *The Sovereignty of the People's Court in Athens in the Fourth Century B.C. and The Public Action Against Unconstitutional Proposals* (1974). I am greatly indebted to all these studies. Among the primary sources, in addition to the histories of Thucydides and Xenophon, the orations ascribed to Demosthenes and Lysias are of the greatest value for the specific cases involving accountability trials which have come down to us; for questions of law, the most valuable sources are, again, the Demosthenic corpus, the Aristotelian *Athenaiôn Politeia*, the lexicon of Harpocration, and the *Onomasticon* of Pollux. Throughout, I have used the names "Demosthenes" and "Lysias" to signal the authors of works commonly attached to these names; I do not mean to argue by doing so that each and every oration so marked is to be ascribed to either of these authors.

I have already cautioned the reader about the dangers of speculative history; clearly I think the effort is, nonetheless, worthwhile. A few more words of caution are necessary. These regard the pitfalls of language. I have used the word "impeachment" throughout this book to refer to any form of accountability trial. I think this usage corresponds to what the word connotes in modern English; accordingly I see no reason to make a special point of calling only trials by εἰσαγγελία impeachment. I have also used the word "party" quite loosely, for lack of a better general term to describe a variety of political groupings. Reverdin pointed out many years ago the unfortunate tendency of modern scholars to imagine that parties in classical times functioned in the same way as parties in modern Europe and the United States.[22] Most recently Connor has called attention to this problem in his important study of Athenian political life in the late fifth century. "It is difficult," Connor writes, "to measure the full harm which the casual use of this word has brought about, both in contributing to misconceptions of classical antiquity among the general public and in misleading classicists and ancient historians themselves."[23] He is right, of course. But it is awkward to say "political group" with great frequency. The best solution, I think, is to stick with the word "party" while bearing in mind that an Athenian party might be a longstanding group with profound ideological convictions or it might be a fleeting group whose political fortunes were tied for the moment to those of some influential man. Context, I hope, will clarify meaning; the interpretation of vocabulary must always depend to some extent on context.

II ATHENIAN OFFICIALS AND THE LAW: THE MACHINERY OF CONTROL AND THE KNOWN CASES OF ITS APPLICATION

ONE method of registering discontent with an official was by a challenge at his δοκιμασία, the scrutiny which all Athenian officials, whether elected or chosen by lot, had to undergo before proceeding to office.[1] Comparatively few candidates were rejected at this scrutiny since at the time it was held they had not yet had opportunity to abuse their offices, and in the case of newly elected generals, such a swift drop in popularity was not likely. That στρατηγοί who had been reelected were subjected to repeated δοκιμασίαι is improbable.

Δοκιμασία consisted of a review before a regular Athenian jury, a dicastery; some officials, including the nine archons and the members of the incoming βουλή, underwent their δοκιμασίαι before the (outgoing) βουλή and subsequently before a regular court.[2] During the δοκιμασία the prospective official had to bring witnesses to affirm that he had met basic civic requirements — that he was a third generation Athenian citizen; that he treated his parents with proper respect; that he had a family tomb; that he had fulfilled his military obligations and paid his taxes; and that he followed the cult of Apollo Patröos and of Zeus Herkeios.[3] The ten στρατηγοί had also to demonstrate that they were fathers of legitimate children and that they owned property in Attica.[4] In addition, the floor was thrown open to complaints from any citizen. If a complainant appeared, the candidate would be permitted to reply to his accusations. The matter could then be put to a vote; a vote on a candidate was obligatory even when no complaints had been lodged. The decision to reject a candidate did not entail any further penalty beyond prohibition from assuming office.

Ten times a year, moreover (at least during the fourth century, if not the fifth), the scrutiny of the officials formed part of the agenda of the ἐκκλησία. At the chief assembly, the κυρία ἐκκλησία, of each prytany, the officials were to make reports, and their conduct was subject to review. A motion would be made to enter a vote of confidence in the magistrates if the assembly was satisfied with the way in which they were conducting their duties, and the floor would be thrown open to complaints. If any official did not receive a vote of confidence — we can only guess that a simple majority decided the issue — he was considered to have been deposed from office by a vote of ἀποχειροτονία.[5] Like an official prevented at his δοκιμασία from assuming office, an official removed by ἀποχειροτονία did not stand convicted of any crime. But unlike an official deposed at his δοκιμασία, he did stand accused, and his removal was only temporary, pending his trial before a regular dicastery by public prosecutors.[6] Over this trial the θεσμοθέται would generally preside, as in most trials for crimes against the state.[7] If acquitted, the official was permitted to resume his office.[8] No doubt a speaker who favored the deposition of an official would offer specific reasons for his views, but we do not know whether it was necessary to enter any formal charge at the ἀποχειροτονία. The resulting trial however, would deal with a specific charge.

At the same κυρία ἐκκλησία a complaint might be lodged by εἰσαγγελία against any citizen whose actions appeared to his accuser gravely to compromise the welfare of the state. Εἰσαγγελία, which is usually translated into English as "impeachment," was indicated in the case of all high crimes against the state and was probably mandatory, at least in the fourth century, for several offenses: attempts to overthrow the government, the betrayal of military forces, and the acceptance of bribes as an orator.[9] If a complaint by εἰσαγγελία was lodged at the κυρία ἐκκλησία, the βουλή would immediately formulate a προβούλευμα indicating whether the case should be tried by the assembly or by a dicastery and what the penalty would be in the event of conviction. This προβούλευμα would then be voted on by the ἐκκλησία.[10] Complaints by way of εἰσαγγελία might also be lodged with the βουλή. Εἰσαγγελίαι to the βουλή were generally restricted to magistrates, whereas εἰσαγγελίαι to the assembly could be preferred against private citizens, but there are some exceptions to this rule.[11] If an εἰσαγγελία was presented to the βουλή, then the βουλή might choose to try the case itself, if the penalty was not likely to exceed the maximum fine of five hundred drachmas that it could impose. But this was rarely the case with those accused of high crimes against the state, and more frequently the βουλή would propose to the ἐκκλησία a decree passing the case on to the assembly itself or, more frequently, to a dicastery: the large majority of εἰσαγγελίαι were tried not in the assembly but by dicasteries. A trial by εἰσαγγελία was an ἀγὼν τιμητός during the period under discussion, although this practice may have changed towards the end of the fourth century. In other words, if the jurors passed a verdict of guilty, they would normally vote again to choose between the penalty sought by the prosecutor and that proposed by the defendant. But on occasion the decree of the ἐκκλησία which passed the εἰσαγγελία on to a dicastery would also specify the penalty in the event of conviction.[12] If the decree was passed in the assembly, as was customary, the case would be tried, either in the assembly or in a dicastery over which the θεσμοθέται would preside. The prosecutors would usually include the original complainant.[13]

Shortly after the death of Philip, Hyperides was to complain that accusers had come to employ εἰσαγγελία for offenses increasingly trivial and removed from the wellbeing of the state.[14] It is not hard to understand why εἰσαγγελία was a popular procedure; for although it is not clear precisely how this was achieved, εἰσαγγελίαι were tried with the greatest dispatch, and plainly the principal purpose of the εἰσαγγελία, as Harpocration (s.v.) points out, was to bring those accused of grave crimes against the state to trial as swiftly and easily as possible. In addition to the speed with which complaints by way of εἰσαγγελία found their way to a verdict, moreover, trial by εἰσαγγελία afforded the plaintiff a number of other advantages in comparison with regular trials. Except perhaps during a brief period towards the end of the fourth century — probably after 330 — the prosecutor in a trial by εἰσαγγελία would not have to pay the fine of a thousand drachmas imposed in regular trials in the event that he failed to obtain a fifth of the votes.[15] Sureties seem to have been taken for the appearance of the defendant, and if the charge was one of treason or conspiracy to overthrow the government, the defendant was held in custody until his trial.[16] In addition, the opportunity of addressing the assembly which was offered to the plaintiff (except in minor cases handled exclusively by the βουλή) was advantageous to a skilled speaker. If the assembly handled the case itself, moreover, then the plaintiff had the opportunity to stir up all the emotions to which large crowds are subject — as appears to have taken place in the trial of the generals who had failed to rescue the shipwrecked Athenian sailors after the battle of Arginusae. And the assemblymen were not bound by the heliastic oath taken by all dicasts, in which they swore to follow the laws strictly and impartially in their verdicts.[17] Even when an εἰσαγγελία was held in a dicastery, an eloquent complainant might hope to influence the assembly in its proposal of a penalty.[18]

As if the threat of ἀποχειροτονία or εἰσαγγελία (or both) were not sufficient, at the end of his term every official was required to submit to εὔθυναι, a review of his conduct.[19] Within thirty days of laying down his office, each official had to present his records for audit or be liable to prosecution.[20] Even officials to whose hands no public funds had been entrusted had to have a statement to that effect approved.[21] During the first portion of the review, the outgoing official's records of the public funds he had received and expended were carefully checked against relevant documents in the state archives, in the case of the ten generals by the θεσμοθέται, and in the case of other officials by a board of λογισταί, Athens' public accountants.[22] If the λογισταί found cause for suspicion in the accounts of any officeholder they would pass the information on to the συνήγοροι, who would arrange the delinquent official's prosecution before a regular court.[23] An official convicted of embezzlement or taking of bribes would have to pay ten times the amount involved. If the charge was simply one of maladministration, the penalty was only twice the amount mismanaged. If no irregularities appeared, it would be proposed to the court that the official's accounts be cleared, but the ultimate verdict lay with the court itself, and any citizen had the right to appear before the court and challenge its recommendation.[24] Even if the financial portion of the audit passed uneventfully, however, a second period of scrutiny followed. For three days a board of ten state examiners chosen by lot, the εὔθυνοι, sat to hear charges of misconduct of a nonfinancial nature. These could be brought by any citizen who felt that the magistrate had been guilty of malfeasance. He might accuse the magistrate of having wronged him personally or of having acted detrimentally to the welfare of any other person or of the state. Offenses committed by an official against a private citizen might result in a regular δίκη; if a public wrong was suspected and a *prima facie* case seemed to exist, the charge was referred to the θεσμοθέται, who in turn brought it before a court.[25] Only when these examinations and any prosecutions arising from them had been completed was an outgoing official permitted to lay down his office with honor. Only when his εὔθυναι were complete, we read, was it legal for a man to set out on a journey, transfer his property to anyone else, be adopted into a different family, or even make a votive offering to a god.[26] In other words, the state had a lien on the property and civic freedom of all officials until their accounts were settled.

In addition to this elaborate machinery, Athenian law recognized a variety of public actions which might be used against delinquent officials. Vinogradoff has assembled a formidable list of the pitfalls of Athenian officials. Athenian procedure, he writes, took cognizance . . . of a great variety of specific delicts, for which members of the administration could be sued. Failure to conform to laws or rules in the exercise of the duties of a πρόεδρος or an ἐπιστάτης gave rise to a γραφὴ προεδρική or to a γραφὴ ἐπιστατική; failure to present accounts within the prescribed times to a γραφὴ ἀλογίου; misconduct of ambassadors to a γραφὴ παραπρεσβείας; failure to inscribe the name of a public debtor on the list of persons liable — to a γραφὴ ἀγραφίου; failure to render an account of the exploitation of mines — to a γραφὴ ἀναπογράφου μετάλλου; the acceptance of bribes — to a γραφὴ δώρων corresponding with a γραφὴ δεκασμοῦ in the case of corruption of judges. The γραφὴ ἀδικίου was directed against the misuse of judicial or administrative authority, while the γραφὴ κλοπῆς δημοσίων χρημάτων was used to prosecute officials guilty of embezzlement.[27]

Some of these γραφαί we know only from the lexicographers. Hansen has inferred from the silence of the sources, indeed, that since there are no attested cases of either the γραφὴ δώρων or the γραφὴ προδοσίας (indictments for taking bribes or for treason) consequently εἰσαγγελία must have been the regular and most common form which a trial for such an offense would take. Similarly, we know of no legal reason why a προβολή, a preliminary registering of complaint that might be laid before the assembly at the κυρία ἐκκλησία of the sixth prytany, could not be used against an official of the state, but it seems to have been reserved for accusations against private citizens, chiefly for sycophancy.[28]

It is difficult to know just how frequently the Athenians made use of this elaborate machinery devised to ensure the accountability of their officials. During the interval between the Persian Wars and the Battle of Chaeronea, we know of fewer than a hundred cases of what seem to be accountability trials — accusations at the δοκιμασία, depositions by way of ἀποχειροτονία, impeachments by εἰσαγγελία, accusations at εὔθυναι, and accusations of uncertain format against office holders and citizens performing a public charge, such as a trierarchy. Demosthenes maintained that every general was tried for his life two or three times in his career and that the danger of being sentenced to death by an Athenian court was greater for a στρατηγός than the risk of dying in battle.[29] It is hard to believe that Demosthenes' first contention is correct, for most trials of Athenian generals were probably by εἰσαγγελία; most εἰσαγγελίαι seem to have ended in conviction; and death or exile was most often the penalty. But it may be, as Hansen has argued, that Demosthenes was quite correct on the second point; Hansen has collected data which show indeed a higher proportion of Athenian generals being sentenced to death than meeting their deaths on the battlefield![30]

Lysias' writings alone reveal several examples of accusations brought at δοκιμασίαι. In 405 Theramenes, who had been elected to the στρατηγία, was rejected at his δοκιμασία.[31] We do not know the nature of the complaints against him, although they may have had something to do with the role he had played in the now unpopular condemnation of the victors of Arginusae the year before. A few years afterwards, one Philon, a would-be βουλευτής, was accused at his δοκιμασία of having plundered and otherwise abused senior citizens of the Attic countryside; the outcome of his δοκιμασία is unknown.[32] In 382 Leodamas (the elder) was rejected at his δοκιμασία for the archonship. One of his accusers was Thrasybulus of Collytus. His place was taken by Evander, who, with the help of Thrasybulus, successfully answered an accusation of oligarchic leanings at his δοκιμασία. The data provided by Lysias, though limited, are interesting. They demonstrate that the alleged purpose of the δοκιμασία — determining that the candidate indeed possessed all the legal qualifications for his new job — was often ignored and that the δοκιμασία was often used instead to try to bar a political, or perhaps personal, enemy from office. They suggest too that some of the Athenians of the early fourth century capitalized on the general nature of the δοκιμασία to get around the terms of the amnesty of 403, which forbade formal prosecution for specific actions prior to that year. Finally, the evidence of Lysias confirms that, as Harrison has argued, the δοκιμασία was in no way intended as a scrutiny of a man's general competence; it would appear that issues of stupidity, ignorance, or political inexperience did not arise in δοκιμασίαι.[33]

Deposition by ἀποχειροτονία was particularly common in the case of στρατηγοί. To be sure, the word appears in the sources in connection with the impeachment of only four generals: Alcibiades (406), Timotheus (373), Autocles (361), and Cephisodotus (359).[34] But the circumstance of deposition from office makes ἀποχειροτονία seem probable in numerous other cases: in those of Pericles (430), Laches (426/25), Alcibiades (415), Phrynichus and Scironides (412/11), the victors of Arginusae (406), Callisthenes and Ergophilus (362), and Timotheus, Iphicrates, and Menestheus (ca. 355).[35] In addition, ἀποχειροτονία was used in some other impeachment cases — in that, for example, against the θεσμοθέται of 344/43.[36]

Εἰσαγγελία was also a common method of impeachment. We know of several cases in which it was clearly used to proceed against στρατηγοί: against Miltiades (489), the victors of Arginusae (406), Timotheus (373), Timomachus (361/60), Leosthenes (361), Theotimus (360), and Cephisodotus (359).[37] It is likely too that most other impeachments brought against Athenian generals were εἰσαγγελίαι: thus Hansen writes that the εἰσαγγελία "was a weapon used primarily against generals although presumably not forged for that specific purpose" and concludes that "for the Athenian generals the eisangelia was the sword of Damocles."[38] Εἰσαγγελία was, however, also used commonly against other officials. Callippus, Timomachus' trierarch, was impeached along with his superior in 360, and Leosthenes' trierarchs were also impeached.[39] It is probable that these trials took the form of εἰσαγγελία. In 357/56, moreover, the former trierarch Theophemus was impeached by εἰσαγγελία for his failure to hand over his equipment to the trierarchs of that year.[40] Antimachus, Timotheus' treasurer, was impeached by εἰσαγγελία along with his superior in 373.[41] Gylon, the commander of a garrison at Nymphaeum, was impeached by εἰσαγγελία some time between 411 and 405.[42] At some point between 420 and 410, Philinus, Aristion, and the ὑπογραμματεύς to the θεσμοθέται were

impeached by εἰσαγγελία for embezzlement.⁴³ In 404 some
generals were impeached along with some taxiarchs and some
other citizens.⁴⁴ An ambassador might well be the object of an εἰσαγγελία.
In 411/10 an indictment was brought, probably by way of
εἰσαγγελία, against Onomacles, Antiphon, and Archeptolemus after they had been sent by the Four Hundred to treat
for peace with Sparta.⁴⁵ During or shortly after the Corinthian
War Callistratus brought an indictment probably by
εἰσαγγελία against Epicrates, Andocides, Eubulides, and Cratinus, who had gone to Sparta to discuss peace and had recommended its ratification.⁴⁶ In 367, on their return from Persia,
Leon accused his fellow envoy Timagoras of treason and corruption by way of εἰσαγγελία.⁴⁷

Most εἰσαγγελίαι were brought before the assembly. In
general, these involved high crimes such as treason and the
taking of bribes; the man impeached might or might not hold
public office. As we have seen, however, it was also possible
to initiate an εἰσαγγελία in the βουλή; these seem to have been
largely restricted to attacks on those who held office (including
a public charge such as a trierarchy). Thus the probable cases
of εἰσαγγελίαι of officials before the βουλή include the impeachment of Ampelinus, Aristion, Philinus, and the anonymous ὑπογραμματεύς to the board of θεσμοθέται on a charge
of embezzlement; the impeachment of the πορισταί, the
πωληταί, the πράκτορες and their secretaries; the impeachment of the ambassadors Antiphon, Archeptolemus, and
Onomacles in 411/10 for treason on embassy to Sparta; the
impeachment of Cleophon in 404; the impeachment of Nicomachus, the ἀναγραφεὺς τῶν νόμων, in 399; the impeachment
by Aristophon of Leosthenes' trierarchs in 361; the impeachment of the former trierarch Theophemus in 357/56 for interfer-
ing with the navy and defying public authorities by refusing to
hand over his trierarchic equipment; and the abortive impeachment of Timarchus for prostitution and embezzlement in 361/
60.⁴⁸ Most of these cases were referred by the βουλή to a
δικαστήριον: this is true of the cases of Ampelinus, Aristion,
Philinus, and the ὑπογραμμετεύς to the θεσμοθέται; of the

case of the ambassadors Antiphon, Archeptolemus, and Ono-macles; of the case of Nicomachus; of the case of Leosthenes' trierarchs; and of the case of the former trierarch Theophe-mus. We do not know the format of the trial of the πορισταί, the πωληταί, the πράκτορες and their secretaries; Cleophon was tried in an unusual and probably unconstitutional proce-dure before a court that included the members of the βουλή.

Why do we hear of no εἰσαγγελίαι brought before the βουλή after the impeachment of Theophemus in 357/56? Chance may explain it; εἰσαγγελίαι to the βουλή had never been common. But perhaps it is to be connected with some change in the law. Now it has commonly been alleged that during the fourth cen-tury the ἐκκλησία was more likely to refer εἰσαγγελίαι to a δικαστήριον than during the fifth.[49] This theory will not, I think, bear the weight of the evidence. The only officials whom we know to have been tried by εἰσαγγελία before the assem-bly during the fifth century are Miltiades and the victors of Arginusae; during the fourth century, on the other hand, Ergo-cles, Thrasybulus of Collytus, Timotheus (at his first impeach-ment in 373), Timotheus' ταμίας Antimachus, the ambassador Timagoras, and the generals Callisthenes and Ergophilus were all judged by the assembly.[50] But it has also been argued that at no time after 360 was an εἰσαγγελία tried in the assembly, and this argument is more persuasive. We know of no εἰσαγγελίαι after 360 which took place in the ἐκκλησία; we know of many which were referred to a δικαστήριον. Lipsius and Thalheim consequently have concluded that a legal reform around 350 institutionalized this change, and in this they have been sup-ported recently by Hansen, who dates the change to 355, after the Social War, and argues persuasively that it is to be con-nected with the Athenians' limitation of the number of extraor-dinary assemblies.[51]

The precise relationship between ἀποχειροτονία and εἰσαγγελία remains unclear. The sources are often vague on the subject of legal technicalities. Thus, for example, while we know that the generals who commanded at Arginusae were deposed by ἀποχειροτονία immediately afterwards, and while scholars agree that their subsequent trial, since it took place in

the ἐκκλησία, must have been an εἰσαγγελία, neither Diodorus' account nor that of Xenophon makes it possible to determine which came first, ἀποχειρονοτία or εἰσαγγελία; likewise,
in the case of Timotheus, Iphicrates, and Menestheus, Diodorus merely states that the Athenians indicted them and removed
them from the command; according to Dionysius of Halicarnassus, the procedure against them culminated in an
εἰσαγγελία, but we can only guess at whether, or when, a vote
of ἀποχειροτονία was passed against the generals.[52]

We know of several cases in which officials were charged at
their εὔθυναι. Plutarch tells how Themistocles attacked Aristides at his εὔθυναι.[53] The trial of Cimon in 463 arose, according to Aristotle, out of his εὔθυναι. He was accused of having
taken bribes not to invade Macedonia.[54] Similarly, according
to Demosthenes, Callias was accused at his εὔθυναι of taking
bribes on embassy.[55] According to the scholiast on Aristophanes' *Peace*, Phormio, towards the end of his career
(428?) was fined a hundred minae at his εὔθυναι, and shortly
afterwards, in the spring of 427, Paches, who had presided
over the surrender of Mytilene, allegedly killed himself in
court either at his εὔθυναι or at a trial arising from it; the
charges against these men are unknown.[56] Lysias records
attacks at εὔθυναι for Polystratus (410), Eratosthenes (403),
and Epicrates (some time during the Corinthian War).[57] The
trial around 360 of Melanopus, who according to Demosthenes
was convicted of embezzlement after sitting on the congress of
the Second Athenian Confederacy, probably arose from his
εὔθυναι.[58] Timarchus, according to Aeschines, was accused of
embezzlement after he had served as inspector of the mercenary troops in Eretria in 348; probably this took place at his
εὔθυναι.[59] So, it is likely, did the attack on Theodorus the following year.[60] Finally, the celebrated trial of Aeschines in 343
for treason in connection with the Peace of Philocrates arose
out of the accusation lodged against him at his εὔθυναι by his
fellow envoy Demosthenes.[61]

It is clear that comparatively little use was made of annual
εὔθυναι as a forum for the accusation of Athens' most important officers, the στρατηγοί. Rather, an attack on a general

was likely to lead to deposition in the course of his term. Probably no more than a third of the στρατηγοί who were impeached filled out their terms.[62]

The deposition of a στρατηγός might have been followed by immediate εὔθυναι (as appears to have been the case, for example, with Timotheus, Iphicrates, and Menestheus during the Social War), or it might not. We do not know whether this was customary. But we do know that it was not the custom of the Athenians to wait until the regular εὔθυναι in the summer to bring an accusation against a general whose conduct had displeased them. About the frequency with which εὔθυναι were used to bring accusations against other officials, we cannot really tell.

Unfortunately the data shed little light on the question of the regularity of the εὔθυναι of Athenian στρατηγοί. A number of scholars have suggested that a general who was continued in office would not be required to submit to εὔθυναι until the year came in which he was not reelected.[63] This argument is supported by Diodorus' account of Pericles' anxiety when his accounts were called in.[64] Kagan is probably right in suggesting that Pericles' distress was due to the fact that as a result of his prolonged tenure of the στρατηγία, his accounts had long gone unexamined.[65]

The evidence of Plutarch concerning Pericles' accounts is inconclusive. According to Plutarch, the Athenians had accepted Pericles' expenditure "for necessary expenses" when he gave his accounts for the στρατηγία of 446/45.[66] Hauvette has argued that this passage in Plutarch points clearly to the existence of regular annual εὔθυναι for continuing στρατηγοί, but in fact the evidence is not at all decisive, for it is perfectly possible that the account which Pericles rendered for the campaign of 446/45 was given in 443, when he was not returned to office.[67]

Somewhat more helpful is Aristotle's contention that the attack on Cimon took place at his εὔθυναι, for since Cimon did go on to serve in the following year, then if Aristotle is correct we have a clear instance of a general's submitting to εὔθυναι between two consecutive terms.[68] It may well be, however, that such εὔθυναι took place only when someone called for them, out of either political animosity or genuine suspicion of wrongdoing.

Because of the variety of resources available to Athenians who were dissatisfied with their officials and because of the sketchiness of many of our sources, we do not know in every case what form an impeachment took. We know of nearly fifty Athenian στρατηγοί who were impeached;[69] but as we have seen, the use of a specific method (ἀποχειροτονία, εἰσαγγελία, εὔθυναι, some sort of γραφή) is attested in only about half the cases known to us. Some time between 420 and 410 the πορισταί, the πωληταί, the πράκτορες and their secretaries were impeached; the machinery used is not clear. Around 399, Nicomachus was prosecuted for failure to render his accounts, but whether his trial took the form of a γραφὴ ἀλογίου is uncertain. During the Corinthian War, Aristophanes and Nicophemus, friends of Conon who were assisting in the campaign to aid Evagoras, were impeached by unknown means.[70] Probably in 377/76 the treasurers of Athena and of the other gods were impeached and charged with some crime in connection with the burning of the Opisthodomos, dated by Dinsmoor to this year, but we do not know the precise format of their trial.[71]

Not all cases of impeachment, of course, ended in conviction. Our evidence regarding δοκιμασίαι and εὔθυναι does not help determine how often accusations in those contexts led to conviction; naturally we tend to hear chiefly about cases in which things went badly for the incoming or outgoing official. Of the nearly fifty στρατηγοί whose impeachments in some manner or another are attested, about a quarter appear to have been acquitted. We know specifically of the acquittals of Cimon (463), Anytus (408), Thrasybulus of Collytus (380s), Timotheus (373), Chabrias (365), and Iphicrates and Menestheus (355).[72] It seems that Xenophon, Hestiodorus, and Phanomachus (430/29?) were also acquitted.[73] Many others are known to have been convicted — Miltiades (489), Pericles (430), apparently Phormio (at his εὔθυναι, ca. 428), Sophocles, Eurymedon, and Pythodorus (424), the historian Thucydides

(423), Alcibiades (415), Phrynichus (posthumously [sic] in 411/
10), Aristarchus (between 411 and 406), the victors of Arginusae (406), Pamphilus (389/88), Ergocles (388), Agyrrhius (387),
Dionysius (ca. 386), the anonymous generals of 378 who
had assisted the return of the Theban exiles, Callisthenes and
probably Ergophilus (362), Leosthenes (361), Timomachus
(361/60), Cephisodotus (359), Timotheus (ca. 355), and Lysicles (338/37).[74] In many cases the verdicts are not known to
us. Most impeached ambassadors were convicted; Aeschines
is the only one known to have escaped. Other categories of
officials probably had a mixed rate of conviction as well, but
we know chiefly of cases which were successfully prosecuted.
Philinus, Ampelinus, and Aristion, and the ὑπογραμματεύς to
the θεσμοθέται, accused of embezzlement some time between
420 and 410, were found guilty, as were the πορισταί, the
πωληταί, the πράκτορες and their secretaries, tried soon
afterwards on an unknown charge; also found guilty were
Timotheus' treasurer Antimachus and the recalcitrant ex-
trierarch Theophemus.[75] In many cases the verdict is unknown
to us.

The penalties handed down to those successfully impeached
were quite severe. We know the charges against about half of
them, and the overwhelming majority concern treason, embezzlement, the taking of bribes, or some combination of these.
Eleven generals were put to death: Aristarchus, six of the
victors of Arginusae, Ergocles, one of the generals of 378,
Callisthenes, and Lysicles. In addition, the ambassadors Antiphon, Archeptolemus, and Timagoras were executed; so were
the assorted generals, taxiarchs, and other citizens accused in
404, as well as Timotheus' treasurer Antimachus. Some were
sentenced to death *in absentia*: two of the victors of Arginusae, for example, and one of the generals of 378. Phrynichus
was impeached posthumously — a uniquely attested case. His
corpse was disinterred, his property confiscated, and his house
razed. Demosthenes includes Dionysius and Timomachus on a
list of generals who were sentenced either to death or to a
substantial fine.[76] We do not know, in general, whether those
who wound up in exile — the historian Thucydides, for

example — had been sentenced in their absence to exile or had chosen exile because a sentence of death hung over them at home; Hansen argues that *all* these men were sentenced to death *in absentia*.[77] Eight generals were fined in varying and often substantial amounts: Miltiades (fifty talents), Pericles (amount uncertain), Eurymedon (amount unknown), Pamphilus (five talents), Agyrrhius (amount unknown), Ergophilus (amount unknown), Cephisodotus (five talents), and Timotheus (one hundred talents, commuted after his death to ten talents for his son Conon). The ambassador Callias was also fined, according to Demosthenes, fifty talents.[78] Philinus, Ampelinus, Aristion, and the ὑπογραμματεύς to the θεσμοθέται were evidently fined, and Theophemus was fined twenty-five δραχμαί.

An impeachment trial did not necessarily spell the end of a man's public career if he was acquitted. The prestige of Cimon remained high enough immediately following his trial to enable him to prevail over Ephialtes in the hotly contested debate over whether to send aid to the Spartans facing a Helot revolt. Xenophon, and perhaps Phanomachus as well, went on to serve as στρατηγός in the year following his trial. Anytus and Thrasybulus both continued to take a prominent part in politics after their acquittals; so did Aeschines. Timotheus saw fit to leave Athens soon after his trial in 373, but his departure was probably due in part to the Thebans' attack on Plataea, which made his fundamentally pro-Theban, anti-Spartan stand a considerable embarrassment to him, especially in respect to the ordeal of his trial; he soon returned to Athens and to the στρατηγία. There is no evidence that the prestige of Chabrias suffered as a result of his trial. In 344/43 the board of θεσμοθέται was suspended by ἀποχειροτονία but, acquitted at the trial, was reinstated in office; this is the one documented case of a trial by ἀποχειροτονία actually being followed by reinstatement. The charge against them is unknown.

The consequences of conviction, on the other hand, were grave. Naturally exile or execution terminated a career. Unfortunately the data do not suffice to enable us fully to understand the position of those men who were convicted but only fined.

The case of Callias does not seem to admit of any certainty. Timotheus and Miltiades, the two στρατηγοί who appear to have been most stiffly fined, died soon afterwards. There is no indication of continued activity on the part of Pamphilus, Agyrrhius, or Cephisodotus. It is likely that the time he spent in debtor's prison weakened the political influence of Agyrrhius.

What kinds of motives could have led the Athenians to impeach so many prominent public servants?

It is this question which the following chapters attempt to answer. I have derived from the evidence a model — or, more properly, several models — which could explain what moved the Athenians in their use of the machinery they had designed to control their officials. The inferences I have drawn are not always inescapable, but I believe that these models are more faithful to the realities of Athenian political life than the only model that has hitherto been put forward — the model of a fickle and irrational mob hounding its chosen leaders out of envy, temper, and blindness to political and military necessity.

III POLITICS AND POLICY

IT is commonly realized that the trial of Aeschines in 343 for misconduct in connection with the peace of Philocrates was in part at least a contest of strength between the pro-Macedonian party on the one hand and the enemies of Philip on the other. What is not so commonly recognized is that Athenian impeachment trials frequently served as arenas of this nature. A wide variety of impeachments can, I think, be shown to have arisen at least in part out of genuine policy differences among the Athenians, and can be shown to have served as arenas in which these disputes might be aired. I speak not of personal political squabbles (although factional considerations often played their part as well, as we shall see below in Chapter IV) but rather of sincere and deep divisions over important issues of policy.

Probably the most striking example of the way in which issues of policy might figure in an impeachment trial is the deposition of Pericles in 430. In the summer of 430, when the Athenians were greatly afflicted by both the war and the plague, they deposed the στρατηγός Pericles and tried him, probably on a charge of κλοπή (embezzlement). He was convicted, fined, and perhaps temporarily disfranchised. Several months later, when the elections were held in March, he was elected once more to the στρατηγία.[1]

None of the ancient sources ascribes Pericles' removal from office to ἀποχειροτονία, although it seems likely that this was the route chosen by the Athenians. Plutarch and Diodorus record only that the Athenians deposed Pericles (Plutarch: ἀφελέσθαι τὴν στρατηγίαν; Diodorus: ἀποστήσαντες αὐτὸν τῆς στρατηγίας), and Thucydides merely implies Pericles' dismissal by mentioning his fine and subsequent reelection.[2] The charge of κλοπή is reported by Plato. Gomme, however, does not accept Plato's word and suggests a charge of deceiving the people or of mismanaging the expedition to the Argolid. He argues that Plato was confusing this episode with the earlier attack on Pericles in connection with Phidias' trial.[3] But Plato says that Pericles was actually convicted and narrowly escaped being sentenced to death; the latter may be an exaggeration, but certainly Plato's account points to the accusation of 430. Plutarch, Diodorus, and Thucydides all agree that Pericles was fined.[4]

Thucydides says that the Athenians returned Pericles to office ὕστερον δ'αὖθις οὐ πολλῷ.[5] Certainly these words can be interpreted to mean that a special election was held, as Miltner and Wilamowitz maintain, but there is no evidence for this; probably Pericles was returned to office at the regular March elections.[6]

The particular offense which formed the pretext for Pericles' trial is unknown. Neither Plutarch nor Thucydides has anything specific to say about it. Diodorus merely calls the charge "some trivial accusation," perhaps in order to throw into relief the staggering size of the fine he reports — eighty talents (Plutarch says that his own sources vary between fifteen and fifty talents, and Thucydides does not record the amount).[7] No doubt accounts were not in the best of order after twelve years: Diodorus' anecdotal account suggests that Pericles was not subjected to audit during this time, and it was an easy matter for the Athenians to find some irregularity to countenance a charge of κλοπή if they wished to bring one. Diodorus tells the tale, evidently popular in antiquity (it appears also in Plutarch), of how Alcibiades happened by one day and, on being told by Pericles (who was greatly alarmed) that he was busy considering how to render his accounts to the Athenians, suggested that his time would be better spent considering how to avoid doing so; clearly Alcibiades was for burning the tapes.[8] But there can be no question about the real purpose of the trial: whatever the pretext, the goal of Pericles' accusers was surely to remove him from office and hence from the leadership of the war.

The situation in 430 makes clear who some of these accusers must have been. According to Plutarch, the various sources named alternatively Cleon, Simmias, and Lacratidas as Pericles' accuser.[9] Idomeneus names Cleon; Theophrastus, Simmias; and Heracleides Ponticus, Lacratidas. The obscurity of Simmias and Lacratidas makes it unlikely that their roles in the attack on Pericles are fabrications; Cleon may have been a conjecture — one would certainly hate to have to reconstruct Greek history from the evidence of Idomeneus — but it is certainly a good one. Whatever the truth of these specifics, it is plain that the aggressive war party, led by Cleon among others, had a great deal to complain of in the summer of 430.[10] Pericles' strategy — a fundamentally defensive one despite the attempt against Epidaurus — did not appear to be winning the war. The frustration of the plague-ridden populace, shut up by Pericles' strategy within the city walls, suggested that the time might be at hand for another attack on him; and his return from the unsuccessful campaign against Epidaurus provided precisely the occasion for the accusation.[11]

The political views of Simmias and Lacratidas are not known. They may have shared the opinions of Cleon. But the war party did not by any means comprise the entire opposition to Pericles in 430. On the contrary, Pericles' last recorded speech before his deposition addresses itself exclusively to the advocates of peace, who had gone so far as to send an embassy to Sparta. According to Diodorus, the Athenians made further overtures to the Spartans after Pericles' deposition, but when "nobody paid any attention to them" they decided to return Pericles to the στρατηγιά.[12] To be sure, this allegation contradicts the explicit statement of Thucydides, who claims that after this speech the Athenians sent no further embassies to the Spartans. Surely Thucydides was in a position to know. But he may be referring to a temporary cessation in the sending of embassies.[13] Even if Diodorus is mistaken about the actual sending of an embassy to Sparta at this time, however, he has caught accurately the purpose of a large body of the men who voted against Pericles in 430.

Thucydides ascribes Pericles' reelection in 429 to the fickleness of the multitude, just as he had portrayed Pericles' deposition as the product of simple resentment. Plutarch takes an equally dim view of the self-control of the Athenian δῆμος when he writes that its anger subsided after Pericles' deposition because "once the multitude had stung Pericles, its anger was left in the sting," and portrays the Athenians as apologizing to him for their ingratitude.[14] The view that the Athenians' attitude to Pericles was determined primarily by emotion has been echoed by several modern historians. Curtius for example envisions Pericles magnanimously condescending to return to office, "free from anger or petty exultation, or ignoble desires of revenge; instead of which he displayed an anxiety generously to pardon the instability of the multitude."[15] Bury has written that the Athenians "had been cast into such despair by the plague that they made overtures for peace to Sparta" and that when these overtures were rejected, "they turned the fury of their disappointment upon Pericles, who had returned unsuccessful from Epidaurus." And the notion of both fury and despair is taken up by Laistner, who writes that "the desperation of the Athenians . . . caused them to sue for peace at Sparta, but without success," and that "their disappointment, added to the misery that they had endured and were enduring, then turned to fury against their leader, whom with pardonable lack of logic they regarded as the cause of all their troubles."[16] In fact, the Athenians had concrete motives for deposing Pericles, and their decision to return him to office was the result of developments during the fall and winter of 430/29.

Sparta proved to be no more willing to come to a settlement with Pericles out of office, and peace did not materialize. Consequently, with Pericles and his moderate, fundamentally defensive strategy discredited, policy fell into the hands of the more aggressive party led by Cleon and others. No doubt there were many in the peace party who at once decided that a return to Pericles' leadership was advisable, if there was to be war; and so the coalition between the two groups who had combined against Pericles began to dissolve. Doubtless other members of the peace party waited to see if the men now in power might move the war to a successful conclusion. Predictably, the aggressive war party was unable to score any dramatic successes before the March elections. The disintegration of the unnatural alliance between the two parties was complete; the majority of the peace party must have withdrawn its support from the coalition, and Pericles was returned to office. The events of 430/29 are easily enough explained without reference to the fickleness and ingratitude of the mob. Two groups had sought the removal of Pericles in order to implement their own policies, and together they had succeeded. When one group found that its policy would not work and the policy of the second group proved less acceptable than that of Pericles, then Pericles regained his office. The trial of Pericles in 430 served indeed not merely as an arena in which men might take sides about these issues but as the very instrument of policy itself.

Issues of policy may well have been involved too in the accusation made a few months later against Xenophon, Hestiodorus, and Phanomachus, the three generals who accepted the surrender of Potidaea. The instigator of the attack on them was evidently Cleon.[17] Thucydides alleges that the Athenians thought that the generals should not have accepted the terms of the surrender offered by the Potidaeans without consulting them, and this may, as Kagan suggests, have been the formal charge against them.[18] But it is not necessarily the case that the formal charge and the genuine grievance were identical, and it may be, as Gilbert and Hauvette both maintain, that the charge was one of δωροδοκία or προδοσία.[19] Thucydides says ambiguously that the Athenians ἐπῃτιάσαντο the generals. Pritchett writes that ἐπαιτιάομαι "probably means not a formal charge, but blame," whereas Kagan claims that "the language leaves no doubt that a formal accusation was made."[20] I would compare 6.28, where Thucydides writes that the metics and servants questioned about the mutilation of the hermae ἐπῃτιῶντο Alcibiades, among others. Thucydides seems to mean that they laid information against him to an official body, but he is not referring to the formal accusation made in a trial.[21]

Aristophanes makes reference to an alleged ten talents received by Cleon in connection with Potidaea.[22] Since Xenophon and Phanomachus were elected to the στρατηγία for 429/28 the inference is natural that at some point the attack on the generals was withdrawn, giving rise to the rumor that Cleon had been bribed to this end.[23] Cleon may, as Gilbert claims, have been the prosecutor in a formal trial, but the accusation could have been abandoned at an earlier point.[24]

The dissatisfaction of Cleon and his associates was not entirely unwarranted. According to Thucydides the Athenians blamed the generals for accepting the Potidaeans' terms because they felt that they could have had the city on any terms they wished. Thucydides alleged that the three generals accepted the Potidaeans' terms — i.e., that the people should depart under a truce, with a fixed amount of clothing and funds for the journey — because of the army's distress in the Thracian winter and the enormous expense of the long siege.[25] But whereas Thucydides has presented the decision of the generals in such a way as to make it appear patriotic and unexceptionable, the facts he presents suggest that the Athenians were justified in questioning their decision. Thucydides concedes that the Potidaeans' grain had given out and that they had been reduced to cannibalism. In view of these circumstances, the generals might well have taken the city on much stiffer terms without a substantial delay, perhaps with no delay at all. Thus the decision of the generals may have been motivated not by concern for the men and money of the Athenians, but by the desire to take a lenient stand with the Potidaeans — a stand which they may well have known would not be approved by the party in control at home. The position of Cleon concerning the fate of the Potidaeans would probably have been the same as his stand on the fate of the Mytileneans soon afterwards, and the recent murder of the Peloponnesian ambassadors, if it was known at Potidaea, may have given the generals an inkling of just what this would be: they may have shared the views later expressed at the Mytilenean debate by Diodotus and preferred to present the Athenians with a *fait accompli*, swallowing their own anger at the Potidaeans and judging that the length of future sieges might be cut short if leniency was employed at the capitulation of Potidaea.

Xenophon, Hestiodorus, and Phanomachus then probably did exceed their authority in negotiating with the Potidaeans, for normally στρατηγοί were empowered to make truces but not to conclude a peace in the field.[26] If this was indeed the charge against them, it may have been based on solid legal grounds. But the real source of the accusation, I believe, was the fundamental disagreement over the policy to be followed in dealing with capitulated rebels which was soon to be debated so hotly in the case of Mytilene.

In the winter of 412/11, the Athenians deposed (παρέλυσαν τῆς ἀρχῆς) the generals Phrynichus and Scironides; they were removed from office, as Thucydides states plainly, because of a major disagreement over policy: Phrynichus, and presumably Scironides as well, stood in the way of Alcibiades' recall.[27]

The generals were deposed at the suggestion of Peisander, on the grounds that they had betrayed Iasus to the Peloponnesians. It does not appear that either general was tried on any criminal charge or received any punishment beyond the loss of his office. The story Thucydides tells suggests that there may have been some substance to the charge, although he calls it false, labeling it διαβολή.[28] That winter Phrynichus, Scironides, and Onomacles were in command off Samos and Miletus; when the Athenians had been victorious at Miletus and were persuaded by Phrynichus to withdraw to Samos, Tissaphernes persuaded the Peloponnesians to attack Iasus, which the Athenians, by taking Phrynichus' advice, had left unguarded. The account of Thucydides is designed to make

Phrynichus' attempts to persuade the Athenians appear not merely patriotic but indeed heroic.[29] On hearing from Alcibiades of the approach of a large enemy fleet towards Miletus, the Athenians, Thucydides writes, were all in favor of going to the aid of Miletus at daybreak; but Phrynichus, although he had ascertained that the report of Alcibiades was true, "refused to do this himself and announced that he would not let anyone else do it either if he could help it."[30] After a speech in which he maintained that it was better to withdraw than to fight a risky battle, Phrynichus persuaded the Athenians of the prudence of his thinking, Thucydides claims, and "in general in whatever circumstances he found himself, on both this and later occasions," he was considered to be a man of wisdom.[31] The Peloponnesians promptly took Iasus.

Phrynichus' course may have been a wise one, but it was certainly not the only one open to the Athenians. His colleagues originally disagreed with him, Thucydides says, and it is not clear to what extent they were won over.[32] Surely the Argive allies who promptly sailed home, indignant at Phrynichus' decision, were not impressed by his arguments.[33] All this is not to say that Phrynichus' arguments for withdrawing to Samos were necessarily treasonous in intent; but it must be stressed that Thucydides' assessment of his policy colors his account of the episode.

In fact Phrynichus was probably loyal to the democracy at this time in his career. To be sure, during the summer of 411 Phrynichus was to be among the leaders of the oligarchic plot to betray Athens to the Peloponnesians.[34] During the previous winter, however, he appears to have behaved as a democrat, which argues against any discernible philolaconian inclinations. Lysias accuses him of sycophancy and claims that he was associated with the demagogues at this time.[35] As McCoy has pointed out, this evidence is difficult to refute. For why would Lysias label Phrynichus a democrat "when he could just as well have called him an oligarch — a term even more hateful to him?" Moreover, McCoy goes on, "Phrynichus surely would not have been elected general in 412/11 and entrusted with the important mission to Miletus if he had been at odds with the democracy.''[36] Phrynichus' open identification with the oligarchic cause seems to have followed his removal from the στρατηγία, not preceded it.

It is easy to understand, however, that the loyalty of Phrynichus may have been suspect at the time of his deposition, for his conviction that the recall of Alcibiades would mean the ruin of Athens had led him to send letters to the Spartan admiral Astyochus in which he revealed the embryonic negotiations then in progress between Alcibiades, Tissaphernes, and the Athenians. Astyochus had promptly presented the letter to Tissaphernes and Alcibiades, who made public Phrynichus' alleged treachery. Phrynichus temporarily restored his credit with the Athenians by luring Astyochus and Alcibiades into accusing him on a charge of which he had prepared a refutation, but the episode no doubt left a bad taste in the mouths of many Athenians.[37]

Combining Phrynichus' treacherous correspondence with Astyochus with the intensity of the opposition among the fleet to his proposed withdrawal from Miletus, it is not hard to see how he might reasonably have been held responsible for the loss of Iasus, despite Thucydides' efforts to make the charge appear ridiculous. In fact, however, the loss of Iasus was simply a pretext for the attack on Phrynichus. Thucydides states the purpose of Phrynichus' deposition plainly: Phrynichus was removed from office because of his opposition to the project of recalling Alcibiades.[38] Here Thucydides' view does not appear to be colored by his sympathy for Phrynichus, for Scironides was deposed at the same time and, presumably, on the same charge, despite his original — and perhaps persistent — opposition to Phrynichus' proposal to withdraw from Miletus.[39]

In the winter of 412/11 Peisander was sent to Athens to carry a message from Alcibiades, who suggested that if the Athenians were to recall him and accept an oligarchy he might involve Tissaphernes in the war on the Athenian side. At first many Athenians opposed the plan and were indignant at the idea of abandoning the democracy and negotiating with Alcibiades. But when Peisander invited other proposals for win-

ning the war and none was forthcoming, the Athenians resigned themselves to their circumstances and voted that Peisander and ten others should sail and negotiate with Alcibiades and Tissaphernes in whatever way seemed best to them.
"At the same time (ἅμα)," Thucydides writes,

> they deposed Phrynichus and his colleague Scironides when
> Peisander brought a false accusation (διαβολή) against Phry-
> nichus, and they sent out Diomedon and Leon instead to take
> charge of the fleet. For Peisander alleged that Phrynichus had
> betrayed Iasus and Amorgos, and he slandered him because he
> did not believe him to be friendly to the negotiations with
> Alcibiades.[40]

We can only assume that Scironides was associated with Phrynichus in his opposition to Alcibiades while Onomacles, the
third commander at Miletus, was not. It is not clear whether
the deposition of Phrynichus and Scironides preceded or followed the vote of the assembly dispatching Peisander and the
others to negotiate with Alcibiades and Tissaphernes, but in
either case Peisander and his partisans had good reason to feel
that Phrynichus' continuation in office would be an obstacle to
Alcibiades' return. He had argued vigorously that Alcibiades'
recall would accomplish nothing for the Athenians. Alcibiades,
he maintained, sought his reinstatement with a view only to his
own welfare; in fact, all στάσις was to the detriment of the
Athenian war effort. Nor, he added, was there any good
reason to think that the Persians would switch their allegiance
to the Athenians, or that the proposal to grant oligarchic gov-
ernments to subject states would stem the tide of rebellion.[41]
When Alcibiades had learned of Phrynichus' correspondence
with Astyochus he had called for Phrynichus' death.[42] Probably the downfall of Phrynichus formed part of Peisander's
mission at Athens. Even if it was not engineered by the express command of Alcibiades, it may be that Peisander hoped
by deposing Phrynichus to consolidate his own position with
Alcibiades, which may have been shaky in view of his role in
Alcibiades' exile; for Peisander had been among Alcibiades'
enemies in the scandal of 415.[43]

No doubt the assemblymen who voted for the deposition of Phrynichus and Scironides believed that Phrynichus might otherwise hinder the return of Alcibiades, which they had come to decide was Athens' only possible recourse. But, as I have suggested, the record of Phrynichus was not spotless; some men may have considered him genuinely guilty if not of treason then at least of incompetence.

The deposition of Phrynichus and Scironides is one of very few cases — perhaps, indeed, the only case — in which removal from office at Athens, presumably by ἀποχειροτονία, was not followed by a trial. The explanation is not far to seek. It is not without meaning that Phrynichus' enemies had accused him in the matter of Iasus rather than using the potentially far more compromising correspondence with Astyochus against him: Phrynichus' dealings with the Spartans would inevitably call before the Athenians' minds those of Alcibiades. It was because of Alcibiades' long sojourn in the Spartan camp, after all, that Phrynichus' correspondence with Astyochus had been uncovered in the first place. The trial of Phrynichus and Scironides would have provided a forum for the discussion of Alcibiades' aid to the enemy that would have been most unwelcome to him and to his supporters. It was probably for this reason that Phrynichus and Scironides were never brought to trial after their deposition. Clearly their removal from office was a political, not a punitive measure.

One of the most outstanding instances of the role of policy questions in impeachment trials is the attack on Timotheus in 373. At first sight it might appear that Timotheus, the victim of irrational expectations, was tried because he failed to raise troops and money for the relief of Corcyra. In fact, the attack on him almost certainly concerned other issues entirely — fundamental issues of Athens' relations with Sparta. In the summer of 373 Timotheus was deposed by ἀποχειροτονία following his delay in relieving Corcyra. In November he was tried before the assembly by εἰσαγγελία on an unknown but serious charge. Timotheus was acquitted, but Antimachus, his treasurer, who was tried at the same time, was convicted of κλοπή and executed.[44]

In April of 373 the Athenians had appointed Timotheus to lead an expedition to Corcyra, which was under siege by the Spartans. Timotheus, however, lacked both funds and personnel to man his ships at Athens. He was accordingly forced to undertake a preliminary cruise in search of men and money. He proceeded first to Thessaly, where he evidently persuaded Jason of Pherae to ally with the Athenians and to assist a division of six hundred Athenian peltasts under Stesicles in their march across Thessaly. The peltasts were further assisted by Alcetas of Molossia, a vassal of Jason, who conveyed them by night to Corcyra. Timotheus himself went on to Macedonia and Thrace. In the course of his cruise he won a number of valuable allies for the Athenians and also acquired some sailors and funds with which to pay them.[45]

Timotheus had arranged to join those of the Athenians' allies who formed part of the Corcyrean expedition, including the Boeotians, at Calauria. But by the early summer these allied troops, still unpaid, became restless. When the Athenians heard of the resentment and began to hear too that the Corcyreans could not hold out much longer, they deposed Timotheus at the instigation of the professional general Iphicrates and the orator Callistratus, who replaced him in the Corcyrean command together with Chabrias. Timotheus finally put in at Calauria. There he apologized for his long delay, paid the Boeotian trierarchs with money he had borrowed on his own credit, and distributed to the allied troops the partial salary which he had managed to collect. There he also learned of his deposition, and he duly returned to Athens.[46]

Meanwhile Iphicrates and his colleagues swiftly gathered a fleet of seventy triremes. It would be a mistake, however, to imagine that this alacrity reflects on Timotheus' previous efforts, for the Athenians were now more cooperative. They permitted Iphicrates to impress sailors at Piraeus, to employ all the ships reserved for the coast guard of Attica and even to press into service the state triremes the *Paralos* and the

Salaminia.[47] It may be too, as Beloch suggests, that an εἰσφορά was rushed through the assembly to expedite the relief of Corcyra.[48] When Iphicrates was off the coast of Laconia, he learned that the Corcyreans themselves had defeated the Spartans. He proceeded to Corcyra nonetheless. There he managed to capture ten Syracusan triremes with all their crews, which he ransomed or sold bringing a total of no less than sixty talents into the Athenian war chest.[49] It appears that Iphicrates did not return to Athens, but Callistratus did, and there he served as the principal accuser in the trial of Timotheus, which now took place in November.[50]

None of the speeches delivered at Timotheus' trial is extant. But an attack on Timotheus' conduct of his finances as στρατηγός is included in a speech written perhaps by Demosthenes for the use of Apollodorus, son of the banker Pasion, in his suit to recover a debt owed by Timotheus to his late father.[51] The speech makes clear that Timotheus' ledgers must have been in a chaotic condition. He does not, however, appear to have been guilty of embezzlement of any kind; it is more likely, I think, that the confusion of his accounts was due precisely to the personal nature of his effort to meet the expenses of the Corcyrean campaign.[52] Could it be that Antimachus capitalized on the complexity of Timotheus' finances to drain off funds for his own use in the expectation that his embezzlement would go undetected in the confusion?[53]

It does not appear that Timotheus in fact delayed unnecessarily in relieving Corcyra. The Athenians had put him in an extremely difficult position, for while they were concerned to prevent a Spartan victory at Corcyra, they were not willing to assume the financial consequences of intervention, and the vote to acquit Timotheus may have reflected in part the Athenians' awareness of his predicament. Doubtless other events contributed to his acquittal as well. When the trial took place, the Corcyreans had already expelled the Spartans; their plight therefore was a dead issue. Indeed, the anger of the Athenians had probably subsided already in the summer when Timotheus had appeared at Calauria, having collected a good deal in the way not only of men and money but of new allies for the

Athenians as well. No doubt the verdict was also affected by the presence at Athens of Jason of Pherae and Alcetas of Molossia, who came to testify in Timotheus' behalf.[54]

The Athenians' behavior regarding Timotheus' expedition to Corcyra shows a strong ambivalence. This ambivalence must be viewed in the context of the events of 374, events in which Timotheus played a vital role. By the winter of 375/74, the Athenians had begun to feel that their new maritime alliance was not all they had hoped it would be. In particular, they were distressed that the Thebans, their most powerful ally, had not taken a more enthusiastic part in the activities of the confederacy. Consequently they decided to conclude a peace with the Spartans. Diodorus names Callistratus as one of the negotiators of the peace. The terms were basically the same as those of the peace of Antalcidas, for the agreement rested fundamentally on the principle of autonomy.[55] Word was then sent to Timotheus, who had wintered with his fleet in the west, to return, as peace had been concluded. Timotheus returned, although not perhaps with the promptness that might have been preferred by the proponents of peace. He had with him some Zacynthian exiles, the victims of civil strife in their native city, and at their request Timotheus landed them on Zacynthus before sailing home. When the Zacynthian government complained to the Spartans of Timotheus' interference, the Spartans determined to take action and set about preparing a fleet.[56]

According to Plutarch, Timotheus was a member of the pro-Theban party at Athens, and his behavior at Zacynthus suggests that Plutarch was right, for such an action was likely to provoke the Spartans.[57] Rice goes so far as to call Timotheus the leader of this faction.[58] Timotheus' action in restoring the exiles has been compared by both Beloch and Rice to the unauthorized raid of the Spartan Sphodrias on Piraeus in 378. "Both," Rice writes, "were unauthorized adventures which endangered peaceful relations between Athens and Sparta. In each case the result was a victory for the war party and a renewal of the war."[59] Certainly the unofficial nature of Timotheus' action recalls not only the raid of Sphodrias on the

Piraeus but the seizure of the Cadmeia by Phoebidas in 382 as well; but a better analogy, I think, would be Pericles' decree against Megara in 433/32.

For whereas the raid of Sphodrias was an act of open aggression, the landing of the exiles on Zacynthus, like the decree against Megara, can be viewed as a test of Sparta's willingness to abide by peace terms which pledged her to a policy of noninterference in the Greek world as a whole. It is not probable that in passing the decree which barred Megara, a member of the Peloponnesian League, from trading within the Athenian empire, Pericles was blind to the dangers of war. Nor is it likely that he wished to bring on a war by passing the decree, for the best way to initiate hostilities would surely have been an attack on Megara of a far more direct and bloodier nature. Rather, Pericles conceived the decree as an acid test of Sparta's willingness to refrain from interference in the Athenian Empire as the terms of the Thirty Years' Peace required. Sparta did not pass the test, and war resulted. Similarly, the landing of the exiles on Zacynthus in 374 tested Sparta's willingness to abide by the principle of noninterference set forth in the peace of 375/74, for as Rice acknowledges, "Sparta had a right to interfere only if she continued to assert the hegemony over all of Greece which Timotheus and his faction vigorously rejected." Probably in fact all Athenians rejected the idea of such a hegemony, and "when the Spartans indeed objected," Rice goes on, "Timotheus was able to show the Athenians" that the Spartans were "plainly insincere in agreeing to the peace."[60]

That the action of Timotheus was not repudiated at once suggests that a majority in the assembly was persuaded that the Spartans were not to be trusted. There remained a strong pro-Spartan peace party, however, led probably by Callistratus; and when the financial implications of the renewed hostilities began to dawn on the Athenians, whose financial difficulties throughout the fourth century are notorious, the balance of power between the two parties who favored alternatively the Thebans and the Spartans became increasingly delicate. This ambivalence was reflected in the actions of the assembly when it decreed that the expedition should be sent and that it should be commanded by Timotheus himself but did not provide any means for its support.

Woodhead has argued, in attempting to date Timotheus' recall precisely, that since "the needs of his fleet were presumably evident to all, and his preliminary Aegean expedition was to be regarded as an indispensable necessity," consequently "since Timotheus did not leave Athens until Mounychion [June] it strains probability that his absence through no more than Thargelion and Skirophorion should have moved the Athenians to such extreme agitation and anger."[61] But this argument overlooks the fact that, precisely because the needs of the fleet were so evident, other factors must have contributed in large measure to the deposition of Timotheus. In truth, Timotheus' delay in relieving Corcyra was probably a pretext seized upon by Callistratus, who opposed Timotheus' policy, and by Iphicrates, whose aid Callistratus had evidently enlisted, presumably on the promise of military glory in the Corcyrean campaign. These opponents of Timotheus were enabled to incite the Athenians to anger because of the extreme delicacy of the balance between the proponents of alliance with Thebes and the war with Sparta on the one hand, and the advocates of peace with Sparta on the other. The impeachment of Timotheus in 373, I would suggest, was then at least in part an attack on his policy. It was instigated by those who opposed the anti-Spartan stand suggested by his restoration of the Zacynthian exiles and by those who blamed him for the consequent renewal of hostilities with Sparta.

Issues of policy, I think, were also involved in Timotheus' second trial, which took place some time shortly after 356. In 356 Timotheus and his relatives by marriage Iphicrates and Menestheus were deposed following their refusal to join battle in the Hellespont and were tried for προδοσία following their εὔθυναι. Their principal accusers were Aristophon and Chares. Iphicrates and Menestheus were acquitted; Timotheus was convicted and fined a hundred talents. He died soon after the trial, and his son Conon was allowed to discharge the debt by remitting only one tenth of the fine.[62]

Two years before, in 358, Chios, Rhodes, Cos, and Byzantium had announced their secession from the Athenian confederacy. The Athenians sent out a fleet with Chabrias and Chares to Chios, where they had to contend not only with the four rebel states but with the rebels' ally as well, Mausolus of Caria. The Athenian fleet was unable to achieve a victory, and in the fighting Chabrias himself was slain.[63]

Encouraged by these developments, the rebels terrorized the Aegean for several months, pillaging Imbros, Samos, and other islands in the confederacy and adding Sestos and other Hellespontine cities to their cause. Finally, the Athenians sent a fleet of 120 triremes — the largest Athenian fleet since Aegospotami — to the Hellespont under the joint command of Chares, Iphicrates, Timotheus, and Menestheus.[64] When the Athenians came face to face with the enemy fleet, however, either in the straits or by Embata, near Erythrae, a storm arose, and Iphicrates and Timotheus refused to join battle until it subsided.[65] Menestheus presumably followed his father and his father-in-law, and Chares attacked alone. Without the assistance of his colleagues, Chares was unable to score a victory. He then sent back a dispatch to Athens in which he accused his three colleagues of treason.[66]

The precise course of the events that followed has been much debated, for the sources are contradictory, confusing, and, on the whole, quite late.[67] Diodorus alleges that the three generals were immediately deposed and summoned home for trial, and Nepos agrees; Isocrates writes that Timotheus, having captured many cities for the Athenians and having lost not a single one, "was tried for treason, and again at his εὔθυναι, and when Iphicrates took on himself the responsibility for the conduct of the campaign and Menestheus accounted for the finances, they were acquitted, but Timotheus was fined a larger sum than anyone in the past."[68] Dionysius of Halicarnassus discusses the trial of the generals on two separate occasions. In one case he places it during the Social War, i.e., around the end of 355, but elsewhere he puts it in 354/53, two years after the original accusation by Chares. Dionysius agrees with Isocrates that the second trial was connected with the εὔθυναι of the generals, but he also maintains that Iphicrates, at least, was tried by εἰσαγγελία.[69]

We hear nothing of Timotheus, Iphicrates, or Menestheus between the abortive battle in the summer of 356 and Timotheus' death in 354; the entire command of the fleet during that period seems to have been in the hands of Chares.[70] It is not credible that the three generals were returned to office after their deposition in 356 and continued to serve until 354, when their εὔθυναι were held as they left office; nor is it likely that the many powerful friends of Iphicrates permitted a trial resulting from his εὔθυναι in 355 to remain pending for such a protracted interval.[71] The allegation of Dionysius that the trial of the generals took place in the archonship of Diotimus (354/53) is the only evidence for such a late date, and it probably represents a simple error arising, as Grote has suggested, from confusion with Timotheus' death, which indeed took place in that year; although the chronology is rife with obscurities, it is likely, I think, that the εὔθυναι of the generals were held directly after their deposition, before the end of the official year 356/55.[72]

As to the format of the trial, the agreement of Isocrates and Dionysius suggests that indeed the trial which resulted in Timotheus' condemnation arose from his εὔθυναι. It would seem that either Dionysius is using the expression εἰσαγγελία loosely to describe an impeachment trial or the results of the generals' εὔθυναι moved the Athenians to try them by εἰσαγγελία.[73] Some additional loose ends remain. Why should Isocrates use the word ἔκρινε, which certainly suggests a formal trial, of the proceedings against Timotheus before the occasion of the εὔθυναι at which Menestheus and Iphicrates attempted to take responsibility for the campaign?[74] And why should the willingness of Iphicrates and Menestheus to take responsibility for the campaign be associated not with the initial inquiry at which Timotheus was not convicted of anything but rather with the later trial, at which he was?

We are left with something of a puzzle; but whatever the precise format of the trial, the purpose of the accusation is not difficult to determine. Deinarchus has recorded the precise charge against the generals: Aristophon alleged that they had held back from battle because they had been bribed by the Chians and the Rhodians.[75] There is no reason to believe this accusation; on the contrary, the motive of Chares' charge is transparent. His action in joining battle without the support of his colleagues was reckless in the extreme, even if in fact his assessment of the weather was superior to theirs, and he might well expect to be himself the object of a grave accusation if he did not act quickly to deflect the blame. In large measure, therefore, the attack on his three colleagues was undoubtedly motivated by self-preservation. But the opposition between Chares and his fellow-generals, Timotheus in particular, indeed went much deeper.

Already in 373 Timotheus' refusal to coerce Athens' allies had prevented him from gathering sufficient men and money to relieve Corcyra and led to his deposition. As Beloch points out, however, Timotheus and Iphicrates owed their long popularity at Athens not only to their military skills but also to their experienced diplomacy.[76] Chares, on the other hand, had a reputation of a very different kind. Diodorus tells how, when Chares was sent out to replace Leosthenes, "he spent his time avoiding the enemy and wronging the allies. For, sailing to Corcyra, an allied city, he stirred up such violent civil strife there that many murders and seizures took place, with the result that the Athenian people were discredited in the eyes of the allies."[77] No doubt there were many who saw in this sort of aggressive violence one source of the Social War which erupted in 358.

The issue in 356, then, was not merely the hesitation of Timotheus, Iphicrates, and Menestheus to join battle with Chares, but rather the conflict between the caution and moderation of the two older generals on the one hand, and the headstrong aggressiveness of Chares on the other.[78] Clearly the Athenians were deeply divided about the comparative merits of the different approaches to foreign policy which their generals represented. According to Isocrates, Timotheus' conviction was due in large measure to his aristocratic bearing, which would not permit him to entreat the people's favor.[79] To be sure, Iphicrates' popularity probably contributed to his acquittal. It is to this popularity that the appearance at his trial of large numbers of Iphicrates' soldiers along with their weapons (a phenomenon recorded by Polyaenus) should probably be attributed.[80] As Grote has pointed out, an attempt to intimidate an Athenian jury would probably have done more harm than good.[81] But the difference in the verdicts handed down to the various defendants may have been due as well to Timotheus' far closer association with the policy of tact and moderation in foreign affairs, a policy about which the Athenians were ambivalent and which Chares was evidently assailing with some success.

Probably the most celebrated instance of an accountability trial resulting in large measure from disagreements over policy is the trial of Aeschines which followed on the unpopular Peace of Philocrates. In 346, when the Athenian embassy returned from its second mission to Macedonia, the envoy Demosthenes and his associate Timarchus announced at the ambassadors' εὔθυναι that they intended to prosecute Aeschines for misconduct on the embassy. The case finally came to trial in 343. Aeschines was acquitted by 30 votes out of 1501.[82] The trial of Aeschines is one of the most celebrated impeachment trials of antiquity, and certainly the most famous impeachment of an Athenian ambassador. A good deal is known about this case and its background.

In February of 346, when Athens and Philip were both involved in the Sacred War, the Athenians on the motion of Philocrates sent ten envoys to Macedonia to ascertain Philip's intentions. The envoys included Philocrates, Demosthenes, and Aeschines. They returned from Pella with a courteous letter from Philip offering both peace and alliance.[83]

Two debates took place in Athens following the return of this embassy. At the first, Philocrates proposed an alliance between Philip on the one hand and Athens on the other, spe-

cifically excluding by name both the Phocians and the be-
leaguered Halians. Both Aeschines and Demosthenes, however, supported the request of Athens' allies that *any* Greek state
(including, implicitly, Phocis and Halus, with whom Philip was
at war) might join the peace within three months.[84] On the
following day, however, Aeschines supported still a third form
of Philocrates' resolution which stated simply that the peace
should include Athens' allies, leaving Philip to interpret that
vague phrase as he wished; the resolution was also supported
by Demosthenes and Eubulus.[85] This resolution passed, Aeschines assuring the Athenians that Philip meant the Phocians
no ill; the same ten ambassadors were reappointed and sent
back to Macedonia to take Philip's oath and those of his allies
in their various cities.[86] They were also given vague instructions to accomplish whatever they could for Athens.[87] According to Demosthenes, only he understood the need for haste on
this mission, in order to prevent Philip from continuing maneuvers against Athens' northern allies, and the envoys con-
sumed over three weeks in reaching Pella, where Philip himself
arrived nearly a month later; he had been off in Thrace, and
had captured a number of cities there.[88] In addition to showing
limited determination to make quick contact with Philip, the
Athenian ambassadors disobeyed their instructions in accepting the oaths of the allied cities not by touring the cities themselves but by meeting with a slate of allies magistrates at
Pherae.[89] (Aeschines in the speech he made at his trial was to
argue that the instruction regarding the oaths was trivial compared to the envoys' blanket instructions to advance Athenian
interests.[90]) When all the ambassadors returned to the city
in early July, Demosthenes immediately denounced his colleagues to the βουλή, and the βουλή was sufficiently convinced by his charges to withhold from the ambassadors the
customary vote of thanks and banquet in the Prytaneum.[91]

Despite the protests of Demosthenes, Aeschines and Philocrates persuaded the assembly to believe that Philip had
only the best intentions towards the Phocians and to pass a decree, proposed by Philocrates, extending the peace and alliance with Philip to posterity.[92] A week later Phocis surren-

dered to Philip. Aeschines and other Athenian ambassadors proceeded to meet with Philip, and Aeschines, as is clear from his own words, joined Philip and the Thebans in celebrating the surrender of the Phocians.[93] Philip decided to destroy the towns of Phocis and resettle their inhabitants in villages standing not less than two hundred yards apart and consisting of not more than fifty houses, and he decreed that those who had fled should be pronounced accursed for their sacrilege in plundering the treasures of Delphi and liable to arrest if found.[94] The Amphictyonic Council transferred to Philip the two votes at their meetings which had previously belonged to the Phocians. The Athenians and the Spartans were so indignant at the action of the Council that each refused to send their customary deputations to the Pythian games; but Aeschines was there, evidently as Philip's guest.[95]

According to Demosthenes, Aeschines attempted to avoid his scrutiny after the embassy, and Demosthenes infers that he did so out of consciousness of guilt.[96] If it is true that Aeschines sought to avoid his εὔθυναι, his motive may have been simple fear. In any event, when the εὔθυναι took place, Demosthenes and his associate Timarchus registered complaints against Aeschines and announced their intention of prosecuting.[97] Aeschines attempted to block their effort by prosecuting Timarchus for prostitution in his youth. Timarchus' trial probably took place in 345, and Aeschines won an easy conviction, disfranchising Timarchus and causing considerable embarrassment to Demosthenes, who decided to postpone his suit. In the summer of 343, Demosthenes finally prosecuted Aeschines, maintaining that he had broken the law in several particulars: in accepting gifts from Philip at all, in disobeying his instructions, in making inadequate and inaccurate reports to the assembly about the negotiations, and in betraying Athenian interests in exchange for money. Demosthenes also maintained that the ruin of the Phocians was the fault of Aeschines.

There can be no question that the envoys disobeyed their instructions in not touring the cities of Philip's allies as they had been ordered to do; Aeschines himself, as we have seen, acknowledges this departure from the orders of the ἐκκλησία. Aeschines, then, was technically guilty of παραπρεσβεία. There can be no question either but that the reports of Aeschines about Philip's intentions were indeed inadequate and inaccurate; but whether Aeschines himself knew this — and whether or not his alleged crime at Athens consisted of *knowingly* making such reports — is another story. There remains the crucial question of the alleged taking of gifts or, as the case may be, bribes.

That Aeschines deliberately sold Athenian interests for money is far from clear. In the denunciation of Aeschines which runs through the long account of the Peace of Philocrates in his *History of Greece*, Grote, I think, may have been led by underestimating the man's stupidity into overestimating the degree of his corruption.[98] It appears to me perfectly possible that Aeschines, though he took gifts from Philip and supported his policies, perceived no connection between the two actions. Aeschines' continued friendship with Philip following the destruction of Phocis seems to me hopelessly out of keeping with the hard calculation with which his worst detractors credit him.[99] But any sort of bungling constituted an extra-legal offense which the Athenians took quite seriously — an offense which brought down many a legal judgment on an official's head. There can be no question that Aeschines offended on this count. Even if he was not bribed by Philip, moreover (and it is easy to see how some Athenians could have thought he was), he and his fellow envoys had disobeyed their instructions: if the jury wanted a legal technicality, it lay ready to hand. Furthermore, the envoys' dilatoriness on the route north had enabled Philip to make a number of new conquests. Aeschines showed extremely poor judgment in his dealings with Philip. If he believed the lavish assurance he gave to the ἐκκλησία about Philip, particularly regarding the Macedonian king's intentions towards the Phocians, then he badly misjudged Philip, and his subsequent refusal to abandon Philip's friendship showed a weak understanding of political realities at home. Cawkwell, in an essay on Themistocles, makes some perceptive remarks about Aeschines and the Athenians' view of accountability trials: "The charges," he writes,

> . . . made by Demosthenes in 343 against Aeschines of being in Macedonian pay, or those made against Timagoras in 366 of selling Athens' interests to the Thebans, are not to be taken literally. Such allegations were frequently unverifiable when they were made and in Athens one was not obliged by exacting rules of evidence. The important question is always what in the policies of statesmen could make such an interpretation of their acts remotely credible, and the right answer seems to be again and again that behind . . . "Philippizing," or "Boeotianizing," were policies of avoiding hostilities with . . . Macedon, or Thebes.[100]

To remain the open partisan of Philip after the destruction of Phocis was, beyond doubt, asking for trouble. It is truly astonishing that Aeschines should have escaped with his life.

No doubt the support of Eubulus and Phocion stood Aeschines in good stead at his trial. But when Athenian courts sat in judgment on their officials, as we have seen, they did not suffer fools gladly. Aeschines had acted like a fool. Why then did fully half the jury vote to acquit him? Surely Aeschines' acquittal showed the continued strength of the pro-Macedonian party at Athens. Cloché has suggested that some of the men who voted for acquittal may have been anti-Macedonians who nonetheless felt that the case against Aeschines was weak: I am not persuaded that this number accounts for more than a handful.[101] Fear of Philip may have played a part. It is likely too that the vote to acquit Aeschines was in part a vote against Demosthenes — a vote to support the comparatively ordinary and affable defendant against the fiery and singularly vicious orator whose contempt for Aeschines could be compared with the contempt which he had shown in earlier speeches for the Athenian δῆμος as a whole. Just as Demosthenes no doubt brought the accusation against Aeschines in large part to protect his own position when a botched embassy was followed by an unpopular peace, so many Athenians may have rejected the attack on Aeschines as a way of rejecting Demosthenes.

Because of all its complexity, I have included the case of Aeschines in this chapter rather than, say, in Chapter VI, though it might with equal justice have been placed there. For prominent among the reasons for the attack on Aeschines were not merely the kinds of personal or factional squabbling for which the Athenians were so notorious, but understandable disagreement over grave issues of policy; and this characteristic the trial of Aeschines shares with the other cases treated in this chapter.

IV FACTIONAL STRIFE

I have suggested in Chapter III that Athenian impeachment trials often served as arenas in which men who differed deeply on major policy issues might argue out their disagreements. In at least one case, the deposition of Pericles in 430, an impeachment trial might serve as an actual instrument of policy. Party strife might also play a role, large or small, in an Athenian impeachment trial. Yet it is not always possible to decide when political quarrels concern the kinds of policy issues that would strike most modern Americans and Englishmen as legitimate and when they point to the sorts of personal and factional differences for which the Athenians have so often been censured; thus some readers are bound to feel that the distinctions I have made are on occasion arbitrary.

Factional considerations seem to have played a large part in the impeachment of Miltiades' son Cimon. In 463/62, after his return from Thasos, the στρατηγός Cimon was prosecuted before a dicastery on the grounds that his decision not to use Thasos as a base for an invasion of Macedonia had been taken as a result of a bribe from its king, Alexander. One of his accusers was Pericles. The charge was presumably δωροδοκία (the taking of bribes) or προδοσία (treason), and conviction would probably have meant the death penalty. The trial ended in Cimon's acquittal.[1]

The technicalities of Cimon's trial have been the subject of considerable debate. According to Plutarch's life of Cimon, Pericles "proved the mildest of Cimon's prosecutors and arose only once to press the charge against him, as if his speech were a mere formality."[2] Plutarch also maintains in his life of Pericles that Pericles was one of the public prosecutors appointed by the people.[3] Aristotle, however, casts Pericles in a far more aggressive role, claiming that he made his political debut when as a young man he challenged Cimon's audits.[4] Some scholars have seen a contradiction here, but to my mind the present state of our knowledge about the details of εὔθυναι suggests that Plutarch and Aristotle are both correct. Lipsius assumes that Aristotle in speaking of εὔθυναι is merely making reference to accountability in the most general sense, and that Cimon was in fact impeached by εἰσαγγελία.[5] Bonner and Smith write that "technically Aristotle is in error in calling the case εὔθυνα. . . . It need occasion no surprise that Aristotle in a mere reference to the trial should use εὔθυναι in a broad sense in referring to a trial involving the official conduct of a general."[6]

If, however, Cimon was in fact deposed by ἀποχειροτονία in the course of his στρατηγία, as Busolt and Jacoby maintain, the same principle holds: the man who first brought the accusation was selected to represent the state in the resulting trial.[7] It may well be, moreover, as Glotz suggests, that ἀποχειροτονία would be followed by immediate εὔθυναι.[8]

It is not clear in all cases who would serve as the prosecutor when a complaint that arose in the course of εὔθυναι was referred to a court. In the case of a discrepancy in a magistrate's accounts uncovered by the financial officers themselves, the λογισταί would preside and the συνήγοροι would prosecute. But it is not known what the arrangements were if a charge were brought by a private citizen; and in the case of στρατηγοί, whose εὔθυναι were different from those of other officials, although we know that the θεσμοθέται would *preside* over a trial that resulted from a complaint at the εὔθυναι, it is not clear who would have *prosecuted* the case. I would suggest that the data concerning the trial of Cimon provide the answer:

a public prosecutor was appointed by the people, and in their choice the people were likely to favor the man who had originally brought the accusation at the εὔθυναι. Wilamowitz is correct, I believe, in citing the parallel of the trial of Labes the dog in Aristophanes' *Wasps*; a clear parody of what a trial of Laches by Cleon might have been like, the play shows the man who first brought the accusation at the εὔθυναι being chosen as the public prosecutor in the resulting trial.[9]

Pericles was not the only man who sought to bring Cimon down. Plutarch records that "Cimon's enemies combined against him."[10] The motive of these enemies can hardly have been the genuine suspicion of bribery. Not only did Cimon have a reputation for both incorruptibility and immense wealth; he was also the champion of a pro-Spartan policy, and as such a policy was incompatible with Athenian expansion in mainland Greece, there was no reason to seek a disreputable motive to explain his lack of interest in Macedonia. Nor could the opposition to Cimon have been related to his military operations in Thrace, which had just been crowned with success. Rather, the attack on Cimon must be viewed in the context of both the personal and the ideological struggles of the 460s. As Meiggs has put it, "the main purpose of the trial was rather to provide a political demonstration."[11]

It would be too simple, of course, to imagine that Pericles by his accusation against Cimon was merely perpetuating a generalized hostility between the houses of Miltiades the elder (not, properly, "Philaids," as Wade-Gery has pointed out) and Alcmaeon.[12] After all, Cimon was married to the Alcmaeonid Isodice. But a more localized family feud very probably existed between the sons of Miltiades the younger and of Xanthippus, the man who had brought about the disgrace of the victor of Marathon in 489 after the failure of the Parian expedition. Plutarch and Aristotle both make clear that one of Pericles' chief concerns in his early political life was to find a way to compete with Cimon, whose easy manner and proverbial generosity Pericles found it impossible to rival.[13] Part of Pericles' motive in bringing the accusation must have been to undermine the position of his opponent while at the same time placing himself squarely in the public eye. The issues which erupted a year later, moreover, should properly be read back into Cimon's trial. In 462, when the Spartans requested the Athenians' aid in their struggle with the rebellious helots, Pericles' associates Ephialtes led the opposition to the Spartans' request in the most vigorous language, exhorting the Athenians to "let the pride of Sparta be trampled in the dust."[14] When Cimon, who of course argued the case for the Spartans, carried the assembly and went off to Sparta at the head of an army, Ephialtes and Pericles seem to have taken the occasion of his absence to pass some sort of important democratic legislation, the nature of which has been eagerly debated.[15] The issues of 462 were surely those of 463: Sparta and the democracy. The attack on Cimon was launched by Ephialtes' party to undermine the prestige of a man who was both the ideological opponent of the party leader, Ephialtes, and the potential personal rival of one of its rising members, Pericles.

Cimon both led and symbolized the conservative, pro-Spartan segment of the Athenians, and the attack on him was partly personal, partly an assault on his view about both Sparta and the progress of democracy. Aristotle has recorded that Ephialtes attempted to undermine the prestige of the Areopagus as a whole by attacks on the probity of individual Areopagites, and it is surely in this context that we must see the attack on Cimon.[16] In addition, the trial was meant to offer a forum in which the rising Pericles might distinguish himself at the expense of a hereditary rival.

Pericles, however, who had been expected to prove one of Cimon's harshest accusers, dealt with him very gently. Plutarch attributes Pericles' mildness during the trial to pleas by Cimon's sister Elpinice, recorded in an anecdote gleaned from Stesimbrotus.[17] It is more likely that Pericles came to realize that the time had not yet come for a more severe attack on Athens' favorite general. Perhaps a token accusation had been Pericles' plan all along; perhaps Pericles' mildness was due to the sober cautions of his less impetuous friends; or perhaps when the hour of the contest actually arrived Pericles simply panicked. In any event, Cimon continued to serve as στρατηγός and was able to persuade a majority of the assembly to support the Spartans in their hour of need over the violent protests of Ephialtes. In the contest of 463/62 Cimon was the victor; but Pericles had at least made his mark on public life.

Factional considerations also played a role, I think it can be shown, in the two attacks on Pericles during the 430s — the first, abortive attack, for which I will follow the forceful arguments of Frost in supporting a date of 438; and the second, successful attack of 430.

At some point during the 430s the assembly passed a decree on the motion of Dracontides ordering Pericles to render his accounts to the prytanes and calling for an awesome trial to be held, with the jurors picking up their ballots from the altar on the acropolis. On the motion of Hagnon, the bill was amended to provide for an ordinary trial, whereupon the whole matter appears to have been dropped.

Thucydides does not mention a trial of Pericles at any time prior to his removal from office in the summer of 430. Plutarch and Diodorus both place the first trial of Pericles during the months preceding the promulgation of the Megarian decree, along with attacks on Pericles' associates Anaxagoras, Aspasia, and Phidias, and claim that Pericles brought on the war to extricate himself and his friends from their difficulties.[18] The god Hermes in Aristophanes' *Peace* (601–618) makes the same argument concerning Phidias. Surely Aristophanes was in a position to know, but he was writing fantasy, not history. The astonishment with which Hermes' allegation is heard by the chorus of Athenian farmers and the other actors in the play suggests that no Athenian had ever put forward *that* interpretation of the war before, and I see no need to accept the personal opinions of Hermes as a source for Greek history.

Fortunately a particularly alert scholiast discovered in Philochorus the statement that the dedication of the chryselephantine statue of Athena, and hence the trial and flight of Phidias, took place in the archonship of Theodorus, 438/37.[19] As it seems likely that the trials of Pericles and his associates took place around the same time and were part of a broadly conceived attack on Pericles himself (indeed Pericles was implicated in the accusation against Phidias), I am inclined to accept a date of 438 for the first trial of Pericles.[20]

The abortive attempt to call in Pericles' accounts, though it did not lead to a trial, deserves study from the standpoint of constitutional history, for it suggests that Pericles had in fact not been submitting his accounts regularly throughout his στρατηγία either at annual εὔθυναι or at the monthly κυρία ἐκκλησία. Suspicion had already arisen concerning Pericles' finances in 446, when he entered in the accounts for his στρατηγία an amount of ten talents εἰς τὸ δέον — for necessary expenses. The Athenians, according to Plutarch, connected this entry with the banishment for bribery in that year of the Spartan king Pleistoanax and his adviser Cleandridas, who had withdrawn from the battlefield after an impromptu conference with Pericles. Plutarch reports that the Athenians approved the expenditure εἰς τὸ δέον "without meddling or probing the mystery"; unfortunately, however, he does not make clear whether this audit in fact took place at the end of the official year or only in 443, when Pericles was not reelected to the στρατηγία and his accounts were presumably audited on his departure from office. Moreover, Plutarch goes on, Theophrastus and a number of others alleged that in fact ten talents had found their way to Sparta not only in 446 but in each subsequent year as well, and that with these funds Pericles bought time with which to strengthen Athens' resources for war. This tale seems out of keeping with the importance Pericles was to place on Athens' independence from all Spartan interference, and it has not won wide acceptance among modern scholars.[21]

In addition, Pericles was accused, though perhaps not formally, of complicity in the alleged misdeeds of the sculptor Phidias, who stood accused of ἱεροσυλία (the theft of sacred property, a capital charge) in connection with his work on the great gold and ivory statue of Athena Parthenos; both Pericles' role as one of the ἐπιστάται of the statue and his friendship with Phidias might lend credence to the accusation.[22] Whether

Phidias remained to stand his trial is not known; he left Athens about this time, either by flight before his trial or by exile after.[23] It may have been the popular suspicion that Pericles was involved in the misdeeds of Phidias rather than the alleged payments to Sparta which provided the pretext for calling in his accounts — although it is, of course, noteworthy that any pretext at all should have been sought.

The Athenians either disbelieved the charges against Pericles or, as at the earlier audit cited by Plutarch, did not care. Dracontides had evidently expected that the awesome sacred procedure he had proposed would lead the jurors — superstitiously, as it were — to bring in a verdict of guilty, and Hagnon's amendment hopelessly undermined the prospects for conviction. The accusation was abandoned. If our interpretation of Hagnon's amendment is correct, it is likely that in the following year, when the strategically important colony of Amphipolis was sent out, Pericles returned the favor: the honor of founding Amphipolis fell to Hagnon. Pericles escaped unscathed from these attacks. Nonetheless it is important to understand from what direction the shots came.

Unless these attacks, which I have placed in 438, took place in fact on the very eve of the war, it is not likely that they originated with the conservative opposition to Pericles' democratic programs, for Thucydides, son of Melesias, the leader of the conservatives, did not return from his ostracism until shortly before the war, and as Plutarch records (and we should in any event expect), Thucydides' faction had collapsed with his departure.[24] This collapse leaves us with the aggressive war party which came to be led after Pericles' death by Cleon. We know nothing about Cleon's activities prior to the outbreak of war in 432, but he may himself have been behind the attacks on Pericles. About the same time as the accusations against Phidias and Pericles, Aspasia, for some years Pericles' mistress and the mother of his children, was accused of impiety; she was acquitted. (Whether or not Pericles, as Plutarch maintains, wept at her trial is another story.) A decree was also proposed in the assembly calling for the impeachment of anyone who disbelieved in the gods or taught anything concerning the heavens. Rightly suspecting that this bill was aimed at his friend Anaxagoras, Pericles arranged for the philosopher's sudden departure from Athens.[25] The tone of these attacks certainly looks forward to the attacks on sophistry and on the intellect as a whole which were to mark Cleon's speech ten years later at the Mytilenean debate; the method chosen to arouse the multitude is strikingly similar.[26] Whoever their leaders may have been, however, Pericles' enemies in 438 were disappointed in their effort to discredit him. His popularity was only underlined by their failure, and he continued to guide Athenian policy without effective opposition for several years.

It is likely too, I think, that party strife played its part in the attack on Pericles in 430 and perhaps in the attack on the generals who accepted the surrender of Potidaea in that year as well, since one of them, Xenophon, was an old associate of Pericles. Certainly it must have played a part in the deposition of Phrynichus and Scironides; for as we have seen, these generals were deposed in 412/11 because they stood in the way of the recall of Alcibiades. And it seems to have played a large role as well in the impeachment of Anytus, the future prosecutor of Socrates.

In 409, Anytus was accused of προδοσία following his failure to relieve the Messenian garrison at Pylos. The manner of his trial is unknown. He was acquitted.[27]

Our chief source for the case of Anytus is the narrative of Diodorus. When the Spartans realized how heavily the Athenian forces were committed in the Hellespont, Diodorus writes, they decided that the hour was at hand for an attack on Pylos, which was being held by a Messenian garrison. On learning that the Spartans were having some success in an energetic amphibious attack on Pylos, the Athenians sent out thirty ships to Pylos under the command of Anytus. But since he was prevented by storms from rounding Cape Malea, Anytus sailed back to Athens, whereupon the Athenian people were incensed, accused him of treason, and brought him to trial. But Anytus, being in the greatest danger, saved himself by his money and is reputed to be the first Athenian to have bribed a jury.[28] That Anytus secured his acquittal by bribing the jury is also alleged by Aristotle, who agrees that he was the first man to be discovered doing so.[29]

We cannot tell whether or not Anytus could reasonably have been held responsible for the loss of Pylos. There is no particular reason to think that he was guilty of treason. He was probably an inexperienced commander, not the best man to select for a circumnavigation of the Peloponnesus in winter, and he may have panicked (was it impossible for him to have waited out the storm on Cythera?).[30] Nor is there any way to tell whether his acquittal was in fact secured by bribery, although Anytus was a wealthy man and could certainly have afforded to purchase a verdict, if indeed anyone could.[31] But the year of his trial strongly suggests that he was among the intended victims of the restored democracy.

That Anytus was at all times a moderate democrat is well attested, and in 409 no moderate could afford the slightest mistake.[32] After the restoration of the democracy in the summer of 410 the radical democrats were in control of Athens, and the speeches of Lysias and Andocides give a vivid picture of the ways in which this control was exercised.[33] The accusation of membership in the Four Hundred was leveled at all moderates. Lysias points out that if everyone accused of membership in the Four Hundred had been guilty, the Four Hundred would have been closer to a thousand.[34] The radical democrats, led by Epigenes, Demophanes, and Cleisthenes, "reaped personal gains from the city's misfortunes," for, Lysias writes, "They persuaded you to condemn men to death without trial, to confiscate the property of many men unjustly, and to banish and disfranchise others; some they took money to let go, others they brought before you and accused without justice."[35] Accusers, Lysias complains, "take money to smuggle out the accused."[36] As McCoy has written, the courts "now became an instrument of terror."[37]

It was in this climate that Anytus was accused and it is in this context that his trial must be viewed. Aristotle says that Anytus was brought to trial "by certain men"; the situation of the moderates in the years following the restoration of 410 makes clear what sort of men these were. Grote has written that the accusation of bribery made against Anytus indicates "that the general Athenian public thought him deserving of condemnation and were so much surprised by his acquittal, as to account for it by supposing, truly or falsely, the use of means never before attempted."[38] But is it not just as likely that the Athenians simply imputed to Anytus a different variety of the kind of financial self-preservation which Lysias insists was widespread under the restored democracy? The charge of bribery may have been brought by the same men who brought the original charge against Anytus, as Curtius implies; but if in fact a citizen as officiously civic-minded as Anytus did resort to bribery, it was probably because under the circumstances he did not expect a fair trial.[39]

Anytus' acquittal may have been due in part to bribery, in part to a genuine belief in his innocence. Unfortunately the unsubstantiated allegation of bribery introduces an additional variable into the case and makes it difficult to know what to make of the verdict. But it seems safe to say that the motive of Anytus' accusers in bringing him to trial was primarily political, although his inexperience as a naval commander may well have played into their hands. The attack on him must be seen in the context of the massive campaign that was waged against the moderates by the radicals following the restoration of 410.

It is not the case, as I shall try to show below in Chapter VI, that Alcibiades was deposed early in 406 principally because of factional considerations, as Henderson maintains, but these considerations no doubt fed the fuel of the attack on him.[40] Factional considerations played a part as well in the celebrated impeachment of the victors of Arginusae later the same year.

In the autumn of 406, following the victory off the Arginusae islands in the course of which thousands of Athenian lives were lost through drowning, the eight generals who had been in command were deposed by ἀποχειροτονία so that they could return home and explain the high death toll. Six obeyed the summons to return: Diomedon, the younger Pericles, Lysias, Aristocrates, Thrasyllus, and Erasinides; two, Pro-

tomachus and Aristogenes, did not. Upon the return of the
generals, Erasinides was formally accused by Archedemus on
a financial charge, perhaps κλοπή, and of some sort of more
general misconduct in his στρατηγία. His case, however, never came to trial, for soon afterwards, when the generals had
made their statement in the βουλή regarding the loss of the
men, they were all imprisoned on the motion of Timocrates to
await trial. The generals were tried in the ἐκκλησία itself, and
probably by εἰσαγγελία. The precise charge is unknown. On
the motion of Callixeinus the generals were tried by a single
vote. They were convicted and sentenced to death. The six
who were in Athens were executed at once. Protomachus and
Aristogenes never returned to Athens.

The account of Xenophon is the chief source for the battle of
Arginusae and for the trial of the generals which followed. The
briefer account of Diodorus in some ways differs sharply from
that of Xenophon, but putting the two together it is possible to
reconstruct the outlines of the situation.[41]

Although the Athenians had defeated the Spartans decisively, many Athenian ships lay disabled in the sea, their
crews clinging to them in the hope of rescue. The generals debated whether to proceed at once to attack the Peloponnesian
fleet besieging Conon at Mytilene, as Erasinides proposed,
or to follow the suggestion of Diomedon and remain to
pick up the many drowning sailors by the twenty or so disabled
triremes in the sea. Thrasyllus recommended a compromise: a
portion of the fleet was to be left in the command of the
trierarchs, Theramenes and Thrasybulus of Steiria, to rescue
the sailors, while the remainder was to go to the aid of Conon.
Unfortunately, by the time Thrasyllus' compromise was
adopted, much valuable time had been allowed to slip by. A
storm had arisen, and neither the rescue operation nor the
voyage to Mytilene took place as planned.[42]

The generals then settled on another compromise. At the
suggestion of Pericles and Diomedon they omitted from their
official dispatch all mention of the rescue mission's having
been entrusted to the trierarchs and blamed only the storm for
the failure of that mission — but in private communications

home they alluded to the role of Theramenes and Thrasybulus in the intended rescue operation.[43] The consequences of this compromise were disastrous. The inconsistency in the generals' story appeared to argue against them, and, worse yet, as Diodorus points out, they had made enemies of Theramenes and Thrasybulus.[44]

When the generals arrived at Athens, Archedemus, one of the radical leaders, evidently determined to handle the situation by bringing to trial only Erasinides, a logical choice of victim.[45] Theramenes, however, was determined that there should be an attack on all the generals. In part he was probably motivated by political considerations. The slate of generals who commanded at Arginusae, after all, had been chosen in the wake of Alcibiades' deposition; it was no coincidence that Thrasyllus was among them and Theramenes and Thrasybulus, both friends of Alcibiades, were not. The victory at Arginusae might convince the Athenians that there were other generals who could conduct the war better than Alcibiades.[46] As several scholars have pointed out, by an attack on the competence of the generals of 406/5, Theramenes might hope to pave the way indirectly for Alcibiades' recall from the exile he had wisely imposed on himself.[47] It is possible too, as Beloch has suggested, that the absence of the name of Cleophon from the proceedings against the generals may be due to Cleophon's unwillingness to associate himself with a project conceived by the friends of Alcibiades, whom he bitterly opposed.[48] In part, however, Theramenes was surely motivated by self-preservation. The task assigned to him after the battle had put him in an awkward position, and his friendship with Alcibiades made this position even more precarious. Indeed it may be, as McCoy has suggested, that Thrasyllus, who was commander-in-chief on the day of the battle and could have expected to be blamed if the men were not rescued, had shifted the responsibility onto Thrasybulus and Theramenes precisely because he felt that their association with Alcibiades would make the Athenians singularly willing to place the blame on them.[49]

There is no reason to think that Theramenes ever expected

to bring about the death of the generals. To the best of our knowledge, at no time prior to 406 had an Athenian general ever been put to death at home. But matters soon passed out of Theramenes' hands. At their trial the generals defended themselves so persuasively that several Athenians offered to post bail for them. As it was getting late, however, the voting was postponed until the following meeting on the pretext that the darkness made it impossible to distinguish the vote, but actually no doubt because it was clear that the generals were about to be acquitted.[50]

It happened that before the next meeting of the ἐκκλησία the Apaturia intervened, a traditional yearly festival rich in sentiment, in the course of which family ties were greatly stressed. This occasion naturally heightened the Athenians' sense of loss and called attention to the formidable number of bereaved families. According to Xenophon, some of the alleged mourners were in fact the agents of Theramenes, who hoped by swelling the numbers of the bereaved to excite the Athenians still further in their grief; but Xenophon himself undermines this contention when he makes clear that Theramenes was not among the men later singled out for prosecution when the Athenians came to regret their execution of the generals.[51] In fact there is no need to seek any special explanation for the high emotion that characterized the next meeting of the assembly.

At the second assembly, one Callixeinus proposed that the generals' guilt or innocence be decided by a single vote and that if they were convicted the penalty should be death.[52] Euryptolemus, a relative of Pericles and a friend of Diomedon, pointed out along with several others that the proposal of Callixeinus violated the psephism of Cannonus, a recognized Athenian usage which provided for a regular defense and, presumably, a separate trial for each defendant, and he proposed that the generals be tried according to that psephism in the usual way.[53] But the assembly was in a state of considerable agitation, and a certain Lyciscus proposed that those who attacked the proposal of Callixeinus should be judged together with the generals on the capital charge. The objections were withdrawn.[54] Several members of the presiding prytany then refused to put Callixeinus' motion to a vote because of its violation of the psephism of Cannonus. Under threats, however, they withdrew their opposition as well, and the vote was taken over the objections of one adamant prytanis, Socrates. Cloché has suggested that the threats of men as obscure as Callixeinus and Lyciscus cannot have been very formidable, and that in fact Callixeinus' subsequent escape to Decelea implies that he was the tool not, as Xenophon maintains, of Theramenes, but rather of the philolaconian oligarchs, who saw an extraordinary opportunity in the tragedy at Arginusae for eliminating eight democratic generals in one fell swoop.[55]

The assembly agreed, however, to vote on the motion of Euryptolemus as well, and the majority favored his motion over that of Callixeinus. But when one Menecles lodged an objection on some unknown technicality, a second vote was taken, and the motion of Callixeinus passed. The generals were found guilty and the six who were at hand were executed at once. Subsequently, Xenophon reports, the Athenians had a change of heart and brought προβολαί against Callixeinus and several others on the grounds that they had deceived the people. All these men were evidently imprisoned pending trial, but in the στάσις which erupted towards the end of the war they escaped. Callixeinus returned after the overthrow of the thirty tyrants, but Xenophon reports that he was hated by everyone and starved to death.[56]

The story of the condemnation of the victors of Arginusae is an intricate one indeed, and our ignorance about the precise nature and status of the psephism of Cannonus makes it difficult to know what, from a constitutional point of view, we are to make of these dismal proceedings.[57] But it seems likely that the political motives of Theramenes and his Alcibiadist associates played an important role in the intricate chain of events which led to the execution of the generals, as did the odd alliance in the assembly between radical democrats like Callixeinus and Lyciscus on the one hand and the pro-Spartan oligarchs on the other. The former probably attacked the admirals partly because they (like nearly all Athenian στρατηγοί) were moderates compared to the leaders of the assembly, the latter because, as Cloché suggests, they saw in the predicament of the generals an opportunity to counteract the recent naval victory by striking a blow at the men who had brought it about.

Towards the end of the Corinthian War a rash of impeachments broke out at Athens. It is not likely to be a coincidence, I think, that so many of the men attacked fell into the radical and moderate camps — camps which had by this time indeed merged — and I shall argue at some length in Chapter V that the trials of this period arose in large part from factional strife.

Factional strife also played a part, I think, in the impeachment of the general Chabrias. In 365 Chabrias was brought to trial for προδοσία following the loss of Oropus to the Thebans. His accusers included Philostratus of Colonus and Leodamas. He was acquitted. The orator Callistratus was also brought to trial in connection with the loss of Oropus, and the attacks on the two men were evidently connected.[58]

Oropus was a small town on the northeastern frontier of Attica, adjoining Boeotia. Since the fifth century the Athenians and the Thebans had quarreled frequently about its proper disposition. Never incorporated as a deme, the town had nonetheless been recognized as a dependency of Athens, despite its apparent Boeotian origin, and many of its inhabitants were in fact Athenian citizens, members of the neighboring deme, Graea.[59] In the late 370s some sort of disagreement had arisen between Athens and Thebes concerning Oropus, and as a result the pro-Theban partisans at Oropus were banished.[60] In the summer of 366 some of these exiles appealed for assistance to Themison, tyrant of Eretria, who helped them to gain admission to their native city and, evidently, to seize the reins of government. Perhaps, as Grote suggests, they also banished the leading Athenian partisans.[61] The Athenians promptly marched out in full force. Presumably this expedition was commanded by Chabrias. Chares was at once recalled from his operations around Phlius and Corinth and ordered to meet

Chabrias at Oropus. The Athenians also called for assistance from their allies, including the Corinthians; but the allies did not come. When the Athenians arrived at Oropus, the town was in the possession of the Thebans, to whom the restored exiles had evidently delivered it. The Thebans refused to surrender the city and insisted on taking charge of it pending arbitration.[62]

The Athenians were aggrieved at the loss of Oropus, and they were also frustrated and angry that their allies had not come to their assistance. To make matters worse, the recall of Chares had resulted in the defeat of the pro-Athenian faction in Sicyon, and that state now returned to the league of the Thebans and Arcadians.[63] It soon became evident, moreover, that the Thebans had no intention of submitting the question of Oropus to arbitration. Callistratus may have had something to do with the unsuccessful Athenian effort to negotiate with the Thebans, or he may have simply conferred with Chabrias before he led the Athenians out to Oropus: in an obscure passage discussing the Oropus trial Aristotle contrasts the ideas of Callistratus with the actions of Chabrias.[64] There is no evidence to suggest that Callistratus was στρατηγός along with Chabrias in 367/66.[65]

At the time of the loss of Oropus, the Athenians were exceptionally bitter against the Thebans, and no doubt their frustration played a part in the attack on Chabrias and Callistratus. In 367 a Greek embassy had gone to Susa. Thebes was represented by Pelopidas and Ismenias, Athens by Leon and Timagoras. Pelopidas made the most favorable impression on the Great King and obtained from him a rescript entirely on his own terms. Messene was to be free from Sparta; Amphipolis was to be autonomous; Elis was declared sovereign over Triphylia; the Athenians were to recall their warships and keep them at home on pain of intervention by Persia; and, it seems, the hegemony of Thebes over Greece was recognized.[66] Predictably, the Athenians were displeased with these terms. When the envoys returned to Greece early in 366 Timagoras, at the instigation of his fellow envoy Leon, was tried for misconduct on the embassy; he was convicted and executed.[67]

The Athenians also joined the other Greek cities in refusing to assent to the formal peace proposed by Thebes on the terms of the rescript.[68] The seizure and retention of Oropus followed.

Chabrias, although he had led the Athenian forces against the Thebans in the Peloponnese in 368, had also been friendly with Pelopidas and Epaminondas; these old friendships may have contributed to the resentment against him.[69] The Athenians' dissatisfaction with Callistratus, on the other hand, may well have derived from his role in promoting their connections with precisely those allies who had deserted them when called upon to assist Chares and Chabrias; indeed, the allies' defection had provoked the Athenians into launching an abortive attack on Corinth itself.[70] And yet at least a year or so elapsed before Chabrias and Callistratus were in fact brought to trial, for it was not until 365, probably in the spring, that Plato (whom Diogenes Laertius places at the trial of Chabrias) returned from Sicily.[71]

This delay was probably due in part to the lapse of time necessary for the Athenians to realize that the Thebans' offer of arbitration was not sincere. In part, however, it must have been due to the changing picture in the Greek world. In 373, as we have seen, Timotheus had been deposed from his στρατηγία and tried on the motion of Iphicrates and Callistratus. His replacements in the command against Corcyra were Iphicrates, Callistratus, and Chabrias.[72] Timotheus returned to active service around 370, and in 366 he was sent by the Athenians to assist the rebellious satrap Ariobarzanes, with the idea of pressuring Artaxerxes into reconsidering the terms of his recent rescript favoring Thebes.[73] By the spring of 365 the Persian king had indeed recognized the Athenians' claims to Amphipolis, and possibly to the Chersonese as well; Ariobarzanes also handed Sestos and Crithote over to Timotheus, and Timotheus was able to gain possession of Samos after a long siege. Iphicrates, on the other hand, had been operating on the coasts of Macedonia and Chalcidice for several years, and he apparently had nothing to show for it; he had been unable to take Amphipolis or any other stronghold.[74] Athens, moreover, was now at war with the Thracian Cotys, whose daughter Iphicrates had married. Soon after the trials of Chabrias and Callistratus, the Athenians recalled Iphicrates from the Thracian command and replaced him with Timotheus. Iphicrates demonstrated his awareness that he had fallen from favor by taking service with his father-in-law and possibly even fighting against the Athenians.[75]

That the trials of Callistratus and Chabrias should have taken place at precisely the time when public opinion was shifting and Iphicrates was being displaced by Timotheus can hardly have been a matter of simple coincidence.[76] Rather, it is in this context that we must view the fact that Callistratus and Chabrias were tried not when the Athenians were at the peak of their frustration following the pro-Theban rescript and the loss of Oropus, but instead at a time when the sting of the loss of Oropus had subsided and Artaxerxes' change of heart had put the Athenians in a more hopeful and, one might have thought, more charitable mood. The timing of the attack on Callistratus and Chabrias suggests that the loss of Oropus was seized as a pretext by the faction of Timotheus, who saw that all three men who had replaced him in the Corcyrean command were embarrassed at Athens and concluded that the moment for a much-delayed counterattack was at hand.

The support of Timotheus' faction encouraged the various opponents of Callistratus and Chabrias to organize an attack on them. Some no doubt suspected Chabrias of pro-Theban sympathies. Many must have resented Callistratus' advocacy of the alliance with the Peloponnesian states that had let the Athenians down so badly in the Oropus affair. The pro-Theban party was represented by Leodamas.[77] No doubt this group sought to avert blame from themselves by attacking Callistratus and Chabrias; Chares too may have been among their accusers, and for the same reason.[78] Personal factors may have been at work as well, for Leodamas had opposed the honors bestowed on Chabrias following the battle of Naxos.[79] It is likely too that the pro-Thebans had long opposed Callistratus because of his anti-Theban policy and welcomed an opportunity to embarrass him.

The political background of Philostratus of Colonus, whom

Demosthenes names as bitterest among Chabrias' accusers, is unknown, as is that of Lycoleon, who pleaded on Chabrias' behalf. Diogenes Laertius, however, reports that Hegesippus, a popular democratic leader, attempted unsuccessfully to dissuade Plato from pleading for Chabrias.[80] It would be too simple, however, to assume from the altercation between Plato and Hegesippus that the trials of Chabrias and Callistratus merely ranged lofty would-be aristocrats against sincere democrats, for it is clear that the grievances against Chabrias and Callistratus were many and varied.[81]

The attack on Chabrias, then, arose in large part from his association with Callistratus, which had evidently persisted since Callistratus, Iphicrates, and Chabrias had all been associated in the Corcyrean command in 373 as replacements for the recalled Timotheus. It did not succeed, however, for both Chabrias and Callistratus appear to have been acquitted. The acquittal suggests that while the prestige of Timotheus was indeed high, nonetheless the party led by Callistratus, Chabrias, and Iphicrates was still strong enough to withstand an attack, and during the years that followed, both Timotheus and Callistratus exercised considerable influence at Athens. It also suggests that the two men were innocent, for it is difficult to believe that even the improved position of the Athenians in 365 and the rhetoric of Callistratus would have induced them to forgive Callistratus and Chabrias had there been any sound reason for believing them guilty of betraying Oropus to the Thebans.

It is likely, I think, that factional strife also played a part in the impeachment of Leosthenes. In 361 Leosthenes was tried by εἰσαγγελία on an unknown charge following his defeat at Peparethus by Alexander of Pherae. He was condemned to death and his property was confiscated, but he escaped the death penalty by voluntary exile.[82]

In the summer of 362 the Athenians decided to take action against Alexander of Pherae. Once their own ally against the Thebans, he was now numbered among the Thebans' friends. He had sent troops to assist Epaminondas at Mantinea, and his fleet had captured Tenos, ravaged a number of the Cyclades, and laid siege to Peparethus.[83] Consequently in August the Athenians decreed that a major fleet should be sent to protect Athens' insular allies and to defend Athenian interests in the Hellespont.[84] This fleet was commanded by Autocles, but a detachment was left at Peparethus under Leosthenes. Diodorus tells how Alexander's men attacked Leosthenes unexpectedly and took captive five Athenian triremes, one Peparethan ship, and six hundred prisoners of war.[85] Polyaenus reports that Alexander's sailors then proceeded to stage a daring raid on Piraeus. As the port was unprotected, they pillaged the dock area, took some prisoners, and then retired before a force could be sent out to meet them.[86]

It does not seem possible to determine how far Leosthenes was responsible for his defeat at Alexander's hands. No doubt the frustration of the Athenians at their inability to inflict a setback on Alexander and their alarm at the raid on Piraeus contributed to the vote for Leosthenes' conviction. The motive for the attack, however, appears to have been at least in part political.

The factional constellations of this period have been hotly debated, and scholars have reached a wide range of conclusions. About the same time as the condemnation of Leosthenes, Callistratus was sent into exile for giving the Athenians bad advice.[87] As Cloché points out, most of the evidence that might cast light on the source of the attack on Callistratus is inconclusive, but it is not impossible to say something about the issues.[88]

Throughout the 360s Callistratus espoused an anti-Theban policy.[89] Although Aristophon had fought in the war against the Thebans as στρατηγός, Aeschines claims that he had a long-established reputation for Theban sympathies.[90] Following the flight of Leosthenes, Aristophon brought an accusation against Leosthenes' trierarchs for failure to do their duty, alleging that they had arranged to avoid serving in person and had hired deputies to appear in their places.[91] The high incidence of trierarchs' accusing their commanders, and in particular the developments of the Arginusae trial, must caution us against assuming that an attack on the trierarchs was necessarily an attack on the commanding στρατηγός; an attempt might, of course, be made to shift the blame from one to the other.[92] But the fact that Leosthenes had fled and had been condemned only *in absentia* suggests that Aristophon attacked the trierarchs not to avert the blame from Leosthenes but to obtain a more concrete victory over the men whom he held responsible for the defeat at Peparethus. That Aristophon was integrally involved in the attack on Leosthenes is also suggested by the fact that after the condemnation of Leosthenes, his command was transferred to Chares, a close associate of Aristophon. Aeschines, moreover, attributed the fate of Leosthenes to sycophants, and we may well imagine that Aristophon's notoriously frequent activity in the courts may have laid him open to such a characterization.

In a variety of cases, then, it appears that factional politics as well as ideological policy differences played a role in Athenian impeachment trials during both the fifth century and the fourth. In addition, a special political consideration can sometimes be seen at work: the impulse to self-preservation. Probably the most obvious case is the impeachment of Aeschines by Demosthenes, who had served with Aeschines on the embassies to Philip in 346 and had reason to fear for his own safety after the Peace of Philocrates. But several other cases as well show this consideration playing a role.

We have seen, for example, how Theramenes was probably motivated in considerable measure in his attack on the victors of Arginusae by the need to preserve his own safety. Thrasybulus may have been affected by similar motives. Leon, who accused his fellow envoy Timagoras of corruption on the embassy to Susa in 367, was probably motivated by considerations of self-preservation after the Persian king issued a rescript favoring the Thebans.[93] If indeed Conon ever prosecuted the στρατηγός Adeimantus for his conduct at Aegospotami, it is likely that his action formed part of a plan to justify his own conduct at that disastrous battle, and to consolidate his own position at Athens. The patriotism of Adeimantus, allegedly the only Athenian whom Lysander freed after the battle, might well be called into question by Conon, who had escaped from Aegospotami just in time. But this case is probably a fiction: Conon had amply restored his credit at Athens after his victory at Cnidus, and I find it hard to believe, moreover, that so flagrant a violation of the amnesty of 403 would be known to us just from one casual reference in Demosthenes, who seeks to justify his own attack on Aeschines by listing others who have prosecuted their colleagues.[94]

In addition, concerns of self-preservation may have motivated Apollodorus in his impeachment of Callippus. Callippus' impeachment is surely to be traced to 360, the occasion being the illegal transport of the exile Callistratus. The format, precise charge and verdict in the case are unknown.[95] In the speech for Phormio, the Demosthenic text tells of the impeachment of Callippus by Apollodorus; in the speech against Polycles, Apollodorus tells how Callippus tried to bully him into transporting the exile Callistratus from Methone to Thasos on an official Athenian ship. Callippus was some sort of subordinate of the general Timomachus; Hansen is probably right in supposing that he was trierarch.[96] According to Apollodorus, Timomachus had sent Apollodorus, a trierarch for that year, off to Methone without telling him the purpose of the expedition. When a sailor betrayed to Apollodorus the true purpose of their journey, Apollodorus refused to proceed — perhaps, as he alleges, out of respect for the laws, and probably, too, out of fear, as harboring Callistratus on his ship would have involved Apollodorus in a serious crime. Callippus then tried in vain to persuade Apollodorus to reconsider, Apollodorus maintains; when he failed, Timomachus found another trierarch to help Callippus carry out the mission. Apollodorus subsequently impeached Timomachus by εἰσαγγελία, as we have seen, probably for treason, embezzlement, and harboring an exile. No doubt the impeachment of Callippus must also be traced to this occasion. It is not known whether Callippus was deposed in the course of his term or charged upon (or after) its expiration. But as we can see, Apollodorus had a clear and pressing motive to charge Callippus — the need to make a dramatic show of his innocence in the matter of the transport of Callistratus.[97]

Probably the most striking example of the way in which considerations of self-preservation may have influenced an Athenian politician is the case of Chares. It is not likely to be a coincidence that we know of three military operations in which Chares was involved which led to the impeachment of one or more of his colleagues: the Oropus campaign of 366 and the impeachment of Chabrias; the naval battle in the Hellespont in 356 and the impeachment of Timotheus, Iphicrates, and Menestheus; and finally the battle of Chaeronea, which led to the impeachment of Lysicles.

In 365, as we have just seen, the στρατηγός Chabrias and the orator Callistratus were impeached following the loss to the Thebans of the border town of Oropus; Chares, who had also been involved in military operations at Oropus, was not impeached. Although there is no direct evidence to suggest anything sinister in the fact that Chabrias was impeached and Chares was not, a pattern begins to emerge when we also consider the events following the campaign in the Social War during the 350s led by Chares, Timotheus, Iphicrates, and Menestheus; for, as we have seen in Chapter III, the latter three generals were impeached at this time when Chares accused them of treason.

In 338/37, moreover, Lycurgus prosecuted the general Lysicles, probably for προδοσία, after the defeat at Chaeronea. Lysicles was condemned and executed.[98] His fellow general Chares was not impeached as far as we know, but there is no reason to believe that Lysicles was any more responsible for the defeat than was Chares. Indeed, there is some evidence that Chares' position after the battle was a particularly awkward one. For one thing, he was probably the most experienced general present at the battle, more experienced by far than either of his colleagues, Lysicles or Stratocles. Nevertheless, he had allowed himself to be duped by Philip with extremely unfortunate consequences for the Athenians.

In the summer of 338 Philip marched on Boeotia from Phocis. The allied Greek force held all the passes by which Philip might wish to cross into Boeotia, chiefly the pass of Parapotamii, northwest of the plain of Chaeronea. Philip hit upon the stratagem of allowing a false dispatch to his general Antipater, announcing his intention of returning at once to Thrace, to fall into the hands of Chares and of the Theban Proxenus, who were guarding the road to Amphissa and the Gulf of Corinth. They at once relaxed their watch, at which point Philip attacked them, seized the route to Amphissa, and advanced to Naupactus.[99] With this stroke, Philip gravely undermined the position of the allied forces in Parapotamii and the other passes, for he could now block their retreat. The allies determined to withdraw their line to the plain of Chaeronea. Philip crossed through the Parapotamii pass and met them there.[100]

The choice to fall back on Chaeronea was probably unavoidable once Philip had taken Amphissa and Naupactus, but it would certainly have been preferable for the allies to have tried to turn Philip back in the hills, where their own familiarity with the territory would have proven an advantage. The necessity of dealing with the well-trained Macedonian army on open ground favorable to Philip was forced on the allies by the miscalculation of Chares and Proxenus, of course, who had failed to maintain adequate vigilance on the road to Amphissa when they had opened Philip's false dispatch.

Cavaignac has argued that Chares was able to avoid prosecution on this occasion because of his political connections.[101] Such a view of Chares' role in the events of 338 strikes me as excessively mild and charitable. Rather, it seems probable that questions of self-preservation led him to join in the attack on Lysicles.

Finally, two unusual and dramatic instances of civic self-preservation deserve mention: the impeachment of Miltiades in 489 following the failure of the Parian expedition and the impeachment of the generals who aided in liberating the Theban Cadmeia in 379/78.

Following his unsuccessful siege of Paros, the στρατηγός

Miltiades was impeached, perhaps on a charge of ἀπάτη (deceiving the people), as Herodotus suggests, or of treason and the accepting of bribes, as Nepos claims. His accuser was Pericles' father, Xanthippus. The trial took place before the assembly and was probably therefore by εἰσαγγελία. To be sure, factional considerations doubtless played a part in the impeachment of Miltiades. Aristotle's view of two parties quarreling for supremacy at this time (that of the aristocrats, led by Miltiades, and that of the people, led by Xanthippus) has been attacked by modern scholars as far too simple, but there is general agreement that party strife at this crucial juncture in Athenian history was bitter and intense.[102] But the case of Miltiades also served to lay down some important ground rules in the relations between Athenian commanders and the assembly.

Our most valuable sources for the Parian episode are Herodotus and Nepos, Nepos presumably following Ephorus, part of whose narrative appears in a fragment of Stephen of Byzantium. Herodotus portrays an extraordinary situation. After the Persians had been beaten back at Marathon, he reports, the already high reputation of Miltiades was still more greatly increased, and when he requested a fleet of seventy ships without even telling the Athenians the object of his expedition, merely saying that he would make them rich if they followed him, they were so carried away that they assented. He then set sail for Paros. The expedition was a disaster. Miltiades returned home fatally wounded; he had lost a good deal of money and a number of men, and he had nothing to show for it. He was summoned to trial in the assembly itself. Because of his wounded thigh, which was beginning to gangrene, he attended the trial on a stretcher and was unable to speak in his own defense. The prosecutor Xanthippus sought the death penalty, but the assembly decided to fine Miltiades fifty talents instead. He died of his wound, however, and according to Herodotus, his son Cimon discharged the debt.[103]

That Paros was not named openly in the Athenian assembly as the object of Miltiades' expedition is confirmed in an odd way by the very different account of Nepos.[104] Nepos seeks wherever possible to place Miltiades' actions in the most favorable light. Miltiades was *innoxius*, characterized by *summa humanitas* and *mira communitas*, the innocent victim of the people's jealous fear.[105] In nearly every respect Nepos' account is the inverse of Herodotus'. Nepos imputes no personal motive to Miltiades' desire to attack Paros, nor does he cite a disgraceful episode as the reason for Miltiades' withdrawal, as does Herodotus, who alleges that the wound sustained while desecrating the sanctuary of Demeter made Miltiades abandon the siege. Nepos attributes Miltiades' departure from Paros to the misapprehension that the Persians were coming to the Parians' aid. He claims that Miltiades was accused of treason (wrongfully, his entire narrative suggests) on the grounds that he had been bribed to withdraw from the city by the Persian king, and that instead of capital punishment Miltiades was fined fifty talents, the cost of the expedition. As he could not pay, Nepos maintains, he was cast into prison, where he died.[106]

Whereas Herodotus suggests that the charge was ἀπάτη and that Miltiades was guilty of it (whatever ἀπάτη is supposed to mean), Nepos claims it was *proditio* and the taking of bribes, that Miltiades was innocent, and that it was fear of tyranny which led the Athenians to fear and condemn him.[107] And yet despite this thorough undercutting of Herodotean tradition, Nepos does not directly contradict one of the central theses of Herodotus' argument — that Miltiades himself conceived the expedition to Paros and that he did not lay his plans before the assembly openly. After Marathon, Nepos writes, the Athenians gave Miltiades seventy ships with which to make war on the islands which had aided the Persians. When Miltiades was unable to bring over Paros to the Athenians by his rhetoric, he laid siege to the island.[108]

Many modern historians have accepted the account of Herodotus in its outlines; some have even accepted his allegation that Miltiades acquired his wound while he was on the verge of violating the sacred precinct of Demeter.[109] But it must be asked whether it is inherently probable that the Parian expedition was conceived by Miltiades alone. It seems far more likely that, as Nepos suggests, the fleet was granted to Miltiades for the purpose of general naval operations. Clearly reasons of security would in any event argue against openly naming Paros as its destination.[110]

The melodramatic account of Herodotus, who maintains that Miltiades took an extraordinary responsibility upon himself, suggests that his conviction was a clear statement by the Athenians to future generations both of private citizens and of military leaders about the dangers of the kind of blank check issued to the victor of Marathon. In the future, the check would not be entirely blank. The terms were spelled out: extraordinary commands and secret commissions were to be undertaken in the understanding that extraordinary (and not very secret) consequences would attend on defeat.

Over one hundred years later, the Athenians impeached two στρατηγοί who had helped the Thebans throw off the yoke of Spartan domination in 379/78. The precise charge is not specified in the sources. The general who remained to stand his trial was condemned to death and executed. The other fled, and his banishment was pronounced.[111]

In 382 the pro-Spartan faction at Thebes had betrayed its acropolis, the Cadmeia, to the Spartan commander Phoebidas. Phoebidas had acted on his own initiative in negotiating with the faction of Leontiades, but the Spartans decided to accept the new situation at Thebes, and a regular garrison was installed.[112] The resulting civil strife sent a number of exiles to Athens, and from there, in the latter part of 379, a plot was formed to recapture the Cadmeia. A handful of Theban exiles led by Pelopidas and Melon returned to their native city and by a ruse accomplished the murder of Leontiades and several others.[113] The conspirators then appealed to their fellow Thebans to rise up in arms and, Xenophon writes, "They also sent horsemen to fetch the troops of the Athenians, who were waiting at the border under two of the στρατηγοί; and these, understanding why they were being summoned, went to the aid of the Thebans."[114]

The Spartan governor, confronted by a superior force, abandoned the Cadmeia under a truce. The Spartans put him to death for this action and sent out an expedition under their king Cleombrotus. Alarmed, the Athenians stationed Chabrias on the road through Eleutherae at the head of a force of peltasts, but Cleombrotus did not wish to provoke a confrontation, and he proceeded to Thebes by an alternate route.[115] Meanwhile three Spartan ambassadors were sent to Athens. There is little doubt that the ambassadors made clear to the Athenians that the price for peace was the repudiation of the two generals who had gone to the Thebans' assistance. And the Athenians, Xenophon writes, "seeing that the Lacedaemonians were going right past Attica and invading Thebes, were so frightened that they brought to trial the two generals who had been involved in the uprising of Melon against Leontiades and his supporters. One they put to death; the other, as he did not remain to stand trial, they exiled."[116]

Diodorus also tells the story of the Athenians' role in the Theban uprising, but it appears that he has confused the assistance rendered to the Thebans by the Athenian generals acting on their own responsibility with an official expedition sent out the following summer, for he claims that the men who assisted the Thebans had been sent by an official decree of the Athenian assembly, and he makes no mention of the trial of the generals.[117] Many scholars who have attempted to reconcile the disparate accounts of Xenophon and Diodorus have accepted the notion of both an official decree sending out the generals and their subsequent trial and condemnation, and such scholars understandably find the Athenians' reversal "shameful."[118] In fact, such a conflation of Diodorus and Xenophon is highly unrealistic. As Burnett points out, it is hard to explain "how, after two generals had been sentenced for following the people's will, others could be found to serve as στρατηγοί, nor how two prominent Athenians could have been destroyed by the pro-Spartan party without causing a whisper of invective in the political speeches of the fourth century."[119] Nor is it likely, as Grote has observed, that the Spartan ambassadors would have felt comfortable visiting at Athens had the Athenians voted an official expedition to aid the Thebans — or that the Athenians would have had the confidence to vote such an expedition in the first place.[120] Most important, however, the coup at Thebes could not possibly have hoped to succeed without the greatest secrecy, and a vote in the Athenian open assembly would have destroyed the plot's chances utterly.

It is likely, I think, that a majority of the Athenians supported the Thebans in their attempt to throw off Spartan domination, and no doubt there were many too who supported the generals who went to the Thebans' assistance — many indeed must have accompanied them. But their support of the Theban exiles was an action for which the Athenians were not really prepared to take the consequences. Neither the appearance of Cleombrotus at the head of an army nor that of the three ambassadors from Sparta was particularly surprising under the circumstances, but these developments drove home to the Athenians the dangers of the step which, however unofficially, they had taken. The condemnation of the generals was no doubt supported not only by the minority who favored Sparta over Thebes but by many pro-Thebans as well who were alarmed by the imminent danger of war with Sparta.[121] Although it strains belief that in condemning the generals the δῆμος ignored a decree of their own authorizing them to move against the Spartans at Thebes, it cannot be denied that the generals appear to have been the victims of inadequate foresight on everyone's part and of an irresponsible, if understandable, approach to policy. The nameless generals of 379/78 had broken the law in acting without instructions from the Athenian assembly. But it seems probable that they had the support of many Athenians, and the source of their condemnation lies not in their technical guilt but rather in an extraordinary need for self-preservation on the part of the entire δῆμος: it arose from the Athenians' fear of war with Sparta.

V THE IMPEACHMENT TRIALS OF THE CORINTHIAN WAR

IN 404 the Spartans defeated the Athenians after a long and exhausting war. The Spartans had won a clear victory; but within less than ten years they found themselves at war with a coalition of Greek states of which Athens was one. The Athenians had deliberated for some time over the proper course to take with regard to Sparta. Naturally many Athenians hesitated to undertake a new war against such a powerful foe. Their reluctance continued into the Corinthian War, and by the time Athens was finally defeated in 387/86, a number of her citizens who had been involved in the conduct of the war had been impeached. Several prominent students of Greek history have assumed that these attacks stemmed from the lower classes, who were frustrated by Athens' failure to win the war. Eduard Meyer sees the attacks as the work of the incompetent and ignorant radicals; Glotz and Cohen view the impeached generals as the victims of "la fureur populaire."[1] I would certainly agree that policy questions and factional considerations played a part in the impeachment trials of the Corinthian War. But I would like to suggest in this chapter that perhaps the thrust of these attacks derived rather from men whom we might call conservatives than from those of radical views.

Until 396, the Athenians' formal attitude to the Spartans was strikingly deferential. At the end of the war Athens had become, perforce, a member of the Peloponnesian league, and she was to prove a far more useful ally than Sparta's traditional associates Corinth and Thebes. Athenian forces served under the harmost Thibron in Asia Minor and fought in Agis' campaign against Elis — a campaign with which the Corinthians and Thebans would have nothing to do.[2] In 397 the Spartan Pharax intercepted three Athenian envoys who were en route to Persia and put them to death.[3] The mission to Persia in itself was probably an indication that a significant body of Athenians was attempting to assess the prospects for Persian support in a war with Sparta, but Athens was not yet in a position to challenge Spartan supremacy, and she evidently made no protest against the action of Pharax.[4] The year following, after a secret meeting with the βουλή, one Demaenetus sailed to Asia in a state trireme to offer assistance to Conon. But the Athenians were ultimately unwilling to take the consequences of this provocative action, and it was the mission of Demaenetus which gave the Oxyrhynchus historian occasion to discuss the political situation in Athens at this time. Demaenetus, the Oxyrhynchus historian tells us,

had privately communicated his plan to the βουλή, so they say, and he went down to the Piraeus with some citizens who had conspired with him and, having launched a ship, sailed off to join Conon. In consequence of this an uproar arose, and the notables of the city — the cultivated class — expressed indignation, pointing out that it would give Athens a bad name if they began a war with the Spartans. The βουλευταί, frightened by the uproar and accepting no responsibility for the undertaking of Demaenetus, convened a meeting of the people. When the people had assembled, the supporters of Thrasybulus, Aesimus, and Anytus came forward and pointed out to the Athenians that they would place the state in considerable danger if they did not absolve the government of all responsibility in this matter. The moderate and well-to-do class in Athens was contented with the present state of affairs, while the masses of the people gave way through fear to their advisers. . . .

Consequently the assembly disavowed the actions of Demaenetus and declared to Milon, the harmost of Aegina, that he could punish Demaenetus as he wished since Demaenetus had acted without official authorization.[5]

The Oxyrhynchus historian here distinguished two groups, the "notables of the city — the cultivated class" (οἱ γνώριμοι καὶ χαρίεντες), also, it seems, called "the moderate and well-to-do-class" (οἱ ἐπιεικεῖς καὶ τὰς οὐσίας ἔχοντες) on the one hand and the masses of the people (οἱ πολλοὶ καὶ δημοτικοί)[6] on the other. The latter group, the historian points out, were led by Epicrates and Cephalus.[7] Most historians of the Corinthian War have perceived three categories of opinion in Athens at this time; for, as Perlman points out, "Since here the dichotomy is not based on the attitude to Sparta only but on social and economic grounds, it may be true to say that Thrasybulus, Aesimus, and Anytus are the leaders of the moderate democrats, while Cephalus and his group are radical democrats," and this conception of a tripartite division has been shared by Cloché, Kagan, Bruce, and Hamilton.[8] The evidence of the Oxyrhynchus historian does seem to suggest the existence of a moderate group led by Thrasybulus, Aesimus, and Anytus, which advocated a cautious approach to foreign policy; a conservative group of well-to-do Athenians who wished to avoid conflict with the Spartans; and a radical group, men chiefly from the lower classes, who were led by Epicrates and Cephalus and who dreamed of a war of *revanche* against the Spartans.

And it was not only at Athens that men thought of going to war with Sparta. The Argives were no friendlier to the Spartans than they had been before. Sparta's old allies Corinth and Thebes had not shared in the fruits of the long Peloponnesian War, and they were bitter. After their victory over the Athenians at Aegospotami, moreover, the Spartans had turned their attention to affairs in mainland Greece; they ravaged Elis, expelled the Messenians from Naupactus and Cephallenia, and intervened in a civil war in Trachinian Heraclia, where they executed several hundred citizens.[9] The conduct of the victorious "liberators of Greece" intensified the hostility felt towards the Spartans in many Greek states, and no doubt it weakened the bond which had traditionally tied Athenian conservatives to Lacedaemon. In 395 the Thebans and the Spartans became involved on opposite sides of a border dispute, the Thebans supporting the Western Locrians and the Spartans championing the Phocians, and the Thebans sent to Athens seeking an alliance. According to Xenophon, the Theban envoys appealed to all parties in Athens, not least the conservatives, whom they implored to cast aside their pro-Lacedaemonian affiliation.[10] Obviously the conservative group at this time was a force to be reckoned with. According to Pausanias, the Athenians sought to persuade the Spartans to submit to arbitration but failed.[11] The Athenians then voted — anonymously, Xenophon claims — to ally with the Thebans.[12] Xenophon's contention that all Athenians — πάντες — voted for the alliance strains belief: is it not more likely that fear of being labeled treasonous led the hard-core conservatives to abstain?

Xenophon's account makes clear, however, that the alliance had wide support among the Athenians, and he traces the Athenians' enthusiasm to the appearance of Persian gold in Greece, sent by Artaxerxes on two separate occasions to induce the various states of Greece to make war on the Spartans.[13] Xenophon is correct in stressing the importance of Artaxerxes' gold; but his thesis that corruption was both its purpose and its result is naive and simplistic. The Athenians did not take money in exchange for an undertaking in which they would otherwise have had no interest; they simply accepted the financial backing which would make possible a war in which both the radicals and the moderates had long held a very considerable interest. When the Thebans came to Athens seeking an alliance, consequently, the Athenians were in a position, with military assistance from other disaffected Greek states and financial assistance from Persia, to undertake a war with the Spartans. And that is precisely what they did.[14]

In 395, then, Athens went to war once more with Sparta. The Athenians' allies included Sparta's disaffected friends, Thebes and Corinth, as well as Sparta's old enemy, Argos; and in addition they had the support of Persia. By the beginning of 392 it became clear to many Spartans that they were unable to defeat decisively the coalition of Greek and Persian forces ranged against them, as they lacked sufficient military strength to wage war both in the Aegean against Conon and the Persians and in mainland Greece against the allied Greek states. Many among the allies were also hesitant to continue the war, influenced perhaps by the devastating effect of the long deadlock which had protracted the Peloponnesian War to such an untoward length. Consequently in 392 more than one attempt to conclude peace was made.[15]

It is clear that two peace conferences took place about this time. One, at Sardis, was sponsored by the Spartan Antalcidas and is described by Xenophon.[16] The other took place at Sparta, and we know about it from the speech *On the Peace* made afterwards by Andocides, one of the envoys sent by Athens. Since Xenophon makes no mention of this conference and Andocides makes no reference to the conference at Sardis, the sequence of the two conferences remains unclear, the nature of the terms discussed at each is uncertain, and we do not know who instigated the conference at Sparta. In short, it does not seem possible to determine the precise course of events with any degree of conviction.[17] It is against this muddy background that we must set the following fragment of Didymus:

> . . . in regard to the former restoration some say that he [Demosthenes] is discussing the peace which came down in the time of Antialcidas [*sic*] the Spartan, but this, in my opinion at any rate, is not correct; for not only did the Athenians not accept the peace, but, on the contrary, they rejected it vehemently, judging it an act unholy and illegal for them, as Philochorus says in these words, having set down as the archon Philocles of Anaphlystus, "and the peace which the King sent down in the time of Antialcidas, the Athenians rejected, since it was written in it that the Greeks who dwelt in Asia were all to belong to the King; and, moreover, on the motion of Callistratus, they exiled the ambassadors who had come to terms in Sparta, and who did not stay for their trials, namely Epicrates of Cephisia, Andocides of Cydathenaeum, Cratinus of Sphettus, and Eubulides of Eleusis."[18]

The argument to Andocides' speech *On the Peace* provides some additional information: when the war had become extremely burdensome, we are told, the Athenians sent πρέσβεις . . . αὐτοκράτορες to the Spartans, of whom Andocides was one. These ambassadors took forty days to deliberate with the assembly. According to the Hypothesis, Philochorus reports that the peace fell through when the ambassadors, in particular Andocides, failed to persuade the Athenians.[19] According to Demosthenes, the attack on the ambassadors was sweeping and included the whole range of possible ambassadorial offenses — disobeying instructions, making untruthful reports to the assembly, sending untruthful dispatches, bearing false witness against allies, and taking bribes.[20]

Understandably, many students of Greek history have been disturbed by the apparent insufficiency of the motive for prosecuting the ambassadors. Recently, indeed, more than one scholar has sought instead to place the trial in the context of the negotiations of 387/86.[21] The majority of scholars, however, accept a date of 392/91 and have concluded that Andocides and his colleagues must have been the victims of the impetuous Athenian radicals and were impeached for their efforts to induce the Athenians to accept the Spartans' terms.[22]

It is difficult to see, however, why the aggressive war party should have prosecuted the ambassadors. This party had wanted not peace, but war; what they got was not peace but war. The four men had been sent off with plentipotentiary powers for the conclusion of peace. They might well have signed an agreement that would have bound the Athenians. They did not do so. The radical war party was not the group with the grievance. The aggrieved party was surely the conservatives. It was they who were thwarted after all by the ambassadors' failure to make use of their plenipotentiary powers; it was they who had not gotten what they wanted. Had the ambassadors signed a peace at Sparta, the Athenian war party would have been committed to upholding such a peace; by signing such an agreement, the ambassadors could have forced the hand of the Athenians at home. There is no reason to imagine that the ambassadors were impeached because they tried to make peace. It makes far more sense to conclude that they were impeached because they failed to do so, and the evidence supports this contention.

As we have seen, it is not clear precisely who called the peace conference at Sparta. Whoever took the first step, though, it is clear from the argument to Andocides' speech that a substantial body of Athenians was interested in peace at the time of the conference at Sparta. The course of events seems clear. First, a majority of Athenians was seriously enough interested in peace to dispatch an embassy to Sparta. Second, a majority of the Athenians voted to reject the peace. Third, an indictment was laid against the ambassadors, who then fled Athens. Clearly, the coalition against the ambassadors was strong enough to induce them to choose exile rather than risk trial.

The reason for this sequence of events is not hard to understand. It was probably shortly before the peace conference at Sparta that the tide of war began to shift against the Athenians and their allies. Probably it was the summer of 392 when the Corinthian oligarchs opened the Long Walls to the Spartans, who then gained possession of Lechaeum.[23] Under Herippidas, moreover, the Spartans had regained mastery of the Gulf of Corinth.[24] By autumn the Spartans held a good deal of the Corinthiad — Lechaeum, Sidus, Crommyum, and Epieicea — and had pulled down the Long Walls between Corinth and Lechaeum. The Spartans now had free access by land into Attica. Nor were the allies' fortunes in the east prospering, for the pro-Spartan Tiribazus was now satrap of Lydia and had imprisoned Conon.[25] It is not surprising that a majority of Athenians should have voted to send an embassy to negotiate with the Spartans. Nor is it surprising that Epicrates himself, who had been prominent in supporting the war, was chosen to serve on the embassy; it was not uncommon at Athens to maintain political balance in an embassy seeking peace and to send a member of the current war party to serve as a check on the others.[26] Andocides had once had oligarchical connections, but these were not recent. It may be significant that Agyrrhius was one of the men who had brought the accusation against him concerning the Mysteries.[27] About the political programs or connections of Eubulides and Cratinus, the other members of the embassy, we know nothing. Altogether the political composition of the embassy seems to have been mixed.

The speech of Andocides is the principal source for the terms offered by the Spartans. It does not seem possible to determine precisely what these were. Andocides' speech makes clear that the fundamental conditions of the peace were first, of course, that the alliance against Sparta should be dissolved and, second, that the principle of autonomy should be recognized, with the exception of the Theban hegemony over Boeotia and Athenian control of Lemnos, Imbros, and Scyros. Andocides does not mention the abandonment of the Ionian Greeks to the Persians. That this indeed formed part of the peace agreement is suggested, however, by the fragment of Philochorus cited above, where he gives this as the Athenians' reasons for rejecting peace in 392/91. It is possible that Philochorus is confusing the terms discussed at Sparta with those discussed at Sardis (all the more since he speaks of the Athenians rejecting the peace "which the king sent down" because of their reluctance to abandon the Ionians). But it is also possible that Andocides may for obvious reasons have omitted this condition from a speech which was, after all, not a report but rather an oration in favor of accepting the peace: the Athenians would know the facts from other sources, including perhaps the ambassadors' official report to the assembly.

The Athenians voted to reject the peace. It is probable that we should connect their rejection with another contemporary event: the replacement by Artaxerxes of the pro-Spartan Tiribazus with the pro-Athenian Struthas as satrap at Sardis.[28] It is easy to understand how the return of Persian support might have swung a majority of the Athenians to vote to continue the war. Shortly afterwards Andocides, Epicrates, Eubulides, and Cratinus were impeached on the motion of Callistratus.[29] All four left Athens. No doubt they could expect some votes against them from those who had been appalled by Andocides' exhortation to peace, in which he suggested to the Athenians

that they really had little choice and should be grateful that
they were not being offered worse terms. In particular, Epicrates, if he also encouraged the peace, might expect hostility
from Cephalus and his other associates among the radicals,
who might have felt singularly betrayed. But the party with the
principal grievance was of course the conservatives, who had
wanted peace and had, through the extreme caution of the
ambassadors, gotten war instead.

Much of Andocides' speech, naturally, addresses itself to
the war party, for these are the men who must be convinced.
In a striking passage, however, Andocides speaks of the grievances of the peace party:

> There are those of you who are eager to see this peace con-
> cluded as quickly as possible. They say that the forty days
> during which you may consider things are unnecessary and that
> we have done wrong to obtain them for you; for they say that
> the whole point of our having been sent us plenipotentiaries
> was so that we would not have to come back to consult with
> you. Our eagerness to consolidate our position they call ner-
> vousness, and they say that nobody has ever saved the Athe-
> nian δῆμος by open persuasion and that one can only do some
> good by secret or disguised tactics.[30]

In part, of course, this statement of Andocides is a rhetorical
device designed to draw the sympathy of the war party to the
ambassadors by pointing out that they too are under attack by
the peace party. But there is no reason to believe that Andocides is not telling the truth, and the name of Callistratus
strongly suggests that indeed the thrust of the attack on the
ambassadors came from the men to whose dissatisfaction
Andocides was addressing himself in this passage.

To be sure, there is no absolute necessity that the policy of
Callistratus in 392/91 should have been the same cautious, pro-
Spartan policy which he was to advocate throughout the 370s.
On the other hand, the notion of Callistratus' leading a con-
servative attack on the ambassadors accords far better with his
later policy than does the idea of Callistratus' heading the

radical war party. It is somewhat disquieting to envision in the camp of the hawks of 392/91 the man the use of whose name was sufficient to gain audience with the pro-Spartan Leontiades at Thebes in 379, who would take the lead in negotiating peace between Athens and Sparta in both 375/74 and 371, and who would lead the attack on the pro-Theban Timotheus in 373.[31] It is interesting to note too that Demosthenes mentions Callistratus' willingness to let his uncle Agyrrhius languish in prison for several years after the end of the Corinthian War when he had been convicted of malfeasance in office.[32] Callistratus' desertion of Agyrrhius is far more comprehensible if in fact the two men stood at opposite ends of the political spectrum. Altogether it makes most sense to see the ambassadors of 392/91 as victims of a concerted attack, one mounted in all probability by the conservative peace party, whose antipathy Andocides makes clear in his speech, but fostered no doubt by the radicals, who had been alienated by the alacrity of Andocides and, it seems, his colleagues in deciding that peace was the best course for the Athenians.

Any Athenians who hoped that the replacement of Tiribazus with Struthas would lead to a swift Athenian victory in the war were disappointed. The war continued. In the winter of 390/89 the Spartan admiral Eteonicus began to incite the Aeginetans to acts of piracy against Athenian shipping. Consequently in the spring of 389 Pamphilus, a στρατηγός for 390/89 whose term had just been renewed at the March elections, was dispatched to Aegina with ten triremes and a force of hoplites. When he arrived he built a fortress from which he could besiege the city of Aegina. Teleutias, however, the brother of the Spartan king Agesilaus, forced the fleet to withdraw, and the Spartan commander Gorgopas managed to besiege the Athenians themselves in their own citadel. Finally, in the fifth month following the departure of Pamphilus, the Athenians were compelled to send out a rescue force to evacuate him and his men. The Aeginetans promptly returned to their old habits, and the Athenians were forced to send out still another expedition in the hope of putting a stop to the piracy.[33] In the fall or winter of 389/88 Pamphilus was deposed and tried on a charge of κλοπή. He was convicted and fined five talents. As he could not pay, his property was confiscated.[34]

Pamphilus' performance in Aegina was hardly a credit to the Athenian armed forces, but it is impossible to judge from the sparse account of Xenophon how far Pamphilus himself was responsible for the embarrassment in which his expedition culminated. Nor is it possible to decide the question of his guilt on the charge of κλοπή. What little we know about Pamphilus, however, suggests that he was a radical democrat. According to the scholiast on Aristophanes' *Plutus*, Pamphilus was a moneylender and a demagogue and was suspected of sycophancy.[35] Without accepting the pejorative connotations of the scholiast's remarks, we may still reasonably infer that Pamphilus' political affiliations were with the radical democrats. It is probably significant too that Pamphilus had a son and a grandson each named Boeotus, a most uncommon name at Athens.[36] Theban sympathies in the early fourth century point to a radical.[37] If our interpretation of the role of the conservatives in the impeachment of the ambassadors in 391 is correct, then Pamphilus' political orientation may well explain the attack on him. As we have seen, the heavy-handedness which the victorious Spartans had demonstrated throughout the Greek world at the end of the Peloponnesian War had weakened the traditional bond which had tied Athenian conservatives to the Lacedaemonians. But the impulse to war had not, of course, originated with these conservatives, and when the peace of 392/91 was rejected by the majority of Athenians and the war dragged on with no end in sight, naturally most of the blame fell on the heads of the radicals. Pamphilus was only one in a long string of generals with radical connections who found himself under fire at home. It is likely that the attack on these generals came at least in part from the conservatives, all the more since around the time of the peace negotiations of 392/91 — whether before or after, we do not know — an εἰσφορά was passed in order to finance the war, and, predictably, the burden of this tax fell chiefly on the rich.[38]

It was probably at about the same time that Conon's friends Nicophemus and Aristophanes were put to death at Athens. Lysias seems to suggest that they were executed without trial: ἄκριτοι ἀπέθανον, he writes.[39] This would certainly be an astonishing phenomenon if true, and one which makes the end of the victors of Arginusae look quite tame, although it strains the imagination a good deal.[40] The precise charge against the two men is unknown, but the Athenians' dissatisfaction with them is not entirely incomprehensible.

Nicophemus, a family friend of Conon, had served with Conon in Asia shortly before the battle of Cnidus and may have shared with Conon some of the credit and glory for that battle.[41] Shortly afterwards he was installed by Conon as governor of Cythera after Conon had seized that island; then he evidently returned to Cyprus, where, like Conon, he had a wife and child.[42] Meanwhile Nicophemus' son Aristophanes had been sent by Conon to Sicily in order to detach Dionysius of Syracuse from his friendship with the Spartans.[43] Our principal source for the careers of Nicophemus and Aristophanes is a speech of Lysias in which they are favorably presented, and we need not place too much value on Lysias' praise of Aristophanes for having dissuaded Dionysius of Syracuse from sending some ships he had been planning to dispatch to the aid of the Spartans; for in fact Dionysius remained an ally of the Spartans and was indeed instrumental in the campaign of Antalcidas in the Hellespont which brought the war to a close. Following his dubious performance in Sicily, Aristophanes became involved in the disastrous campaign by which the Athenians attempted to aid Evagoras, though he was fighting against their ally Artaxerxes, and ended by losing all their ships to the Spartan navy.[44] Whether Aristophanes had any role in the naval encounter by which the ships were lost we do not know; according to Lysias he simply put up most of the funds for the ships and went to Cyprus as an ambassador.

It is likely that both Aristophanes' failure in Sicily and his advocacy of the campaign to assist Evagoras — a campaign badly conceived and badly executed — contributed to the sentiment against him, though why he and his father should immediately afterwards have been put to death is not clear. Shortly after the campaign to aid Evagoras, the pro-Athenian Struthas was replaced with the pro-Spartan Tiribazus as satrap of Lydia.[45] The action of the Athenians may have been taken in anger against one of the backers of that expedition; that Aristophanes' father shared his fate suggests that he too was involved in the campaign. It may be significant that at around the same time Philocrates, commander of the squadron of ten ships seized while en route to Evagoras, was impeached ostensibly in connection with the attack on Thrasybulus and Ergocles.[46] Nicophemus and his son may also have suffered because of their affiliation with Conon.[47] Clearly we cannot say just what was in the minds of the Athenians. But it is not likely to be a coincidence that each one of the men who were impeached toward the end of the Corinthian War seems to have had connections with a particular political faction — that of the radical war party.

The dangers of Athenian naval imperialism had been driven home when their expedition to aid Evagoras had cost them Persian support. It is not likely that all the hostility to Nicophemus and Aristophanes derived from the frustrated hawks who had favored the expedition in the first place; surely some derived from the conservatives who had doubtless opposed the campaign from the start.

Continued Persian support must now have seemed unlikely to the Athenians, for in the early months of 389 they had sent Thrasybulus of Steiria to Asia at the head of a substantial force.[48] With him went Ergocles, an old associate from the days when they had fought together on the side of the democrats in 403.[49] The expedition did not end well. Thrasybulus was killed, and in the summer or fall of 388 Ergocles was tried on several counts — probably δωροδοκία, κλοπή, and προδοσία. He was condemned and executed. After his death, his property was confiscated by the state.[50]

Thrasybulus had been expected to stop first at Rhodes; presumably he had reason to believe that pro-Athenian elements were firmly in control there, however, for he decided that control of the grain route from the Black Sea was Athens' first priority, and he altered his course accordingly. In the north he made many stops. He was successful at Thasos, where the inhabitants overthrew their Spartan governor, and he was warmly received at Samothrace, Tenedos, and Byzantium. His attempt to conquer Lesbos met with only partial success, and from there he continued south, with the idea in mind of attending at last to Rhodes, his original destination.[51] In the course of his στρατηγία Thrasybulus seems to have reinstated the εἰκοστή, the five-percent tax that had been levied during the Decelean war, in the cities he had won over.[52] On his journey to Rhodes he also augmented this income by enforced contributions from the coastal cities of Asia Minor. Some of these contributions were collected by means of pillage and murder — whether at Thrasybulus' instigation or through the uncondoned excesses of his soldiers is not clear.[53]

At the March elections in 388 the terms of Thrasybulus and Ergocles were not renewed. Before their terms expired that summer they received a summons to return home to give an accounting of the funds they had collected, and perhaps to answer charges of general misconduct as well.[54] It is not known whether the Athenians also deposed them by ἀποχειροτονία. Possibly they did not bother, since the end of their terms was so close. But the pointed request that they return home to render an accounting shows that Thrasybulus and Ergocles were under suspicion (and it strongly suggests too that there were some generals who did not automatically return home to render their accounts when their terms had expired).

But Thrasybulus and Ergocles did not return. According to Lysias, they remained in Asia because Ergocles was at work trying to persuade Thrasybulus to declare himself in open rebellion from the Athenians, to marry the daughter of the Thracian prince Seuthes, and to seize Byzantium.[55] These projects, however, came to nothing, for Thrasybulus was soon murdered in his tent by the inhabitants of Aspendus in retaliation for the excesses which his soldiers had perpetrated there.[56] Ergocles then returned to Athens. There he was tried, convicted, and executed.[57]

The principal speeches delivered at Ergocles' trial are not extant. All that remains is one supplementary speech for the prosecution composed by Lysias.[58] In it Lysias appeals to the jury to defend the city against lawlessness and licentiousness in its commanders by bringing in a verdict of guilty. The earlier speeches had dealt with the particulars of the charge against Ergocles; although Lysias alleges that it was Ergocles who urged Thrasybulus to ignore the summons to return home, fundamentally his speech is an attack on the corruption of the Asian commanders as a whole.[59] Ergocles clearly was tried as the representative of the Asian expedition — and as the longtime associate of Thrasybulus.

The last months of Thrasybulus' life pose a considerable embarrassment to his champions both ancient and modern. Xenophon tries to portray Thrasybulus as an innocent victim of his soldiers' spontaneous abuses of the Aspendians, but his frank account of Thrasybulus' fund-raising cruise along the Asian coast casts doubt on this interpretation. By Xenophon's own admission — appearing in the same paragraph in which Thrasybulus' death is recounted — ''Thrasybulus brought over some of the cities, and those which he could not bring over he plundered to collect money for his men; meanwhile he was eager to get to Rhodes. But to strengthen his army yet further he collected money from various cities and came to Aspendus. . . .''[60] Grote and Bury have both attempted to refute suspicions that Thrasybulus was not in fact a perfect gentleman to the last on the grounds that such suspicions rest only on the insinuations of the prosecutor who delivered Lysias' speech against Ergocles.[61] This is not true. In point of fact, the speech of Lysias probably distorts the truth to Thrasybulus' advantage, for Lysias tries to throw as much as possible of the blame for wrongs committed in Asia onto Ergocles himself. The truth is that Thrasybulus' behavior in Asia had laid him open to a variety of complaints. Although Xenophon does not say so specifically, it certainly seems that

Thrasybulus' projected expedition to Rhodes had been agreed upon at home; thus his decision to take on himself the authority to alter that strategy was risky — and his unofficial raids along the coast, however necessary from a financial point of view, were politically dangerous. Finally, Thrasybulus' refusal to return home with his accounts was a clear violation of the law.

It is not difficult to understand Thrasybulus' behavior. Convinced of the best course to follow in Asia, he felt secure in acting on his own authority in advancing Athenian imperial interests and did not anticipate an attack by his enemies at home. Evidently genuine financial need prompted his lawless fund-raising expedition along the coast.[62] His refusal to obey the summons to return home strongly suggests that he saw in that summons the hand of his personal enemies — Agyrrhius, among others, as several scholars have imagined, who was soon sent out to replace him — and of those who opposed his imperial policy.[63] The speech of Lysias gives indirect support to this notion, for he puts into the mouth of Ergocles just such ideas: Ergocles, he claims, "advised Thrasybulus to occupy Byzantium, keep the ships and marry Seuthes' daughter: 'in this way,' he told him, 'you will put a stop to their slander-mongering; for you will make them stop sitting around plotting against you and your friends and begin to be afraid for themselves.'"[64] I am inclined to accept Accame's interpretation of Thrasybulus' actions following his summons to return home. Accame suggests that Thrasybulus saw that an attack was being launched by his political enemies, and that his political position had been made precarious by the fact that his forays along the Asian coast had resulted in many irregularities in his accounts, which might furnish grounds for an accusation against him. Consequently, Accame maintains, he decided to follow the precedent of Conon after Aegospotami and not to return until he had scored some striking success for Athens, and for his policy, on his own.[65]

Thrasybulus' situation was also comparable to that of Demosthenes in 426. Demosthenes had been sent to support the Acarnanians in joint maneuvers with Athens' western allies.

Without any authorization from the government at home, he had acceded to the suggestion of the Messenians at Naupactus that he attack Aetolia. The Corcyraeans and Acarnanians would have nothing to do with the expedition. The Aetolian campaign ended in a horrible rout. Demosthenes, Thucydides reports, did not come home until he had redeemed his reputation by more auspicious campaigns, for "he feared the anger of the Athenians after what had happened."[66] Thrasybulus, however, did not live to redeem his reputation, and when the attack on him and his associates reached the trial stage at Athens, it focused on Ergocles.

The motives for the attack on Thrasybulus were extremely complex. Xenophon suggests that he supported in the assembly the alliance with Thebes which had led to the outbreak of the war; Xenophon may have been exaggerating when he maintained that the alliance was passed without a single dissenting voice, but clearly entrance into the war had wide support at that moment.[67] As we have seen, however, a large body of Athenians was sufficiently interested in peace in 392/91 to send plenipotentiaries to Sparta, and some, Andocides makes clear, were resentful that the ambassadors did not conclude a peace at once. By 388 many Athenians from all social and economic groups had lost patience with the war. Athens' economic situation had deteriorated gravely. According to Lysias, some of the most traditional ancient sacrificial rites had to be omitted through lack of funds, and the docks and walls could not even be kept up.[68] Property taxes were required to pay for the war. Charges that a defendant had been enriched by the war that was impoverishing the citizenry could be counted on to arouse strong feelings in the courtroom.[69] It was clear, moreover, that the war was not going well. If anyone was on the brink of victory, it was the Spartans; for during the early months of 388 the Persian king had once more replaced Struthas with Tiribazus. No doubt the campaigns of Thrasybulus had something to do with the king's decision: and the Spartans had responded to this diplomatic signal by appointing as navarch for 388/87 Antalcidas, who had of course taken the lead in the abortive peace negotiations of 392/91.[70] The Athenians correctly foresaw the peace of 387. In part, the attack on Thrasybulus was emotional in its origin and derived from resentment against him for having helped to persuade the Athenians to go to war and for leading an aggressive campaign in Asia Minor which alienated Artaxerxes; certainly it is ironic that the plundering and taxation abroad by which he had hoped to ease the burdens of the Athenians at home should have provided the matter for the attack.

The hostility to Thrasybulus, however, went much deeper than this. For Thrasybulus occupied an ambiguous position at Athens. As we have seen, after the Peloponnesian war, the Oxyrhynchus historian suggests, there were three parties at Athens. Thrasybulus, along with Aesimus and Anytus, led the moderate party. This party advocated a cautious approach to foreign policy and opposed itself on the one hand to the conservatives, well-to-do men who preferred to preserve the *status quo* by shunning the unpleasantness of conflict with Sparta, and to the radicals on the other, men from the lower classes on the whole who desired a war of *revanche* against the Spartans. The passage of time, however, made clear that the reservations of the moderates arose in large measure from a gloomy assessment of Athens' economic situation. As the economic situation improved, the distinction between moderates and radicals gradually disappeared and the moderates came increasingly to support the idea of fighting Sparta. By 389 the distinction between moderates and radicals was so defunct that Thrasybulus was a logical choice as a commander for the imperialist expedition to Asia, and Curtius can refer to him at this time as the "leader of the war party."[71] Thrasybulus, then, a man of good family and a man of means — a man who had once been a friend of Alcibiades, and who had once stood so far from the radical democrats that the Thirty had considered offering him a position in their cabal — found himself in odd company as the leader of the aggressive, imperialist war party.

The consequences of this anomaly were two. First, the men of property saw in him a renegade, and when the war dragged on and became an increasing burden, they felt that he had

singularly betrayed them.[72] The lower classes, however, suspected him of aristocratic, oligarchic, and even tyrannical
inclinations — and these suspicions were of course greatly
heightened by his refusal to return home. Lysias does his best
to play on these fears when he warns the Athenian jurors that
"there is one thing you can count on: any man who, in these
straits you are in, would betray your cities or steal your money
or accept bribes — a man like this will surrender your walls
and your ships to the enemy, and will replace democracy with
oligarchy."[73] In Aristophanes' *Plutus*, Penury even accuses
the youth Chremylus of comparing Thrasybulus with Dionysius, the tyrant of Syracuse.[74] Like Theramenes, Thrasybulus
won enemies at both extremes of the political spectrum through
his attempts to adapt his policy to changing circumstances.
Thrasybulus, then, had through his aggressive independence in
Asia not only alienated Artaxerxes but brought to the surface
the latent hostility of two large groups of Athenians as well. By
his death they were disappointed of their retribution — but not
entirely, for their wrath descended on the head of Ergocles. It
descended too on that of the trierarch Philocrates, a political
associate of Ergocles who had served on the Asian expedition
and was accused after Ergocles' death of having embezzled
thirty talents from the estate of his late commander.[75] The
verdict in his case is unknown to us. No doubt the Athenians'
irritation was aggravated by the fact that Philocrates had commanded the ill-fated expedition to assist Evagoras.[76]

Soon afterwards, both Thrasybulus of Collytus and a certain
Dionysius were brought into court. Dionysius was condemned
to death or a stiff fine for treason in Thrace.[77] Thrasybulus was
tried on a charge connected with the betrayal of ships, and
perhaps also for charging a fee of thirty minae to Athenian
prisoners of war as a condition for arranging their release. The
verdict in the trial or trials of Thrasybulus is unknown.[78] Probably the trials of Thrasybulus and Dionysius were the product
of the fiasco in the Hellespont in the spring of 387, when Antalcidas succeeded in cutting off the Athenians' grain supply by
eluding the fleet commanded by four generals, of whom one

was named Dionysius, and capturing a squadron of eight ships commanded by Thrasybulus of Collytus.

In the spring of 387 Antalcidas, having been assured the support of the Persians through the satrap Tiribazus, determined to bring the war to a close by cutting Athens off from the Black Sea grain supply on which she was so profoundly dependent. Although the Athenians at that time had the entire passage from the Black Sea to the Aegean under their firm control, Antalcidas' project was a success.[79] When Antalcidas arrived on the coast in the spring, the Bosporus was guarded by Iphicrates, who was occupying Byzantium and Chalcedon with eight ships. Thrasybulus of Collytus was stationed at the western entrance to the Hellespont with another eight ships. The bulk of the fleet was operating in the Hellespont and the Sea of Marmara, under the command of Demaenetus, Dionysius, Leontichus, and Phanias, and this division, amounting to thirty-two ships, put the twenty-five ships of Antalcidas under a virtual blockade at Abydos. Antalcidas had been assured the support of Tiribazus' ships from Ionia and of Dionysius of Syracuse, who had sent him twenty ships, but with the Athenian force guarding him there was no way to combine the Spartan fleet with the auxiliary ships. Consequently Antalcidas spread the report that his assistance had been requested at Chalcedon, and he set sail in that direction, pursued, of course, by the Athenian fleet. At Percote, however, he lay at anchor in a concealed spot and watched the Athenians continue their eager pursuit in the direction of the Bosporus. When they were safely past he turned swiftly back to the Hellespont. There he encountered Thrasybulus' eight ships in the narrows; for Thrasybulus, not realizing that the fleet was no longer at Abydos, had determined to join them before the ships of Dionysius arrived to threaten his small squadron. Naturally he had assumed that the narrows were secure from the ships of Antalcidas. Once more Antalcidas concealed his ships until the Athenians had sailed by. Then he set his fastest ships to work overtaking the lead Athenian ships, ignoring the slower ones, on the premise that if the swifter Athenian ships were taken, the slower ones would lose heart; and that is precisely what happened. By this coup, Antalcidas was enabled to join his fleet with those of the Syracusans and the Persian ships, swelling its number to eighty ships, and with this force he was able to blockade the remainder of the Athenian fleet in the Bosporus. The Black Sea grain route was closed to the Athenians. The war was over.[80]

It is not surprising that the men of Athens were bitter against some of the commanders of this expedition — particularly so since the στρατηγοί had evidently been warned of Antalcidas' plan to double back to Abydos; for a certain Phanocritus of Parium had somehow gotten wind of Antalcidas' design and had reported it to them, as we know from an inscription passed by the Athenians in Phanocritus' honor.[81] In view of Phanocritus' story, the charge of treason against Dionysius is comprehensible, although it is impossible, of course, to know whether he was in fact guilty. One is reminded of the reckless — or treasonous — way in which the generals at Aegospotami disregarded the advice of Alcibiades.[82] As we know nothing whatsoever about Dionysius, it is not possible to judge what other factors may have contributed to the Athenians' dissatisfaction with him. It is possible that his colleagues Demaenetus, Leontichus, and Phanias were tried as well; there is no record of any of them serving subsequently as στρατηγοί.

The grounds for the accusation against Thrasybulus of Collytus, who led the squadron of eight taken by the narrows, are less clear and probably more complicated. Demosthenes lists Thrasybulus along with Agyrrhius as one of those who took a strong stand for the democrats against the Thirty in 403 — a statement which would be pointless if there were not some truth to it. Probably these democratic traditions contributed to Thrasybulus' difficulties; for if, as I have suggested, the attacks of these years can be traced in no small measure to the conservatives, his strong stand with Thrasybulus of Steiria and the democrats in 403 must have aggravated the feeling against him.

Finally, Agyrrhius was charged following his στρατηγία of 388/87 with having misappropriated state funds. He was con-

victed and, as he did not have the missing funds in his possession and was unable to pay his debt to the state, spent some
time in prison as public debtor.[83]

The source for Agyrrhius' trial is Demosthenes. As we have
seen, Demosthenes claims, perhaps by way of exaggeration,
that Agyrrhius languished "for many years" in prison, but
unfortunately he does not tell us which years these were. As
we know of no public position held by Agyrrhius after his
στρατηγία, it seems a reasonable inference that he was accused of mismanaging or embezzling state funds while he was
στρατηγός. Presumably, then, his trial took place not long
after the end of the Corinthian War.

Naturally, nothing is known about Agyrrhius' accounts for
388/87. It is possible that the attack on Agyrrhius had some
connection with his conduct of the war in Asia. Perhaps the
fact that we hear nothing of him after his arrival in the vicinity
of Asia Minor in the summer of 388 indicates that he accomplished nothing of note. Perhaps one factor in the accusation
against him was the hostility of the partisans of Thrasybulus of
Steiria, who may have seen the rivalry between Thrasybulus
and Agyrrhius as one source of Thrasybulus' summons to return home and sought retribution for the cloud under which
Thrasybulus had ended his life.[84] But it is likely that the principal motive for the attack on Agyrrhius derived from his
prominent position in the radical democratic faction.

It was Agyrrhius after all who had instituted pay for attend-
ance at the assembly, and the ridicule which Aristophanes
heaps on the μισθὸς ἐκκλησιαστικός may show how it was
received in conservative circles. It was Agyrrhius too who
raised the amount to three obols after it had gone up from one
to two, and who restored the θεωρικόν as well.[85] Before that,
he had fought, like Thrasybulus of Steiria, Thrasybulus of Collytus, and Ergocles, for the men of the Piraeus in 403.[86] Demosthenes includes Agyrrhius and Thrasybulus of Collytus in
a list of men whom the Athenians convicted of wrongdoing
despite their strong democratic backgrounds; but he has
missed — or perverted — the point.[87] This was precisely the

sort of political background which invited an attack in the courts at the end of the Corinthian War.

In the political backgrounds of the men impeached in connection with their conduct during the Corinthian War a clear pattern is visible. Only one man, Andocides, is known to have had connections with the oligarchs, and these were not recent. Only one man, Thrasybulus of Steiria, is known to have had connections with the moderates; and by the time of the attack on him, he had come to lead the aggressive war party. Thrasybulus had fought with the democrats in 403 along with Ergocles, Thrasybulus of Collytus, and Agyrrhius. Definitely Epicrates and almost certainly Pamphilus and Ergocles' associate Philocrates belong in the radical camp; Nicophemus and Aristophanes were political allies of Conon and espoused an aggressive Athenian naval policy. Of twelve prominent men impeached in the course of the Corinthian War, fully nine can be placed in the radical camp; and it is possible, of course, that the names of Cratinus and Eubulides should be added to the list.

It would be odd indeed if the thrust of these attacks derived entirely from the radicals. It was, after all, their war, conducted by their leaders. It was not the war of the conservatives, who had sought to end the hostilities in 392/91 and had, I have suggested, impeached the envoys who failed to do so. There is no reason to believe that the men who were impeached during the course of the Corinthian War were simply the victims, in the words of Glotz and Cohen, of "la fureur populaire." Rather, the political background of the victims suggests that the attacks on them derived in large measure from the conservatives.

VI GUILT AND INADEQUACY

POLICY questions and factional considerations were not, of course, the only issues involved in Athenian impeachment trials. The Athenians sometimes had reason to be dissatisfied with an official's performance. The evidence points, I think, to several cases in which Athenian officials seem to have broken the law. As we have seen, it appears that Xenophon, Hestiodorus, and Phanomachus broke the law when they negotiated with the surrendered Potidaeans without consulting the Athenian assembly; the anonymous pro-Theban generals of 379/78 probably acted without authorization when they assisted in the liberation of the Cadmeia from Spartan control; and Aeschines had disobeyed his instructions on the embassy to Philip in 346. In addition, the law seems to have been broken by the ambassadors of 411/10 and by the στρατηγός Timomachus in 360.

In 411/10 the Board of Generals impeached Antiphon, Archeptolemus, and Onomacles for treason in connection with their peace embassy to Sparta.[1] We happen to know a good deal about the format of this trial from a decree preserved by Caecilius:

Voted by the βουλή on the twenty-first day of the prytany. Demonicus of Alopece was secretary, Philostratus of Pallene was president. Andron moved concerning the men whom the generals denounce for acting to the detriment of the state while on embassy to Sparta and for sailing from the camp on an enemy ship and for going by land through Decelea, to wit, Archeptolemus, Onomacles, and Antiphon, that they be arrested and handed over to the court for trial. And the στρατηγοί with those members of the βουλή whom they shall coopt up to the number of ten, must produce them in court for the trial. And the θεσμοθέται shall summon them tomorrow, and when the summonses have been returned to the court, the θεσμοθέται shall propose that the chosen συνήγοροι and the στρατηγοί and anyone else who wishes shall accuse them of treason; and whoever is convicted shall be treated in accordance with the law which exists concerning traitors.

Caecilius goes on:

Archeptolemus, son of Hippodamus, of Agryle, and Antiphon, son of Sophilus, of Rhamnus, both being present, were found guilty. They were sentenced to be handed over to the eleven [for execution] and to have their belongings confiscated and ten percent thereof given to the goddess. Their houses were to be torn down and boundary-stones set up on their sites inscribed "of Archeptolemus and Antiphon the two traitors." The two demarchs were to make a declaration of their property. It was forbidden to bury them in Athens or any place over which the Athenians ruled; and their descendants, legitimate and illegitimate, were disfranchised; and anyone who adopted any of their descendants would be disfranchised as well; and this was all to be inscribed on a bronze tablet which was to be set up in the same place as the decrees about Phrynichus.[2]

Theramenes took the leading role in the prosecution. Antiphon and Archeptolemus were executed, and the other provisions of the decree were carried out against their families and property.[3] Onomacles did not remain at Athens to stand his trial, and we do not know the verdict in his case. Xenophon lists an Onomacles among the Thirty Tyrants of 404; very possibly this was the same man.[4]

There is little room for doubt concerning the motivation for the impeachment of the envoys. In the summer of 411, the oligarchy of the Four Hundred ruled Athens. The position of the Four Hundred, however, was not what the Athenian oligarchs, led by Antiphon, Peisander, and Phrynichus, had hoped it would be. A democratic government persisted at Samos, where the Athenian fleet was stationed; the cooperation of Persia promised by Alcibiades had not materialized; and consequently the moderate wing of the Four Hundred, led by Theramenes and Aristocrates, had begun to pressure the extreme oligarchs to establish, as promised, the more broadly based government of the Five Thousand.[5] Fearing for their position and for their lives, the oligarchs sent several embassies to Sparta seeking peace. The first of these embassies never arrived, for the crew of the state trireme *Paralos* intercepted their mission; but a second embassy arrived safely.[6] This second embassy was composed of twelve men, including Antiphon, Archeptolemus, Onomacles, and Phrynichus.[7] We do not know just what went on at Sparta; the oligarchs cannot have been willing to purchase peace at any price, for no peace materialized. What Thucydides has to say on the subject is obscure: the ambassadors, he claims, returned to Athens without having made a general agreement: οὐδὲν πράξαντες ἀνεχώρησαν τοῖς ξύμπασι ξυμβατικόν.[8] Did the ambassadors make some kind of a deal with the Spartans concerning their own fate?

At the same time, the oligarchs began fortifying Eëtioneia, a mole extending from the Piraeus. Thucydides, despite his great admiration for Antiphon, has this to say about their motives in fortifying Eëtioneia and in sending envoys to Sparta:

> Theramenes said that [the Spartans] were en route not to Euboea but rather to help those who were fortifying Eëtioneia, and if they were not careful, their cause would be lost. And indeed this was not mere slander, for there was some such thing being done by those whom Theramenes accused. For those people wished above all to rule as oligarchs in Athens and over the allies, and, failing that, at least to be independent, keeping

their ships and their walls; and if this was impossible at least not to be themselves the first to be destroyed by the restored democracy, but indeed to bring in the enemy and, giving up the walls and the ships, make any terms at all about the affairs of the city, if only they themselves could have immunity.[9]

This is pretty strong stuff from a man who has described Antiphon as a man inferior to none of his Athenian contemporaries in ἀρετή; and so I think we must accept Thucydides' judgment.[10]

The envoys had no encouraging news to report to the citizens of Athens on their return, and στάσις in the city worsened. Phrynichus was murdered in the marketplace.[11] For reasons still incomprehensible to historians, the Spartan fleet, though it sailed by Piraeus, did not seize this moment to attack: the Spartans contented themselves with sparking the revolt of Euboea.[12] The affairs of Athens had worsened considerably under the Four Hundred, and in September the Athenian δῆμος replaced the Four Hundred with the Five Thousand.[13] Most of the Four Hundred wisely fled; one of them, Aristarchus, managed to place the border town of Oenoe in Boeotian hands before doing so.[14]

In September of 411 the position of Theramenes and his fellow moderates was extremely precarious. All along, the moderates had been afraid not only of what the extreme oligarchs might do to the city as a whole but also of what the city as a whole might do to the moderates if the democracy were restored. Once the overthrow of the Four Hundred had been accomplished, it was crucial for its moderate wing to dissociate itself from the extremists; and the impeachment of the extremist leaders was an obvious means to this end. The impeachment was made easier by the fact that the treasonous intentions of Antiphon and his associates were manifest; as we have seen, even Thucydides, no lover of Athenian democracy and a particular admirer of Antiphon, states plainly that the extremists were willing to betray the city to the Spartans in exchange for their own lives.[15] Lysias tells us that Theramenes took the lead in prosecuting the envoys; Harpocration reports that Andron, who moved the decree against the ambassadors, had also been one of the Four Hundred.[16] As virtually all the other oligarchic extremists had fled, and Phrynichus was dead, Theramenes and Andron had to content themselves with trying those on whom they could lay hands. Yet it would be wrong to see Antiphon and Archeptolemus as scapegoats in any meaningful sense; although they might have seen patriotism in a different light from that in which their compatriots viewed it, from a legal standpoint their guilt seems clear.[17]

The στρατηγός Timomachus seems also to have broken the law in his conduct of his στρατηγία. In 361/60, Timomachus was impeached by εἰσαγγελία on an unknown charge following his στρατηγία in Thrace. He did not appear at his trial and was convicted *in absentia*. He was sentenced either to death or to a substantial fine.[18]

In the late summer of 361 Timomachus was sent out to take over from Menon. One of Timomachus' principal duties was to provide a convoy to ensure the safe conduct of the ships carrying corn from the Euxine. This task he performed successfully.[19] In other respects, however, his στρατηγία did not go well, for during his tenure of office Cotys sent him a letter the arrogant tone of which made the Athenians realize that all their efforts to restrain him had been futile.[20] There is some reason to believe that Timomachus may have been partly responsible for this state of affairs, for his efforts as στρατηγός did not occupy his entire energies: he also devoted some time, and at least one ship, to rendering illegal assistance to his exiled relative by marriage Callistratus.[21]

Bonner is correct, I think, in seeing Timomachus' transport of Callistratus as "almost certainly" the charge against him.[22] Not only was the assistance rendered to Callistratus illegal by virtue of Callistratus' exile; worse yet, Timomachus, in order to assist his exiled relative, had deployed the Athenian armed forces and deflected at least one ship and a number of sailors from their official duties.

Other motives besides Timomachus' actual abuse of his office may have contributed to the attack on him. He had once before exercised the στρατηγία — not, it seems, gloriously. In 366, Timomachus and his fellow general Nausicles were guarding Oneum, the mountain range southeast of Corinth which might block the road from northern Greece into the Peloponnesus, when Peisias the Argive, an ally of Epaminondas, seized the hill above Cenchreae for the Thebans, thus assuring them entrance into the Peloponnesus. According to Xenophon, Peisias was enabled to do this in part by the carelessness of the Athenian guard.[23] Xenophon's assessment, while it may not be accurate, probably reflected popular opinion, and it is probably a testimony to the strength of Callistratus' faction that in the spring of 361 Timomachus was elected once more to the στρατηγία despite his past performance.[24] Clearly the balance between political parties was extremely delicate at this time, for Callistratus was probably exiled about the time Timomachus was elected.

The Athenians were not prepared to countenance a second mistake on the part of Timomachus. It may be too that they saw a connection between Timomachus' preoccupation with Callistratus and the seizure of Sestos from Theotimus, which took place while Timomachus was at Thasos; perhaps Timomachus had not taken sufficient care to leave an adequate force with his colleague. Finally, Apollodorus' complaint that Timomachus had not forced Polycles to meet his obligation of relieving him in the trierarchy may have contributed to the Athenians' view of Timomachus as careless of his duties.[25]

Apollodorus' grievance against Timomachus was clearly personal. A political motive also appears to have been involved in the attack on Timomachus, for as we have seen above in Chapter III, some of the backers of the attack were among the enemies of Callistratus. But this does not change the fact that Timomachus had abused his office and broken the law.

Political factors also played a part in the impeachment of Aeschines in 343. But he too seems to have broken Athenian law. For as Aeschines himself acknowledges, the Athenian ambassadors disobeyed their instructions by meeting with a slate of Philip's magistrates at Pherae instead of touring the individual cities as they had been instructed.[26]

In a handful of cases, then, it seems clear that those who were impeached had indeed broken the law. But most cases show no such thing, and we are forced to conclude that probably few Athenian officials were guilty as charged. The evidence will show, however, that the Athenians often had reason to be dissatisfied with the performance of their officials, and this dissatisfaction, I believe, often manifested itself in an impeachment.

The cases of Callisthenes and Cephisodotus are particularly outstanding. In 362 Callisthenes along with his colleague Ergophilus was deposed by ἀποχειροτονία and brought to trial following the failure of their military operations in the Hellespont and the Chersonese. The precise nature of the charge and the names of the accusers are unknown. Callisthenes was convicted and executed. Ergophilus appears to have gotten off with a stiff fine.[27]

In the summer of 363, Ergophilus and Callisthenes had been sent to aid Timotheus in guarding Athenian interests in the north. Timotheus had carried on the war with moderate success and had acquired considerable plunder for the Athenians. But the new alliance between Thebes and Alexander of Pherae, formerly Athens' ally against the Thebans, made operations in the north more difficult, and neither Ergophilus in the Hellespont nor Callisthenes at Amphipolis met with great success. It is not clear precisely what Ergophilus did during his στρατηγία. Nor are the actions of Timotheus during this year accounted for. Callisthenes' activities are somewhat better documented. The Macedonian Perdiccas, who had formerly fought on the side of the Athenians, accepted an invitation from the Amphipolitans to assist them in their defense against the Athenians. After some fighting, Callisthenes was able to force Perdiccas to promise to abandon his support of Amphipolis in exchange for a truce. But Callisthenes had rested content with the mere promise and returned to Athens, informing the people of his victory — whereupon Perdiccas, who had regained some of his strength during the truce, made clear that in fact he had not the slightest intention of relinquishing Amphipolis.[28]

Callisthenes' trust in Perdiccas' good faith showed poor judgment, and the Athenians were understandably displeased with him. Cephisodotus too showed poor judgment in his conduct in the north. In 359 Cephisodotus was deposed by ἀποχειροτονία and tried on an unspecified but serious charge after concluding an unfavorable treaty with Charidemus. He was found guilty and fined five talents.[29]

When Cephisodotus first took office, Athenian affairs in the north appeared to be taking a turn for the better. The powerful mercenary leader Charidemus, hard pressed by the Persian satrap Artabazus, offered to destroy Cotys' power in the Chersonese if Cephisodotus would provide Athenian ships on which he might cross his troops to Europe. An unexpected truce, however, enabled Charidemus to cross without Athenian assistance, and his promised aid never materialized. When Cotys died, Charidemus entered the service of Cotys' teenaged son Cersobleptes. Charidemus aided Cersobleptes in his struggle against the pretenders who had arisen in the form of two Thracian chieftains, Berisades and Amadocus, and together Charidemus and Cersobleptes made war on the Athenians, attacking them at Perinthus and assisting the pirates at Alopeconnesus whom the Athenians were besieging.[30] By spring, Charidemus had forced Cephisodotus to conclude a treaty. According to Demosthenes, the terms of the treaty were so dishonorable that the Athenians at once repudiated it and deposed Cephisodotus. Unfortunately, Demosthenes says nothing more substantial about the terms of the treaty. The Athenians must have been extremely displeased with Cephisodotus, for Demosthenes reports that he escaped the death penalty by only three votes.[31]

The principal source for Cephisodotus' στρατηγία is Demosthenes' oration 23, *Against Aristocrates*. It must be borne in mind, however, that as his speech is devoted in large meas-

ure to demonstrating the unworthiness and perfidy of Charidemus, and as there were old ties of friendship between the
families of Demosthenes and of Cephisodotus, its testimony is
tendentious.[32] Demosthenes gives the impression that Charidemus abused Cephisodotus shamefully by his failure to hon-
or his offer of friendship. In fact, Cephisodotus had no reason
to have any expectations of Charidemus. There is no evidence
that he ever concluded an agreement with Charidemus and, in
any case, the truce unexpectedly granted by Artabazus which
enabled Charidemus to cross the straits without Athenian
assistance would certainly seem to invalidate any notion of a
quid pro quo. Moreover, Charidemus' and Cersobleptes'
attack on the Athenians at Perinthus was made possible because Cephisodotus had come there with a weak force of only
ten ships in order to talk matters over with Charidemus. Demosthenes implies that Charidemus' enmity to the Athenians
on that occasion was astonishing and unforeseeable; but a sober consideration of the evidence presented by Demosthenes
himself suggests that Cephisodotus exercised extremely poor
judgment throughout in dealing with Charidemus. The treaty
which he finally concluded in the spring of 359 may have been
in fact dictated by his military situation at the time; we do not
know. But that situation itself appears to have arisen in large
measure because Cephisodotus blundered in trusting Charidemus. It is possible, of course, that Cephisodotus harbored the
treasonous intentions of which the Athenians probably accused him, but the fact that he was fined rather than executed
or exiled makes it unlikely that there was any real evidence of
treason.[33]

These are the most striking cases, I think; but there are other
instances in which it seems distinctly possible that the Athenians had good reason to be dissatisfied with their officials, and
instances as well in which the suspicion of guilt, even if not
justified, is understandable. In 424, for example, the generals
Sophocles, Pythodorus, and Eurymedon were tried on their
return from Sicily on the grounds that their withdrawal had

been prompted by bribes. The charge was δωροδοκία. Sophocles and Pythodorus were exiled. Eurymedon was fined in an
unknown amount.[34]

In 426 Pythodorus had been sent out to Sicily to take over
from Laches, who had been recalled.[35] With the same forces at
his disposal as his predecessor, who had taken Messina,
broadened Athens' base of support in Sicily, and sparked
enough enthusiasm among the islanders so that they sent an
embassy to Athens requesting additional assistance, Pythodorus lost Messina and very nearly Rhegium and Camarina as
well, and he was unable to maintain the morale of his allies
until the arrival of the reinforcements.[36] Sophocles and
Eurymedon were to follow after stopping at Corcyra to deal
with the civil disturbances there.[37] Thucydides stresses the
fact that by the time Sophocles and Eurymedon arrived — in
the summer of 425, for the Pylos campaign had intervened —
it was too late to prevent Athens' war-weary allies in Sicily
from reaching a settlement. This may be so; but Thucydides
has deliberately arranged his narrative so as to obscure the
conclusion, which can be easily enough derived from the facts
as he himself reports them, that Sophocles and Eurymedon
were in fact responsible for their delay in arriving. For it was
probably they, as Kagan suggests, who had been counted on to
keep watch over the Peloponnesian fleet from Zacynthos but
had failed to do so. As a result the enemy fleet proceeded
unhindered to Pylos, where it endangered Demosthenes and
made it necessary for Sophocles and Eurymedon to sail with
their own forces to Pylos and pass the summer there blockad-
ing the Peloponnesian fleet.[38] Thucydides conspicuously
makes no mention of the connection between Sophocles' and
Eurymedon's failure to keep track of the Peloponnesian fleet in
425 — a failure duly recorded in its place — and their unpopularity a year later, but in fact his narrative makes clear that
these two generals might well have seemed to the Athenians to
be culpably negligent in arriving late.[39]

The Athenians had an additional grievance, for when the
generals arrived they did not merely consent to a peace upon
which the warring city-states of Sicily had agreed; they con-

sented to a peace which was put forward by the eloquent Hermocrates of Syracuse in a long speech which stressed the need for union — against Athenian aggression. The Sicilians must recognize, he argues,

> that, if we are prudent, the subject of our conference will be not our private interests merely but rather the question whether we will still be able to save Sicily as a whole, for it is against all Sicily, I think, that the Athenians are plotting. . . . And so now, taking alarm . . . , let us send out of the country the enemy who is upon us, and if possible let us make peace among ourselves.[40]

It was no ordinary internal agreement to which the Athenian generals assented, but rather an accommodation predicated on the assumption of Athenian aggression, present and future, and to this sort of settlement no Athenian official could give his blessing with dignity.

The punishments meted out by the Athenians on this occasion were severe. Sophocles and Pythodorus were banished and do not seem to reappear; Eurymedon was fined but went on to serve in the Decelean war.[41] The comparative leniency shown to Eurymedon may have been the product of his affiliation with the aggressive war party during the mid-420s as a whole, but it may also be connected with his conduct in Sicily, for Timaeus reports efforts on his part to rouse the allies to action.[42] In retrospect the punishment seems excessive.[43] But the censure of the Athenians in itself does not appear incomprehensible.

The Athenians' conviction of Thucydides himself at his impeachment during the following winter is also understandable. In the winter of 424/23, Thucydides, who was one of the two generals assigned to Thrace, was exiled following the fall of Amphipolis. The charge was probably προδοσία, and the accuser may have been Cleon. It is not clear whether Eucles, Thucydides' fellow general for the Thracian district, was banished as well, nor whether Thucydides returned to Athens to stand his trial.[44] The account of Thucydides is virtually our only source for the loss of Amphipolis, and he is remarkably reticent about the episode. Diodorus also tells the story, but he adds nothing.[45]

On a cold and snowy night in December 424, the Spartan general Brasidas moved down on the town of Argilus, where he knew that a faction would make it easy for him to gain admission. His partisans there guided him to the bridge that led over the Strymon river to Amphipolis. He found the bridge poorly guarded and he succeeded in crossing to the outskirts of Amphipolis, where he encamped, hoping that his friends within the city would make a military contest unnecessary.[46] Within Amphipolis, the people were divided. The pro-Athenian party, acting in concert with Eucles, the Athenian general in charge of the city, sent a summons for aid to Thucydides, who shared with Eucles the responsibility for the Thracian district and who was with his fleet off Thasos, half a day's sail from Eion.[47] Brasidas, fearing the arrival of new troops under Thucydides, offered the residents of Amphipolis the freedom to remain, in full possession of civic and property rights, or to depart within five days. After some hesitation, his terms were accepted. When Thucydides sailed into Eion that evening, Amphipolis was in Brasidas' hands. There was still time, however, for Thucydides to fortify Eion, and consequently the attack which Brasidas launched that night was repelled.[48]

Surely Thucydides' absence from Eion must have been a central issue at his trial. And yet his narrative does nothing whatever to explain it. Some historians — Busolt and Grote among them — not surprisingly have taken a harsh view of Thucydides' performance as στρατηγός in the north. Grote has written:

> Had [Thucydides and Eucles] a difficult position to defend? Were they overwhelmed by a superior force? Were they distracted by simultaneous revolts in different places, or assailed by enemies unknown or unforeseen? Not one of these grounds for acquittal can be pleaded. . . . Having . . . ample warning for the necessity of a vigilant defense, Thucydides and Eukles withdraw, or omit, both the two precautions upon which the security of Amphipolis rested — precautions both of them obvious, either of them sufficient. The one leaves the bridge under a

feeble guard . . . the other is found with his squadron, not at
Eion, but at Thasos — an island out of all possible danger,
either from Brasidas (who had no ships) or any other enemy.
The arrival of Brasidas comes on both of them like a clap of
thunder. Nothing more is required than this plain fact, under the
circumstances, to prove their improvidence as commanders.[49]

More recently, Thucydides' performance as general has been
criticized by Bauman and by Kagan.[50]

Thucydides' account of the fall of Amphipolis is not an
adequate one. It does not even include any mention of the
accusation against him. His banishment he records only in an
aside in Book V, where he writes (on the subject of his opportunities for research) that "it happened that I was banished
from my country for twenty years following my command at
Amphipolis."[51] Another conspicuous feature of his account of
the loss of Amphipolis is his failure to explain his presence at
Thasos. Thucydides' journey to Thasos might, of course, be
explained in any number of ways.[52] But the fact remains that
Thucydides puts forward none of these explanations. It has
been argued that Thucydides' silence on this point is to his
credit as an impartial historian and demonstrates nothing more
than his refusal to permit the intrusion of autobiography into
his history, just as elsewhere he refuses to allow the intrusion
of biography.[53] But in fact Thucydides' reasons for going to
Thasos are not merely relevant but requisite in an account of
the fall of Amphipolis. Surely it is odd that while we are given a
running commentary on the thinking of Brasidas, we are let
into the mind of the general Thucydides only when he has
determined to set sail full speed for Eion, wanting to save
Amphipolis or at least to establish himself at Eion.[54] We are
never told what was in the minds of the two Athenian generals
when it was decided that Thucydides would go to Thasos.[55]
Nowhere does Thucydides outline the Thracian strategy by
which he and Eucles intended to execute their command. As
de Romilly has pointed out, it is characteristic of Thucydides
to stress the role played in the outcome of a military confrontation by the thinking on either side.[56] This is missing from

Thucydides' account of the fight to hold Amphipolis.[57] In addition, Thucydides tells us nothing about the size of the forces at Eucles' disposal. The entire account of the collapse of Amphipolis certainly suggests that Eucles did not have much of an army. The guard at the bridge was a light one, and once Brasidas had crossed, Thucydides reports, the general impression was that he could have taken the city had he not preferred to wait in the expectation of its betrayal.[58] And yet it is hard to believe that Thucydides would not have said so if he and Eucles had been sent on an important mission without sufficient resources: he had just written concerning the impeachment of Sophocles, Pythodorus, and Eurymedon the year before that the Athenians had impeached the generals because "to such an extent . . . did the people expect to be disappointed in nothing, and believed that, regardless of the size and strength of their forces, they could equally achieve what was easy and what was difficult."[59]

All these omissions in Thucydides' narrative make it impossible fully to understand the reasons for his conviction at Athens. But the mysterious reticence of his account is hardly a good sign. If Thucydides gave the Athenians no better rendering than this, it is no wonder that he found himself in trouble.[60]

Nor should the deposition of Alcibiades towards the end of the war occasion surprise or be laid squarely at the door of "political enemies at home . . . too numerous and too bitter," as Henderson would have it.[61] In fact Alcibiades had given the Athenians good reason for complaint — reason above and beyond the rather subtle and esoteric nature of his patriotism.

In the late winter of 406, Alcibiades and his colleagues were deposed by ἀποχειροτονία following the defeat of Alcibiades' forces at Notium. After Alcibiades' removal from office, many private complaints were lodged against him and he was indicted by Cleophon, evidently for προδοσία; but he never returned to Athens, and the Athenians may not have troubled themselves to try him *in absentia*.[62]

In the fall of 407, soon after his reinstatement at Athens, Alcibiades sailed for Asia Minor. On his way he stopped to attack Andros, now held by the Spartans, where he had mixed success.[63] From Andros he proceeded to Samos, where he learned to his dismay that the influence which Lysander had won with Cyrus had put an end at least for the time being to any hopes that he could bring the Persians over to the Athenian side.[64] To restore his credit with the Athenians, Alcibiades tried to provoke to battle the fleet of Lysander, which was stationed at Notium, but Lysander wisely held back.[65] Alcibiades then decided to move northward with part of his fleet to attempt to win back lost cities for Athens and to raise money.[66] On this expedition he evidently plundered the allied city of Cyme, which promptly sent ambassadors to the Athenians to complain of him.[67] The remainder of his fleet he left at Notium under the command of Antiochus, his personal pilot, with strict orders not to engage the enemy.[68] Antiochus, however, deliberately provoked Lysander's fleet, and in the ensuing battle the Athenians were defeated, losing fifteen triremes and a large number of men, of whom Antiochus was one.[69] When Alcibiades learned of the battle he hastened south and attempted to draw Lysander into another contest, but to no avail.[70]

Word of the defeat at Notium soon reached Athens. At the same time the Cymean ambassadors arrived with their complaints.[71] Soon Thrasybulus of Collytus arrived at Athens.[72] He had served in the fleet, and he alleged that Alcibiades' excursion along the coast had been a pleasure trip of the most disreputable kind and that Antiochus had won his command not through any military ability which he possessed, but by his capacity for drink and skill at gossip.[73] In addition, the Athenians were disturbed to hear that Alcibiades had fortified a castle in Thrace as a refuge in case of emergency, and they could not but wonder what sort of emergency he foresaw: there were the inevitable rumors that he intended to betray them to the Spartans.[74]

Doubtless all these factors contributed to the Athenians' decision to depose Alcibiades. It was not the case, as Bury maintains, that "a slight incident" at Notium "completely changed the current of feeling in Athens."[75] Indeed, even before the debacle at Notium the Athenians must have conceived some second thoughts about Alcibiades. Immediately after his reinstatement it became obvious that he could not fulfill his promise of bringing the Persians over to the Athenian side. Doubtless many Athenians considered the hope that he might do so the only excuse for countenancing his return to grace, and the support of these men collapsed immediately with the death of that hope. It remained for Alcibiades to recoup some of this lost support by consolidating the Athenians' position in Asia Minor and the Aegean. This, however, he failed to do during the several months between his departure from Athens and the defeat at Notium. During this period he had wasted much valuable time in his unsuccessful attempt to take Andros; in the course of his expedition along the coast of Asia Minor, he had either, as Nepos alleges, failed in his attack on a presumably revolted Cyme, or, as Diodorus claims, plundered an allied city; and, finally, he had left his fleet in the command of a personal friend whose unworthiness was proved in the event.[76] In view of Alcibiades' record during the months that had passed since his reinstatement, it is not reasonable to conclude with Henderson that his removal from office was the product of "party spirit."[77] Inevitably Alcibiades' failure to score any military successes, coming on top of the realization that his promise of Persian aid was not to be fulfilled, destroyed the precarious position of the former traitor at home.[78]

Shortly after the deposition of Alcibiades came the impeachment of the victors of Arginusae. As we have seen in Chapter IV above, inadequacy in the στρατηγία was one factor in the complex chain of events which led to the condemnation of these eight generals. It appears that the loss of life immediately after the battle was due not only to the storm but also in part to laxity on the part of the generals. The στρατηγοί do not seem to have dealt swiftly enough with the crisis at hand — a crisis which after all could easily have been foreseen by experienced naval commanders; and as Cloché points out, Thrasyllus, commander-in-chief on the day of the battle, was as experienced an admiral as could reasonably have been hoped for.[79]

It would seem, then, on the basis of the evidence that has come down to us, that suspicions of general inadequacy in the discharge of an office might be a more important factor in an Athenian impeachment trial than actual guilt on a specific count. The charges of bribery and treason which the Athenians leveled against their officials, we must conclude, were intentionally extreme. We must not imagine that the men who brought these accusations necessarily believed that the defendants were guilty as charged. Extreme charges against Athenian officials with whom the people were dissatisfied were evidently something of a formality — a grim tradition intended to remind Athenians of the extremely high standards by which their conduct in office would be judged.

VII THUCYDIDES, PLUTARCH, AND ATHENS' GENERALS

WHEN the στρατηγοί Sophocles, Pythodorus, and Eurymedon were prosecuted on their return from Sicily in 424 on the grounds that their withdrawal had been prompted by bribes, Thucydides wrote that

> to such an extent, because of their current good fortune [i.e., their success at Pylos] did the Athenians expect to be disappointed in nothing, and believed that, regardless of the strength of their forces, they could achieve equally what was easy and what was difficult.[1]

Here Thucydides is not reporting facts. Rather he is interpreting them in a highly subjective manner, and consequently there is no need for any subsequent student of the Sicilian episode to accept his view of the attack on the generals. It is astonishing how many modern scholars matter-of-factly cite Thucydides as a final authority on the significance of this trial — all the more astonishing in light of the fact that Thucydides himself was exiled by the Athenian people later in the same year for his own conduct as στρατηγός. And yet as sensitive an observer as Grote, for example, incorporates Thucydides' views into his account of the trial of the generals as unhesitatingly as he accepts his facts, writing that the Athenians "were at this moment at the maximum of extravagant hopes, counting upon new triumphs everywhere, impatient of disappointment between the means entrusted to, and the objects expected from, their commanders'' — without so much as a reference to Thucydides, as if the interpretation he had adopted from him were an established fact; and John Finley in his discussion of Thucydides' exile after the loss of Amphipolis has described him as "a victim of the people's exorbitant hopes," extrapolating from the case of the Sicilian generals in precisely the way Thucydides had surely intended.[2] In fact, I think, the case histories which I have studied suggest that Thucydides had a fairly consistent bias concerning the impeachment of Athenian στρατηγοί — a bias in favor of the στρατηγοί and against the δῆμος.

The first impeachment of a στρατηγός with which Thucydides deals in his history is that of Pericles in 430. In that year, Thucydides writes, Pericles found it necessary to deliver a long speech in the assembly in the course of which he attempted to persuade the Athenians to persevere in his war policy and to abandon their embassies to Sparta.[3] By such words, Thucydides says, Pericles "sought to cure the Athenians of their anger towards him, and to divert their minds from their present misfortunes."[4] But, he goes on, the Athenians "did not cease their anger against him until they had fined him," and "not long afterwards, as is the habit of the multitude (ὅπερ φιλεῖ ὅμιλος ποιεῖν), they chose him again as general and entrusted him with all their affairs."[5] Thucydides, in other words, implies that the Athenians had no hard-headed intellectual reservations about Pericles' war policy but rather were temporarily swept away by selfish emotions.

As we have seen, however, the facts provided by Thucydides and others make plain that the Athenians had rational motives both for the deposition of Pericles and for his reinstatement. During the summer of 430, the aggressive war party in Athens had much to complain of. Pericles' defensive strategy did not appear to be winning the war. But the war party cannot have comprised the entire opposition to Pericles at this time. On the contrary, Pericles' recent harangue to the assembly had included an exhortation to the advocates of peace, who had gone so far as to send an embassy to Sparta, to give over their attempts to end the war in this way. I have suggested in Chapter III consequently that, as Kagan has argued, the success of the attack on Pericles in 430 was due in all probability to the combination against him of two large groups who opposed his continuation in office for opposite reasons.

During the fall and winter of 430/29, Sparta proved to be no more willing to come to a settlement with Pericles out of office, and so Athenian policy found itself in the hands of the more aggressive party led by Cleon and others. Doubtless, many in the peace party decided that a return to Pericles' leadership was advisable if the war was to continue; and so the coalition against Pericles began to dissolve. When the peace party found that its policy would not work and the aggressive war party had little success in moving the war to a victorious conclusion, the Athenians decided to return to Pericles' moderate strategy, and he regained his office. The events of 430/29, then, are easily enough explained without reference to the mob's fickleness or ingratitude. But these developments are obscured by the narrative of Thucydides.

During the same year the Athenians brought an accusation against Xenophon, Hestiodorus, and Phanomachus, the three generals who accepted the surrender of Potidaea. In the winter of 430/29, Thucydides reports, the Potidaeans were hard pressed and offered terms of capitulation. The generals, according to Thucydides,

> accepted their terms in view of the distress which the army was suffering in such an exposed place and the large amount — two thousand talents — which the Athenians had already spent on the siege. So the capitulation was made on the following terms: the Potidaeans, along with their children and wives and the mercenary troops, were to leave the city with one garment apiece (two for each woman) and with a fixed sum of money for the trip. So they left under a truce and went into Chalcidice or

wherever each one was able to go. The Athenians, however, blamed the generals because they had granted terms without consulting them — for they thought they could have become masters of the place on any terms they wanted.[6]

Thucydides presents the generals' decision in such a way as to make it appear unexceptionable, and his statement that the Athenians "thought they could have become masters of the place on any terms they wanted" may adumbrate his dictum in Book IV that the Athenians came to believe in the course of the war that they could accomplish whatever they wished regardless of the realities of individual military situations. But the facts which he himself presents suggest that the Athenians had rational grounds for questioning the generals' action. Thucydides concedes, after all, that the Potidaeans had run out of grain and that they had been reduced to cannibalism. In view of these circumstances, it certainly seems that the Athenian generals might well have taken the city on much stiffer terms with little or indeed no loss of additional time and men. I have suggested in Chapter III, therefore, that the generals' decision was motivated in fact by their desire to take a lenient stand with the surrendered Potidaeans — a stand which they had good reason to believe would not have been approved by Cleon and his supporters in the assembly. In addition, the generals almost certainly exceeded their authority in negotiating with the Potidaeans. Neither of these issues, however, is treated by Thucydides.

As we have seen, moreover, there is some reason to suspect bias in Thucydides' account of the impeachment of Sophocles, Pythodorus, and Eurymedon. For he has arranged his narrative, I have suggested, in such a way as to obscure the conclusion that Sophocles and Eurymedon may themselves have been in part responsible for their delay in arriving in Sicily. Thucydides' own narrative makes clear that it may have been because they had misplaced the Peloponnesian fleet from Zacynthus that it was able to proceed to Pylos where it endangered Demosthenes — and made it necessary for Sophocles and Eurymedon to delay their voyage to Sicily in order to go to Demosthenes' aid. In addition, the Athenians had another grievance. When the generals arrived, Thucydides says, they consented to a peace for Sicily which Hermocrates had proposed in a speech arguing that the Sicilians needed to unite against the danger of Athenian aggression. Surely this was not the sort of peace in which the Athenian στρατηγοί ought to have concurred.

A case for the possible inadequacy of Sophocles, Pythodorus, and Eurymedon can easily enough be made, then, from the facts reported by Thucydides; but it is far from what his interpretation of their trial would lead us to believe, and indeed the events of the following winter no doubt put Thucydides in a frame of mind increasingly skeptical of the wisdom of the Athenian democracy. For it was during the winter of 424/23 that Thucydides, one of the two generals assigned to Thrace, was blamed for the loss of Amphipolis and forced to leave Athens.

According to Grundy, the "impersonal character" of Thucydides' account of the fall of Amphipolis "is peculiarly illustrated by his omission of anything resembling a defence of his action," and Grundy's view is shared by a large body of scholars of both the nineteenth and twentieth centuries.[7] Meyer, for example, praises Thucydides for recounting the events of his στρατηγία with the same detachment as that of any other general and claims that those who find his account wanting are forgetting that he is writing history, not autobiography; and Gomme in his commentary argues that Thucydides "makes no attempt at self-defence."[8] It is understandable therefore that so many scholars have concluded that Thucydides' conduct at Amphipolis was unimpeachable in every sense: Thirlwall, for example, Classen, Delbrück, Adcock, and Finley.[9] Several others disagree: Busolt, Schmid, and Grote; even Gomme himself; and, most recently, Bauman and Kagan.[10]

It is not surprising that it should be difficult to determine the extent of Thucydides' responsibility for the loss of Amphipolis: military competence is, after all, a hard thing to judge.

What is astonishing, however, is that Thucydides' account should give us no real sense of what must have gone on in the minds of the men who sat on the jury at his trial.

In the case of all the other impeachments with which Thucydides deals, he offers an explanation of the impeachment. We may not agree with his assessment; but in the cases of both the impeachment and the reinstatement of Pericles; in the case of Xenophon, Hestiodorus, and Phanomachus; in the case of Sophocles, Eurymedon, and Pythodorus; and, as we shall see, in the deposition of Phrynichus and Scironides, Thucydides makes perfectly clear the reason for the impeachment *as he perceived it*. This explanation is entirely absent from his account of his own impeachment, which, as we have seen, he does not mention at all in his discussion of the events of his στρατηγία; we learn of his exile only in Book V where he mentions, "I was banished from my country for twenty years following my command at Amphipolis."[11] Holm has observed that "if it were not a Thucydides who is concerned no one would care to waste one single word on the matter in view of our complete ignorance of all the precise circumstances of the case."[12] He is quite right, and the state of our ignorance does not speak well for Thucydides' account of the fall of Amphipolis.

In his essay entitled "Thucydides and the Fall of Amphipolis" H. D. Westlake has analyzed in detail the way in which Thucydides sought by his account of the loss of Amphipolis "to guide the judgment of his readers" and has shown that "his narrative contains *inter alia* a very skillful self-justification against the charges which led to his banishment."[13] As Westlake points out, Thucydides' narrative contains much to suggest that he was innocent and nothing to suggest that he was guilty. Westlake calls attention, for example, to Thucydides' rather selective analysis of the thinking of Brasidas outside Amphipolis. "In a very significant sentence," Westlake writes, "the decision of Brasidas to offer moderate terms to the Amphipolitans is attributed wholly to fears that the approach of Thucydides would stiffen their will to resist." As Westlake goes on to say, Thucydides' own narrative makes perfectly clear that, on the contrary, Brasidas' decision was taken in order "to build up a reputation for moderation and to pose as a liberator"; "fear that the prize might be lost through the instrumentality of Thucydides was certainly not his only motive," although it is a motive "that redounds to [Thucydides'] own credit."[14] Westlake, however, devotes comparatively little space to the one staggering omission in Thucydides' narrative: Thucydides' reason for finding himself, when the crisis of Brasidas' appearance arose, not at Eion, from which help could easily be brought, but rather at Thasos, half a day's sail from Amphipolis.

In fact Thucydides' journey to Thasos might be explained in any number of ways. He may have been using his connections in Thrace to recruit reinforcements; he may have decided to station himself at Thasos because of its superior harbor, generally better than that of Eion. He may have heard of disturbances in Thrace. That Eucles knew where Thucydides could be found implies that the decision for him to go Thasos was taken jointly, which argues against any personal motive Thucydides may have had for going there (perhaps connected with his own holdings in Thrace); besides, the best way to protect Thucydides' Thracian holdings against Brasidas, who had no ships, would have been to hold the line of the Strymon. But Thucydides does not mention any of these possible motives.

A variety of reasons other than Thucydides' betrayal of Athens may have prompted this omission. It may be, for example, that Thucydides does not tell us what he was doing at Thasos because, while his reasons for being there were in his opinion entirely sound, he knew that those reasons had not been convincing to the Athenians, and he felt that his behavior would be cast in the best light if he treated his presence at Thasos as casually as possible. It may be too that in retrospect his sound reasons did not look so compelling to him after all; or it may be that he felt so strongly that, for whatever reasons, Thasos was the right place for him to have been that he would not stoop to discuss the issue. It is also possible that Thucydides did not say what he was doing at Thasos because he did not consider his presence there to be relevant to the loss of Amphipolis. After all, it can be argued, as Gomme has done, that "the only risk he [Thucydides] ran by staying at Thasos was in the ability of Amphipolis, with an Athenian strategos in charge, an Athenian element in the population and the majority of citizens in their favour, to hold out for twenty-four hours," which "he may well have thought . . . a reasonable risk." [15]

Meyer, as we have seen, has argued that Thucydides' reticence here is to his credit as an impartial historian and demonstrates his refusal to permit the intrusion of autobiography into his history, just as elsewhere he refuses to allow the intrusion of biography.[16] But in fact Thucydides' reasons for going to Thasos are essential to any account of the fall of Amphipolis. Surely it is odd that Thucydides has told us so much about what was going on in the mind of the Spartan Brasidas and so little about what was in the minds of the two Athenian generals when the decision was taken to send Thucydides to Thasos. Thucydides' account of the fall of Amphipolis must be judged a poor one, since he omits from it the exposition of the Athenian generals' strategy in Thrace; and if his account of the loss of Amphipolis is poor, his account of the impeachment of the general Thucydides is nonexistent. He does not mention the trial in its proper context, and he omits all explanation of what must almost certainly have been the central issue at his trial, his absence at Thasos. Thucydides' reticence not only speaks poorly for him as a historian; it has created a widespread impression that he was an exceptionally fine sport about his unfortunate fate. On the last page of his *Thucydides Mythistoricus* Cornford praises Thucydides on the grounds that in treating of the events which led to his exile he "neither extenuates the blunder nor complains of the penalty," and a significant proportion of modern undergraduates when asked to study Thucydides' account of his στρατηγία find him amazingly charitable towards the Athenians who blamed him for this loss of Amphipolis — wrongly, they maintain, "since he was not even there." [17] In fact there is nothing admirable about Thucydides' silences concerning his στρατηγία, in the deceptive casualness about his absence at Thasos. There is nothing praiseworthy about either melodramatic martyrdom or deception, however subtly and dextrously executed, in a historian.

Thucydides succeeded in large measure in justifying himself to posterity by a skillful combination of tactics: studied casualness about both his absence at Thasos and his exile itself; juxtaposition of his description of himself sailing full speed to rescue Eion with a description of the Athenians' distress at the loss of Amphipolis; and the earlier adumbration of the theme of the people's irrational expectations. This theme was introduced in a very general way, as we have seen, in Thucydides' discussion of the trial of the στρατηγοί who had accepted the surrender of Potidaea, where he wrote that the Athenians felt that the generals could have become masters of Potidaea on any terms whatever — and did not acknowledge that the facts recorded in his own narrative suggested that the Athenians, if they felt that way, were perfectly justified. The theme reaches its highest pitch in Thucydides' judgment about the reason for the impeachment of Sophocles, Eurymedon, and Pythodorus after their return from Sicily. Now it would certainly have undermined what we might call "the strategy of martyrdom" for Thucydides to have reiterated his views about the irrational expectations of the Athenian δῆμος in his discussion of his own fate; it may be too that Thucydides realized — as several more recent historians have not — that it was meaningless to apply quite the same analysis to an impeachment which took place in the aftermath of the disastrous defeat at Delium as had been applied to an impeachment which took place in the aftermath of the exhilarating victory at Pylos. Judgments such as Busolt's — that in Thucydides' case the δῆμος was unusually sensitive to frustration since their military successes had imbued them with excessive confidence and they wished to find scapegoats — and conclusions such as Finley's — that "like the generals who had been punished for accepting peace in Sicily, he [Thucydides] was a victim of the people's exorbitant hopes" at a time (Finley adds, paying lip service to the change of mood at Athens after Delium) when "there must have been a still greater demand for scapegoats" — cannot, I think have been far from Thucydides' intention.[18]

In the winter of 412/11, we have seen in Chapter III, the Athenians deposed Phrynichus and Scironides at the suggestion of Peisander, on the grounds that they had betrayed Iasus to the Peloponnesians. Thucydides labels the charge false, calling it διαβολή.[19] But in fact the story which Thucydides himself tells suggests that there may have been some substance to the accusation. The account of Thucydides is designed to make Phrynichus' attempt to persuade the Athenians to withdraw to Samos and leave Iasus unguarded — a course which led to the loss of Iasus — appear patriotic and heroic. Indeed, Phrynichus' course may have been a sensible one, but it was certainly not the only one open to the Athenians. Clearly, the Argive allies who promptly sailed home in protest against Phrynichus' decision were not won over by his arguments.

It is easy to understand, moreover, that Phrynichus' loyalty to the Athenian democracy may have been suspect at the time of his deposition. For Phrynichus' conviction that the recall of Alcibiades would destroy Athens had led him to send letters to the Spartan admiral Astyochus revealing the embryonic negotiations then in progress between Alcibiades, Tissaphernes, and the Athenians. Phrynichus managed temporarily to restore his credit with the Athenians by luring Astyochus and Alcibiades into accusing him on a charge for which he had prepared a refutation, but the correspondence with Astyochus no doubt lingered in many Athenian minds. In the light of Phrynichus' treacherous correspondence with Astyochus, and of the intense opposition among the fleet to his proposed withdrawal from Miletus to Samos, it is not hard to see how he might reasonably have been held responsible for the loss of Iasus, despite Thucydides' efforts to make the charge appear ridiculous. In fact, however, as Thucydides well understood, the loss of Iasus was simply a pretext for the attack on Phrynichus. Thucydides states the purpose of Phrynichus' deposition plainly: Phrynichus was removed from office because he opposed the recall of Alcibiades.[20]. The narrative of Thucydides suggests that Scironides was associated with Phrynichus in this opposition. No doubt the assemblymen who voted for the deposition of Phrynicus and Scironides were concerned that Phyrnichus might otherwise hinder the return of Alcibiades, which they had come to decide was Athens' only recourse. But, the record of Phrynichus at any rate was far from spotless, and some men may have genuinely considered him guilty if not of treason then at the very least of incompetence, despite Thucydides' attempt to make the charges against him appear farfetched.

In his history of the Peloponnesian War, then, Thucydides dealt with the circumstances surrounding five impeachment trials — that of Pericles in 430; of Xenophon, Hestiodorus, and Phanomachus in the winter of 430/29; of Sophocles, Pythodorus, and Eurymedon in 424; of Thucydides (and possibly Eucles) in the winter of 424/23; and of Phrynichus and Scironides in the winter of 412/11. The degree to which Thucydides explicitly offers his analysis of the impeachment varies from case to case. But in each instance his treatment of the impeached generals is favorable; in more than one case he is open in siding with the generals; and in no instance does he support the citizens who voted for impeachment. He describes the Athenians who convicted Pericles in 430 as a selfish and emotional mob, although the facts which he himself presents make clear that sensible reasons of policy might have led the Athenians to depose Pericles, and then to reinstate him. He gives the impression that Xenophon, Hestiodorus, and Phanomachus did the only natural thing in accepting the surrender of the Potidaeans on lenient terms, and he implies that the Athenians were unreasonable in contending that they could have obtained Potidaea on their own terms, though his own narrative suggests that this view would have been justified. He states plainly that Sophocles, Pythodorus, and Eurymedon were impeached because the Athenians were entirely unrealistic in what they expected of their commanders, although his own account makes clear that the three generals may not have been blameless in the failure of Athenian operations in Sicily. He treats the circumstances surrounding his own impeachment with studied casualness and has made it difficult for readers of his work to understand this episode. He openly calls the attack on Phrynichus διαβολή, although in fact many Athenians might reasonably have doubted Phrynichus' loyalty and wisdom. In each case Thucydides has been careful to cast the impeached generals as, in one degree or another, martyrs to the unreliable δῆμος, though the stories he himself tells suggest in each instance that another interpretation was also possible.

In general, historians have estimated Thucydides' political insight highly; his views have been accepted by many modern students of antiquity. As Plutarch's views have, on the whole, been held in less esteem, his perspective has had somewhat less influence; but it has reinforced the impression made by Thucydides. In casting doubt on the story which Craterus had told concerning the alleged conviction of Aristides for taking bribes, Plutarch writes that he is suspicious of the tale since it is omitted by "all the others who detail the misdeeds which the Athenian δῆμος inflicted on its leaders."[21] He nowhere names the "others," but clearly the topos had grown up already by Plutarch's day. Plutarch's particular interest was directed not so much to the irrational expectations of the δῆμος as to its tendency to envy and fickleness. The ostracism of Aristides, for example, he attributes not only to the strife between Aristides and Themistocles: he gives equal space to the theory that

> by this time the δῆμος, having become greatly elated because of their victory [over the Persians], and thinking that nothing was too good for them, hated anyone who was above all the others. So they gathered from all over the city and ostracized Aristides — calling their envy of his reputation "fear of tyranny."[22]

The echo of Thucydides' judgment of the impeachment of Sophocles, Pythodorus, and Eurymedon after the Athenian success at Pylos is a strong one.

Plutarch in his life of Pericles, moreover, tells a dramatic tale of Pericles' deposition and reinstatement that stresses emotional factors. Although Plutarch does concede that the δῆμος returned Pericles to his office when they had tried alternative leadership and found it wanting, nonetheless a strain of melodrama runs through his account of the whole affair. When the war was going badly and the plague was raging in the city, he writes, the pestilence "undermined the Athenians in both mind and spirit, and they became quite wild against Pericles and attacked him in their delirium as one maddened by disease will attack his father or his doctor."[23] After Pericles' unsuccessful expedition to Epidaurus, he goes on, the Athenians were even more displeased with him, and

> he did not succeed in appeasing their anger or in changing their minds until they took their ballots into their hands, became master of his fate, took away his στρατηγία and punished him with a fine.[24]

After this, Plutarch concludes, the Athenians got their anger out of their system; the δῆμος, he says, having stung Pericles, had left its anger in the sting.[25] When the Athenians had tried other leaders, therefore, and were dissatisfied and had come to long for Pericles, they summoned him back to office and "apologized for their ingratitude."[26] The view that the Athenians' changing attitude to Pericles in 430 was determined primarily by emotional considerations has been echoed by several historians — Curtius, for example, who envisions Pericles magnanimously condescending to return to office, "free from anger or petty exultation, or ignoble desires of revenge; instead of which he displayed an anxiety generously to pardon the instability of the multitude."[27] But, as we have seen, the Athenians had sound political reasons both for Pericles' deposition and for his reinstatement.

A similar bias may underlie Plutarch's story of the alleged suicide of the στρατηγός Paches. Plutarch claims that Paches was driven to suicide in the courtroom either at his εὔθυναι or at a trial arising from his εὔθυναι. He tells the story of Paches' demise in his lives of both Nicias and Aristides, and on both occasions the purpose of the anecdote is to illustrate the fickleness of the Athenian δῆμος. In his life of Nicias, Plutarch maintains that Nicias attempted to avoid long and demanding campaigns because

he observed that the people, in the case of eloquent and eminent
men, made use of their talents when they wished, but were
always jealous of their abilities and eyed them watchfully, taking all opportunities to humble their pride and abate their reputation, as was manifest . . . especially in the case of Paches, the
conqueror of Lesbos, who, at his scrutiny (εὐθύνας διδούς), in
the very δικαστήριον unsheathed his sword and slew himself.[28]

(Already at the end of the sixth century, Plutarch maintained in his life of Themistocles, Neocles had sought to dissuade his son from politics by showing him hulks of triremes
abandoned on the shore and telling him that this was how the
people treated their leaders when they had no further use of
them.[29]) In his life of Aristides, Plutarch writes that "those
who detail the misdeeds which the δῆμος inflicted on its leaders mention the cases of Miltiades, Themistocles, Pericles —
and Paches, who committed suicide at his trial when he was
found guilty: καὶ τὸν Πάχητος ἐν τῷ δικαστηρίῳ θάνατον,
ἀνελόντος αὐτὸν ἐπὶ τοῦ βήματος ὡς ἡλίσκετο."[30]

What is the meaning of this twice-told tale?

Beloch, Busolt, and Kagan have all seen a political trial as
the source of Paches' downfall. Rightly rejecting or discount-
ing the evidence of a poem written some thousand years later
by Agathias, which attributes Paches' suicide to shame at the
exposure of his violation of two Mytilenean women and the
murder of their husbands, they incline to the view of Plutarch
and see in Paches a moderate brought down by the aggressive
war party, to whom his conduct had evidently furnished some
pretext.[31] It is certainly reasonable to explain an attack on
Paches in 427 as the work of Cleon's party, particularly in view
of the closeness of the vote concerning the fate of the Mytileneans and Cleon's probable bitterness at his defeat. Cleon may
well have felt that Paches was insufficiently aggressive at
Mytilene and that his dilatoriness contributed to the escape of
those Mytileneans who did not perish. Diodorus reports that
Paches was happy when informed of the reversal of the Athenians' harsh decree.[32] Westlake, on the other hand, citing the
rarity of Paches' name and of that of his father (Epicurus)
during the fifth century at Athens, suggests that Paches may

have been "a *novus homo* who obtained his command through the influence of the new politicians, such as Cleon, but subsequently incurred their displeasure" and found himself haled into court.[33]

What could Paches have done to bring down an accusation on his head, or simply to furnish a pretext? It could be, as Busolt and Lenschau have suggested, that he was accused of exceeding his powers as στρατηγός in dealing with the situation in Lesbos, but in fact it seems unlikely, for Thucydides' account suggests rather that Paches made every effort to leave the final decision about the fate of Mytilene to the Athenian ἐκκλησία.[34] As Meiggs has pointed out, Paches may have borne in mind the accusations which had been made against Xenophon, Hestiodorus, and Phanomachus in 430 when they had given terms to the Potidaeans without reference to the assembly.[35] Westlake, on the other hand, has made an ingenious suggestion. Thucydides, he reminds us, had attributed the Athenians' rage at the Mytileneans in part to their anger at the fact that a Spartan fleet had sailed as far east as Ionia in support of their rebellion. Now when the Spartan admiral Alcidas thought better of this expedition and decided to turn swiftly back home, Paches had pursued him as far as Patmos but then decided the chase was hopeless and returned to his base at Mytilene. Thucydides, Westlake points out, claims to know what was in Paches' mind as he turned back from Patmos: since he had not come upon the Spartan fleet in the open sea, Thucydides says, he thought it advantageous that the enemy had not been overtaken in some port and thereby compelled the Athenians to divert their fleet in order to blockade them.[36]

Now Westlake has argued that, since Thucydides does not often offer an insight into undisclosed motives or feelings, it may well be that he learned what Paches was feeling when he decided to turn back from Patmos because Paches was forced to discuss this part of his στρατηγία at his trial. As Westlake points out, "the tone of the views ascribed to Paches is markedly apologetic," and Paches "seems to be trying to justify . . . a rather questionable decision by resorting to rather questionable arguments."[37] He may well be right; and if he is, then I think we may accept the fact that there were indeed accusations made against Paches at his εὔθυναι. Thucydides, however, could certainly have learned of Paches' thoughts through private conversations. In any case, Plutarch explains nothing of the military situation in 428 which might have made Athenian dissatisfaction with Paches intelligible. (I am not saying that the Athenians would have been justified in attacking Paches, only that their dissatisfaction is not necessarily beyond comprehension.) But the story of Paches' suicide is something else entirely. Plutarch's language does not make clear whether he felt that Paches' suicide took place at his εὔθυναι or at a trial arising from them. He says in his life of Aristides that Paches killed himself when the verdict was brought in — ὡς ἡλίσκετο — but in his life of Nicias he says Paches killed himself in the δικαστήριον — *while* undergoing this scrutiny (εὐθύνας διδούς). But εὔθυναι did not take place in a δικαστήριον; *trials* arising from εὔθυναι did. The crucial question is, did Paches' alleged suicide precede or follow the pronunciation of a negative verdict? If the former, what did Paches know of which we today are ignorant? Paches, after all, was allegedly tried in 427: i.e., before the trial of Sophocles, Pythodorus, and Eurymedon; before the trial of Thucydides the historian; before the trial of the victors of Arginusae; before all the impeachments of the fourth century. Our evidence suggests that when Paches' εὔθυναι took place, no Athenian στρατηγός had suffered worse at the hands of the δῆμος than a stiff fine. (I except Themistocles, of course, as the accusation against him was not connected with his στρατηγία.) Paches, after all, did not have the benefit of reading Thucydides, Plutarch, or the historians of the nineteenth and twentieth centuries. If the latter, we must ask if it is likely that Paches was the first Athenian general sentenced to, say, death or exile — and would not this development have been given a prominent place by writers of the classical period? Or would the sentence of a fine which he could not have paid, thus incurring ἀτιμία, have driven Paches to suicide?

In any event, moreover, suicide is a most un-Athenian act — virtually unheard-of. Two inferences follow from this

fact. First, it is not likely that Paches would have killed himself. Second, it is not likely that, had he done so publicly, the
event would not have drawn more attention from writers before Plutarch. Had the story been taken up by Ephorus, for
example, it surely would have appeared in Diodorus, who had
an appetite for melodrama.

More decisive against the authenticity of Plutarch's story,
however, is the *argumentum e silentio* from Thucydides. To be
sure, such arguments are, as a rule, methodologically dubious.
As I have tried to show at some length, however, Thucydides
demonstrated a consistent opinion that the Athenians treated
their στρατηγοί unfairly. If I am right, then does it not seem
unlikely in the extreme that he would have omitted from his
history the story of a στρατηγός hounded by the irrational and
ungrateful δῆμος to the point of public suicide?

Plutarch's vague account of Paches' accountability trial and
death, then, is incoherent and inadequate in a number of particulars. But it is of a piece with the unflattering view of the
Athenian δῆμος which he has presented in passing in a number
of his biographies and in some detail in his account of Pericles'
deposition and trial. In view of the picture of the Athenian
δῆμος and its treatment of its leaders which has been painted
by both Thucydides and Plutarch, it is not surprising that, as
we have seen in Chapter I, modern scholars have taken con-
demnatory views of Athenian accountability trials. Hansen has
concluded that "the numerous eisangeliai cast a shadow over
the Athenian democracy and indicate that a direct democracy
may employ the same judicial methods as a totalitarian state."
The Athenians, he goes on, "behaved as tyrannoi not only
against their allies but also against their own leaders."[38] Another view, however, is possible. Thus for example Cawkwell
has written that "bribery and corruption were common enough
in Greece, if one is to judge by the frequency of the accusation."[39] Indeed Hansen himself is open to two possibilities.
"The astonishingly high number of trials," he writes, "leaves
us with a rather sinister dilemma. *Either* the Athenian people
must have elected and appointed a high number of treacherous

and corrupt generals *or* the Athenian jurors must have convicted a high number of honest leaders on false accusations. . . ."[40] I have tried to suggest in the chapters that have gone before that in reality the explanation of the frequency of Athenian accountability trials is far more complex.

VIII THE ACCOUNTABILITY OF PRIVATE CITIZENS

THE Athenians, as we have already seen, demanded an extremely high standard of performance from their chosen officials. In addition, two principal weapons of the δῆμος were employed in large part against those who held no public office. These weapons were, on the one hand, ostracism, and, on the other, the γραφὴ παρανόμων: the indictment for making an illegal proposal.

The first of these has attracted a great deal of attention because of its unusual and, indeed, bizarre nature.[1] In the sixth prytany of each year the ἐκκλησία would put to a vote the question of whether or not to hold an ostracism. If it was decided that an ostracism should be held, a second vote was taken soon afterwards. At this second meeting, part of the Agora was fenced off and each citizen would cast his vote under the supervision of the βουλή and the archons by writing a name on an ὄστρακον, i.e., a broken piece of pottery. The candidate who received the largest number of votes was sent into banishment for ten years, provided that a certain minimum number of votes had been cast. We know that a quorum of six thousand was required, but whether of six thousand votes cast in total or of six thousand against the leading candidate is not clear.[2] No pretext was called for to justify sending a citizen into banishment by ostracism; the victim was not charged with any crime, and when he returned to Attica after his ten years were up, he resumed the full exercise of his civic and property rights: as Bonner and Smith point out, ostracism "was an administrative rather than a judicial act."[3] It cannot be denied, however, that an exile of ten years was a severe sentence indeed in an age when a man's identity was far more closely tied to his native state than it tends to be today. Even in our own comparatively cosmopolitan age, such a penalty would weigh heavily on many citizens. It is interesting to notice that no opportunity seems to have existed at Athens for removing an official from his post without either charging him with a crime or inflicting a penalty. Only by ostracism could a man be removed from office without being charged (though such, it seems, was neither the intent nor the use of the law); and ostracism entailed what amounted to a serious penalty. But by ostracism the Athenians might remove those who, like the suspected tyrannists ostracized during the 480s, seemed to pose a danger to the democracy, or those who, like later victims, were involved in political rivalries of various kinds: in the latter case, an ostracism might befall the man whose misfortune it was to be the second most popular politician in town.

There are only about ten well-attested cases of ostracism, although a variety of others have been suggested and are discussed by Carcopino under the rubric "Les Ostracisés imaginaires."[4] Over half of these took place during the 480s: that of Hipparchus in 487, of Megacles in 486, of an anonymous friend of the Peisistratids in 485, of Xanthippus in 484, and of Aristides in 482.[5] (Possibly we should add to these the less clear case of the elder Alcibiades.[6]) Themistocles was ostracized at some point in the 470s.[7] Cimon was ostracized in 461 and Thucydides, the son of Melesias, in 443.[8] The last ostracism was that of Hyperbolus about 416.[9]

It is likely, I think, that ostracism was instituted at Athens by Cleisthenes. Such, at any rate, is the contention of Aristotle, Philochorus, Aelian, and Diodorus (following Ephorus, who in turn probably followed an earlier Atthidographer, such as Cleidemus or Hellanicus).[10] Cleisthenes' purpose, it would seem, was to discipline the Peisistratid party; yet the Athenians, Aristotle maintains, did not put ostracism into practice until 488/87, when they ostracized Hipparchus, and Androtion has seemed to many scholars to suggest that the law was passed very shortly before Hipparchus' ostracism.[11] This seeming inconsistency has distressed modern historians and has led some to allege either that Cleisthenes did not in fact institute ostracism or that Aristotle was unaware of victims prior to Hipparchus.[12] But the delay is far from inexplicable; why should Cleisthenes not have preferred simply to hold the new institution in reserve as a threat, by which he might coerce the tyrannist party into cooperation?[13]

To be sure, tension between the two parties was inevitable. But the years prior to the ostracism of Hipparchus indeed give some evidence of a coalition between the parties of Cleisthenes and of Hipparchus. The two parties, after all, shared a common opposition to Sparta and a favorable disposition towards Persia, where Hippias had taken refuge. As C. A. Robinson has argued, "it was inevitable that those who had supported the Peisistratidae should also support Cleisthenes. The tyrants' partisans had included the poorer classes and those of impure Athenian descent, and it was these very persons whom Isagoras as archon had attacked. With Hippias in exile, and the aristocrats oppressive, the people turned to Cleisthenes. . . ."[14] If this view of the relations between the two parties is correct, then, it may be that the archonship of Hipparchus in 496 represented, in Kagan's words, Hipparchus' "reward for support and cooperation" — and that Hipparchus' ostracism, when it came, arose from another quarter entirely.[15] Besides, as A. R. Hands has pointed out, Aristotle nowhere states that no Athenian ever *attempted* to ostracize anyone prior to the ostracism of Hipparchus. For a successful ostracism two preconditions had to be met: first a preliminary vote in favor of holding the ostracism, and then a sufficient number of sherds cast at the second vote.[16] It may be, then, that the ostracism of Hipparchus was not the first to be proposed but rather simply the first to "take." If this is so, then we have another reason for accepting a delay between the institution of ostracism and the first known case.

In any event, Aristotle maintains that the first victims of ostracism were the friends of the tyrants, and that subsequently ostracism was used to remove anyone who seemed to be too great, the first of this latter group being Xanthippus:

> And Megacles, the son of Hippocrates, of the deme Alopece, was ostracized. Now for three years they went on ostracizing the friends of the tyrants, for which purpose the law had been made, but afterwards in the fourth year they used it to remove any other person who seemed to be too great. And the first person to be ostracized who had nothing to do with the tyranny was Xanthippus, the son of Ariphron.[17]

Lenardon has suggested that the man whom Aristotle left unnamed was Callias of Alopece, called Μῆδος or ἐκ Μήδων on a few surviving ostraca, and has suggested the following schema for the ostracisms of this period:

488/87	Hipparchus, a Peisistratid	
487/86	Megacles, an Alcmaeonid	Friends of the tyrants,
486/85	Callias (?), pro-Persian	according to Aristotle
485/84	Xanthippus, an Alcmaeonid[18]	

Lenardon conjectures therefore that these ostracisms represent an attack on the coalition of Cleisthenes' party and that of the tyrannists, and joins a long tradition of scholars who have argued that we ought to see here the fine hand of the rising Themistocles.

Two years after the ostracism of Xanthippus came both the discovery of the great vein of silver at Laurium and the ostracism of Aristides. Aristotle suggests that the ostracism of Aristides should be traced to the conflict at Athens over what to do with the silver, with Themistocles advocating the building of ships and Aristides supporting the distribution of the money among the citizens; most scholars have found this suggestion persuasive.[19] Plutarch suggests that Themistocles had a hand in Aristides' ostracism, and throughout his biographies of the two men he stresses with obsessive persistence the intensity of the rivalry between Themistocles and Aristides, whom Themistocles had just recently accused at his εὔθυναι.[20] Large finds of ostraca bearing Themistocles' name and dated to the 480s suggest that the contest between the two men may have been a close one. Plutarch states plainly too that Aristides was an associate of Cleisthenes.[21] It seems probable, then, that during the 480s Themistocles indeed led an attack on both the tyrannist and the Alcmaeonid parties.

What is not so certain, of course, is how much of Themistocles' motivation was related to the advancement of his naval policy and how much of it derived from his desire to advance his own career; probably both motives were combined. At some point during the 470s, however, probably in 471, Themistocles found himself the "victor" in an ostracism — and worse: while in exile he was impeached for treason by εἰσαγγελία and condemned to death *in absentia*.[22] Some ancient sources even posit an earlier trial for treason at which he was acquitted.[23]

The chronology of this period of Themistocles' life is one of the great cruxes of Athenian history, and much ink has been spilt in the attempt to solve the problem.[24] In vain, it seems; but the extent of our ignorance about the chronology of Themistocles' misfortunes is matched by the ease with which we may understand the source of the Athenians' dissatisfaction. The tale of Themistocles' ostracism reads like a mystery story with an abundance of well-motivated potential villains, and we begin to suspect a denouement rather like Agatha Christie's *Murder on the Orient Express*: they all done it. As Lenardon has written:

> Overweening ambition and tyrannical behaviour are the reasons cited, coupled with the envy of his fellow Athenians for his glorious victory at Salamis. Hostility and fear on the part of political rivals and the anger of Sparta also hastened his downfall; and it is not too difficult to imagine that issues revolving about the formation of the Delian Confederacy were very much at stake. Cimon, backed by Spartan hatred, would be delighted to see the last of Themistocles. . . .[25]

Kagan sees a clear coalition of Aristides, Xanthippus, and Cimon and attributes Themistocles' ostracism to a "union of

Philaids and Alcmaeonids and Kerykes"; and Meiggs concludes that Themistocles was ostracized because "the leading
families in the seventies . . . were too powerful to be effectively challenged."[26] This picture of important families operating
as monolithic blocs may be too simple; after all, it was evidently the Alcmaeonid Pericles who served as χορηγός for Aeschylus' *Persians* around the same time; it is hard to believe (despite some arguments put forward by Lenardon) that the glo-
rification of Themistocles was if not the intent then at least the
foreseeable consequence of the play.[27] But whatever the precise nature of the coalition against Themistocles, the ancient
sources tell a story which, despite the chronological difficulties, is in its outlines both coherent and convincing. Athens'
political leaders, favoring peace with Sparta and a tactful, diplomatic approach towards the allies of the newly founded
Delian confederacy, understandably felt that their interest lay
in getting rid of the man who had tricked the Spartans into
allowing the Athenians to fortify their city — the same man
whose ruthless exactions from the allies had been felt in Carystus, in Paros, in Andros, and even perhaps (if we may believe
Themistocles' evident enemy Timocreon) so far away as
Rhodes.[28] And so Aristides, Cimon, and Xanthippus probably
joined together against their dangerous rival. As for the men of
Athens who inscribed Themistocles' names on their sherds (or
who accepted readily those sherds which finds have suggested
had been prepared in advance *en masse* by Themistocles'
enemies) — what motivated them in their choice of a victim?
Some surely were moved to vote for Themistocles' ostracism by disapproval of his policies and fear of Sparta; others
doubtless had been alienated by that lack of modesty which
had become his trademark after Salamis, if not before. The
reasons for Themistocles' ostracism were, doubtless, multiple,
but they are not far to seek. It is certainly true that the evident
combination against him of representatives of Athens' most
blue-blooded families is a striking one; but there is no reason, I
think, to imagine with Glotz and Cohen, following Busolt, that
the attack on Themistocles turned upon the issue of domestic
politics and to see Themistocles as the victim of a conservative

coalition which opposed the progress of democracy.[29] Should Themistocles have remained prominent among Athens' politicians, a war with Sparta would have lain not far ahead, and for such a war Athens had neither the resources not the appetite.

Neither the ostracism of Themistocles, however, nor his subsequent exile removed the strain between Athens and Sparta. In 462, the Spartans appealed to their allies in the Hellenic league for help in breaking the stronghold of the rebellious helots on Mt. Ithome, and their request led to a famous debate in Athens. Ephialtes exhorted the Athenians to turn a deaf ear to the pleas of a rival city and to "let the pride of Sparta be trampled underfoot." [30] In part, Ephialtes' opposition to the project of aiding the Spartans may have been opposition to the Spartans' champion, Cimon; as we have seen in Chapter IV, Ephialtes' associate Pericles had only recently attacked Cimon at his audits, accusing him of having taken a bribe in exchange for not invading Macedonia. Predictably, Cimon advocated sending help to the Spartans, urging his fellow citizens not to desert their "yokefellow." [31] Cimon's arguments won, and he was dispatched in person to aid the Spartans at the head of four thousand hoplites.

Cimon and his men, however, returned rather sooner than had been expected. For reasons which elude us today, the Spartans had undergone a sudden change of heart and, while accepting the aid of other πόλεις, nonetheless sent the Athenians packing as soon as they arrived, claiming that they had ceased to need their help.[32] Not surprisingly, the Spartans' *volte face* proved fatal to Cimon's position in Athens. As a result of this insult, the Athenians abandoned the alliance which had bound them to Sparta through the Hellenic league; they allied themselves with Argos, Sparta's old enemy, and with Thessaly; they rejected Cimon's attempts to restore the lost powers of the Areopagus; and in the spring of 461 they held an ostracism. We may guess that Cimon was the decisive "victor."

It is likely that Ephialtes proposed the ostracism of 461. But is it true, as Kagan has argued, that "no politician used the weapon of ostracism unless he was altogether confident that his opponent would be ostracized and not himself"?[33] How many political situations in fact admitted of such confidence? Ephialtes in 461 had reason to be confident; so, probably, did the prominent men who had combined against Themistocles a decade before. But when the next documented ostracism was held in 443, could any politician in Athens have been certain of the outcome?

Organized party politics, according to Plutarch, were invented during the middle of the fifth century by Thucydides, the son of Melesias. Thucydides was the first, Plutarch tells us, who made a point of having all his friends — the καλοὶ κἀγαθοί, Plutarch calls them — sit together in the ἐκκλησία. Plutarch claims that Thucydides capitalized on a growing rift in Athens between these καλοὶ κἀγαθοί and the rest:

> From the first there had been a kind of flaw beneath the surface
> . . . but the rivalry and ambition of the two sides cut a deep
> wound in the state and caused it to be divided into two parts,
> one called the δῆμος and one called the ὀλίγοι.[34]

How were these καλοὶ κἀγαθοί to undermine the growing prestige of Ephialtes' successor Pericles? The son of Melesias found several means. First, he suggested that Pericles, who had always found his physical resemblance to Peisistratus something of an embarrassment, was well on the way to establishing a tyranny at Athens. Second, he accused Pericles of extravagance in his building program. Finally, and most important, he attacked the very foundation, as it were, of the building program. It was inappropriate, he claimed, for the Athenians to take tribute money which had been given to them for protecting the allies from Persia and use it instead to "adorn our city like a wanton woman."[35] Pericles in turn pointed out that the Athenians were paid to keep the allies from the Persians — and that the allies *were* indeed safe from the Persians.[36] Consequently, he went on, the Athenians were quite free to spend any moneys not necessary for military preparations in any way they wished; and to the charge of extravagance, he replied that he was willing to pay for the new buildings out of his own private funds — provided, of course, that his name alone would be inscribed on them.[37] The building program went on at the public expense, and it was shortly after this debate that the ostracism was held which ended in the departure from Athens of Pericles' opponent Thucydides. In this way the Athenians resolved the tensions between the two men who commanded the largest followings in the assembly.

Finally, during the troubled interval between the Peace of Nicias and the Athenian decision to invade Sicily, the Athenians ostracized Hyperbolus. Why Hyperbolus?[38] The motive for his ostracism has been spelled out plainly by Plutarch, who discusses it in three of his biographies, those of Aristides, Nicias, and Alcibiades.[39] In his *Nicias*, Plutarch writes that the ostracism was a contest between the young, who wanted war and therefore opposed Nicias, and the old, who wanted peace and therefore opposed Alcibiades. This division, Plutarch says, created an opportunity for the most reckless of the Athenians' leaders, among whom was Hyperbolus: he was a man, Plutarch says,

> whose arrogance was not based on any power that he possessed but who had acquired power through arrogance. He had become a discredit to the city by virtue of the credit he had in the city. He thought that he was safely beyond the reach of ostracism at that time, since he was indeed a more probable candidate for the whipping post. He hoped that when one of the other two was driven out, he would be a match for the one who was left. . . . The supporters of Nicias and Alcibiades, recognizing his worthlessness, met secretly, conferred, combined forces and saw to it that neither of them was ostracized, but Hyperbolus instead.[40]

But Plutarch goes on to admit that Theophrastus attributes the ostracism to the strife not between Alcibiades and Nicias but rather between Alcibiades and Phaeax.[41] In his life of Alcibiades, which was probably composed later, he gives somewhat more prominence to the possible role of Phaeax in the ostracism of Hyperbolus.[42]

Now it has been the traditional view of historians that Hyperbolus was a political nonentity, that the combination

against him of Nicias' and Alcibiades' supporters was positive-
ly comical, and that the Athenians abandoned ostracism precisely because they were horrified to see how it could be perverted in this way. In fact, the research of Connor and also of
Baldwin and Camon makes clear that Hyperbolus was far from
a nobody.[43] It was he, after all, who proposed the ostracism;
and his activity in Athenian politics during the decade before
his ostracism is well documented.[44] What seems to have
alarmed the Athenians, as Carcopino and Hatzfeld have
observed, was rather the way in which aristocratic clubs could
have joined together to produce such an unexpected coup.[45]
The assumption that Hyperbolus was a man of no account
rests in part on the slanders directed against him by Plutarch
and also by Thucydides, who claims that he was ostracized
because of depravity and the disgrace he brought to the city,
but also, as Connor has pointed out, on "the notion so common in late antiquity and in modern times that Athens was a
city where only two or three leaders were active at any one
time."[46] Rather, Connor suggests, the situation was far more
complex, involving rivalry not only between Nicias and Alcibiades but between Nicias and Alcibiades and Phaeax and
Hyperbolus.

Yet the central fact remains that the ostracism of Hyperbolus did represent a departure from previous Athenian practice.
Previous ostracisms (those we know much about, at any rate)
had combined precisely the sorts of factional and policy differences which we have seen playing such a large role in Athenian
accountability trials of a more direct nature. The ostracism of
Aristides seems to have arisen from his constant rivalry with
Themistocles but to have focused in the end on the question of
Themistocles' naval policy. The ostracism of Themistocles
himself arose in part from his provocative personality, in part
from his perilous anti-Spartan stand. The ostracism of Cimon
represented both Ephialtes' attack on his factional rival and a
vote against Cimon's philolaconism. Finally, the ostracism of
Thucydides, the son of Melesias, offered the Athenians a
choice between the head of the καλοὶ κἀγαθοί and their programs on the one hand, and the rising head of the δῆμος on the

other. But the situation at the time of Hyperbolus' ostracism seems to have been different. Unless there is a huge hole in all the accounts which have come down to us, Hyperbolus advocated no special program or policies. As Fuqua has written, the institution of ostracism "was designed to offer the Athenian populace the opportunity to choose between policies and their proponents; but when Hyperbolus proposed an *ostrakophoria* in 416 this was not the case." Rather, "instead of a clear choice between policies, the Athenians were presented with the alternatives of either continuing with an indefinite policy under known and tried leaders or embarking on a new and untested strategy."[47] The latter choice, it would seem, they were not prepared to make. The ostracism of Hyperbolus, then, which Fuqua rightly calls "one of those puzzling minor events in Greek history which upon closer examination take on added importance," would seem to be the exception that proves the rule: ostracisms at Athens arose, like other kinds of accountability trials, not only from factional politics but from policy questions as well.[48]

Why did the Athenians never hold another ostracism? Plutarch thought he knew, and his view has won wide acceptance among modern historians. In his life of Nicias, he explains that the Athenians were so horrified that the ostracism "should have been abased by being applied to such an utterly unworthy creature" that they abandoned the practice. He goes on to cite Plato the comic poet: the man, he said, deserved the fate, but not the fate the man.[49] In his life of Aristides, moreover, Plutarch maintains that the horrified Athenians not only abandoned the practice of ostracism but indeed abolished it legally, but the Athenians seem still to have considered ostracism annually at the κυρία ἐκκλησία of the sixth prytany.[50] Whether or not ostracism was legally terminated at this time, Plutarch's explanation is surely too simple. He ignores another possible motivation for the abolition of ostracism: the case of Hyperbolus may well have been the first instance in which the proponent of an ostracism found himself the victim. As Carcopino and Hatzfeld have pointed out, moreover, the Athenians as a whole can hardly have been pleased by the coalition of oligarchic clubs which would appear to have underlain the ostracism of Hyperbolus.[51]

What is certain is that around the same time as ostracism was either abolished or abandoned, the Athenians began to make use of another device which, like ostracism, could be deployed not only against men in office but against private citizens as well — the γραφὴ παρανόμων, or indictment for illegal proposals.

Any citizen who made a proposal in the assembly might be the victim of such an indictment for an illegal proposal.[52] A citizen who wished to bring an accusation of illegality against the author of a proposal would announce on oath (ὑπωμοσία) in the assembly his intention of doing so at any time after the proposal was made, either before or after it was passed. This ὑπωμοσία had the effect of suspending the validity of the decree under attack until the γραφὴ παρανόμων came to trial. The alleged illegality might concern the form of the proposal — a proposal was illegal, for example, if it had not been properly submitted to the assembly by the council — or its substance, if, for example, it contradicted a previous law which had not yet been abolished. The case would then come for trial before a dicastery of at least a thousand jurors, over which the θεσμοθέται would preside. A γραφὴ παρανόμων was an ἀγὼν τιμητός, and the penalties handed down to convicted proposers of decrees varied; death is mentioned as a theoretical possibility in several speeches of Demosthenes, but all the attested sentences entail only fines.[53] A citizen whose measures were condemned three times by way of γραφὴ παρανόμων was forbidden to bring further proposals before the assembly. After a year had passed, the author of a motion ceased to be liable to prosecution by γραφὴ παρανόμων, but the proposal itself might still be annulled by the same procedure.

Is it a coincidence that the first known case of the γραφὴ παρανόμων followed so quickly on the heels of the last ostracism? We cannot be certain. The date of the origin of the γραφὴ παρανόμων is nowhere stated in the sources. Some, like Bonner and Smith, Glotz, and Cloché, have assumed that it was instituted in 462 by Ephialtes.[54] At opposite extremes, Wilamowitz has sought to trace it as far back as Solon, though his arguments have not won acceptance, and Kahrstedt has argued that it was not instituted until the archonship of Eucleides.[55] It seems by far most likely that the γραφὴ παρανόμων was instituted either during the reforms of 462 or at some point between the reforms of 462 and the year 415, when Leogoras prosecuted Speusippus for proposing and carrying a decree of imprisonment for Leogoras as an accessory to the profanation of the Mysteries.[56] But when? If in 462, as part of Ephialtes' reforms, surely it is odd that we have no documented case of its deployment before 415 (unless perhaps the indictment by Antiphon of the στρατηγός Demosthenes should be placed shortly before this date).[57] If after 462, why do we hear of no constitutional reforms between 462 and 403?

In any event, particularly during the fourth century, the γραφὴ παρανόμων seems to have been used with considerable frequency. According to Diodorus, Demades was convicted by this kind of indictment three times and lost his civic rights for a time.[58] Aeschines mentions in his oration on the crown that Aristophon boasted of having been acquitted on charges brought by way of γραφὴ παρανόμων no less than seventy-five times.[59] Exactly how many of these took place during our time period is not certain. During our time period, we also know of a handful of cases of uncertain date. At some point Antiphon indicted the στρατηγός Demosthenes for an unconstitutional proposal, probably concerning an honorary decree connected with a naval battle; all that can be said for certain about the date is that the indictment preceded Demosthenes' departure for Sicily in 414.[60] Some time towards the beginning of the fourth century Lysias served as logographer for Phanias, who indicted Cinesias for an unconstitutional proposal.[61] Demosthenes' speech against Meidias, written probably in 347, makes reference to the fining of Sciton and Smicrus for illegal proposals.[62] During the period 357–340, Theocrines assumed Charinus' prosecution of Thucydides for an unconstitutional proposal and also brought another γραφὴ παρανόμων against

Demosthenes. The accusations seem to have to do with Thucydides' decree that the Aenians should pay to the Athenian confederacy the contribution on which they had agreed with Chares.[63] During the period 350–340, Theocrines also brought an accusation by way of γραφὴ παρανόμων against Epichares' father, whose name is unknown to us, for proposing an honorary decree for Charidemus, son of Ischomachus. The decree was overruled by the court, and Epichares' father was fined ten talents. As he could not pay, he became ἄτιμος and his fine was doubled.[64] To about the same period must be dated Theocrines' indictment of Antimedon for a decree which he had proposed for the Tenedians, but Theocrines withdrew his accusation before the case came to trial.[65]

In a number of other cases, the date of the prosecution is known to us, but often we know little else. We have already seen how in 415 Leogoras indicted Speusippus for a decree calling for the imprisonment of Leogoras as an accessory to the profanation of the Mysteries. The court overruled the decree.[66] During the attack on the victors of Arginusae in 406, Euryptolemus tried to indict Callixenus for an illegal proposal, and in turn Menecles tried to indict Euryptolemus; but neither γραφή was ever voted on.[67] In 403/2 or 402/1, Archinus indicted Thrasybulus of Steiria for his decree providing that citizenship be awarded to those who participated in the return from the Piraeus. The decree was overruled by the court.[68] About the same time Theozotides was indicted — we do not know by whom — for his decree providing state aid for Athenian children whose fathers had died while fighting for democracy during the civil strife at the end of the Peloponnesian war; the money was to be raised by reducing the pay of the cavalrymen from one drachma to four obols. The decree, however, was upheld by the court.[69]

In 376/75, Leodamas indicted someone for the honorary decree which he proposed for Chabrias after Chabrias' victory at Naxos, but the decree was upheld by the court.[70] Similarly, it is possible that the next year one Athenian indicted another for the decree which he had proposed in honor of Timotheus after his victory at Alyzia but that the decree was upheld; so was the decree which Harmodius attacked in 371/70, a decree honoring Iphicrates.[71]

According to the scholiast on Aeschines 1.64, Hyperides brought an indictment for an illegal proposal against Aristophon in connection with Aristophon's expedition against Keos in 363/62. In 357 or shortly afterwards, Hegesippus indicted Callippus of Paiania for a decree stating that landed property on Cardian territory belonged to Cardia and was held by the Athenians as ἐγκτήματα only. The decree was upheld by the court.[72] In 355/54, Euctemon indicted Androtion for the decree which he proposed for crowning the retiring βουλή; a year or two later Androtion, Glaucetes, and Melanopus indicted Euctemon by way of γραφὴ παρανόμων for a decree calling for the state to collect nearly ten talents from some trierarchs, who might in turn collect it from the ambassadors Androtion, Glaucetes, and Melanopus.[73] In 352/51, Euthycles indicted Aristocrates for the decree which he had proposed honoring Charidemus of Acharnae.[74] Probably in 349 the decrees proposing citizenship to be conferred on Apollonides of Olynthus and Peitholaus of Pherae, which had been passed by the assembly, were challenged by γραφὴ παρανόμων and overturned by the court.[75] In 349/48, Apollodorus' decree, which the assembly had passed, calling for the assembly to decide whether the surplus of the budget should be used as στρατιωτικά or θεωρικά, was challenged by Stephanus, and overturned by the court; Apollodorus was fined one talent.[76] In 348 Lycinus indicted Philocrates for the decree permitting Philip to send a herald and ambassadors to Athens to negotiate peace, but the decree was upheld by the court.[77] In 340 someone attacked a decree of Demosthenes, probably one which provided that νομοθέται be appointed to pass a new trierarchic law; the decree was upheld.[78] In 338 Diondas indicted Hyperides and Demomeles for decrees they had proposed in Demosthenes' honor, but the decrees were upheld.[79] Shortly after the battle of Chaeronea, Aristogeiton attacked Hyperides' decree, which had been passed in the assembly, granting citizenship to metics and slaves and amnesty to assorted persons, and providing for women and children to be moved to the

Piraeus along with the βουλή. The decree was upheld.[80] Around the same time Hyperides indicted Demades for the decree he had proposed honoring Euthycrates of Olynthus.[81]

Now if it is true that Aristophon was acquitted seventy-five times on charges of γραφὴ παρανόμων, the Athenians must have made use of this procedure with considerable frequency, and it must be that only a small fraction of cases is known to us. Even if Aristophon's boast is false, the fact that Aeschines could cite it implies that such a feat did not defy the imagination of an Athenian dicastery. There can be no question, then, that those who undertook to propose decrees in the assembly were, in fact, accountable for their actions. About half the decrees which we know were attacked by γραφὴ παρανόμων were overturned by the courts; of these, about half had been already passed in the assembly, but this clearly did not prevent their being overruled in the court.[82] Several men who had proposed decrees wound up fined for their trouble: Stephanus (one talent), Sciton and Smicrus (ten talents, if we may believe Demosthenes), and Ephichares' father (ten talents). Yet it does not seem that the γραφὴ παρανόμων functioned as the true safeguard of responsible government. Nor is there any comparison between the gravity of an indictment by γραφὴ παρανόμων and an impeachment by way of, say, εἰσαγγελία.

Consider the evidence. About one half of the decrees which we know were challenged by γραφὴ παρανόμων dealt with honorary decrees of one kind or another. It is hard to believe that any significant number of these were brought by men who opposed honorary decrees on principle. Rather it is likely, as Hansen points out, that most attacks on honorary decrees were *ad hominem* attacks on the proposers or on the honorees.[83] This is particularly clear in the case, for example, of Leodamas' attack on the decree honoring Chabrias. As we have seen, it was to be Leodamas who impeached Chabrias and Callistratus ten years later following the loss of Oropus. In addition, some of the γραφαὶ παρανόμων aimed at other decrees seem to have been brought by way of self-defense. Leogoras' attack on Speusippus is one example: Speusippus' decree had called for Leogoras' imprisonment. Another exam-

ple is the attack of Androtion, Glaucetes, and Melanopus on
Euctemon's proposal, which called for the state to collect
nearly ten talents from the trierarchs Archebius and
Lysitheides — who in turn might collect it from Androtion,
Glaucetes, and Melanopus, whom the trierarchs had conveyed
on their embassy to Mausolus of Caria. In the chapters that
have gone before, we have seen how personal considerations
of these kinds might also play a part in other kinds of impeachments. But two central facts are, I think, striking in the Athenians' use of the γραφὴ παρανόμων. First, it does *not* appear
to have been used to ensure orators' responsibility for the
military expeditions they might propose — to make sure, in
other words, that the responsibility for the success or failure of
a mission lay not only with the general chosen to carry it out
but with the man who proposed it in the first place. The only
decree that we know was attacked by γραφὴ παρανόμων that
seems to deal with a military mission was that of Aristophon
concerning the subjugation of Ceos — and it was Aristophon
himself who seems to have led the mission. We do not appear
to have a single obvious instance of a γραφή παρανὸμων being
brought against the instigator of an unsuccessful military expedition. Second, we have not a single clear instance of anyone's career being ruined by conviction on a charge of γραφή
παρανὸμων — as it was likely to be in the case of a conviction
by εἰσαγγελία. As we have seen, Demosthenes suggests that
death might be the penalty in the event of conviction; whether
or not he is telling the truth, we know of no cases for which the
penalty was so severe. Demades, Diodorus tells us, lost his
civic rights after three convictions on the γραφὴ
παρανόμων — but only for a time.[84]

It would be an exaggeration, in other words, to maintain that
the institution of the γραφὴ παρανόμων placed the unofficial
adviser in the same position as the elected official.[85] But it is
important to notice that, as we have seen in Chapter I, the
procedure of εἰσαγγελία could be brought not only against
those who held office but against private citizens as well. And
so it was. In the matter of the mutilation of the Hermae and the

profanation of the mysteries, εἰσαγγελία was the weapon used to proceed not only against Alcibiades, who was, after all, στρατηγός at the time, but also against over fifty other Athenians; Diocleides, moreover, who had denounced forty-two of these, including Andocides, was successfully impeached by εἰσαγγελία when, after the information laid by Andocides, he confessed that his denunciation had been false.[86] Εἰσαγγελία was the weapon used against Hipparchus and Themistocles, both impeached for treason during the first half of the fifth century, although there is no evidence that either man held political office at the time of the accusation against him.[87] It may also have been the weapon used against Cleophon, who was executed in 404 for dereliction of his military duties, a charge which may or may not have been valid but which was clearly brought by those who opposed his strong anti-Spartan stand; he may have held no political office at the time of his trial.[88] In 410/9 the βουλή instituted an impeachment, probably by way of εἰσαγγελία, against some citizens accused of taking bribes in connection with the decree conferring citizenship on Apollodorus.[89] And, as we have seen, the Athenians impeached by εἰσαγγελία in 404 included not only στρατηγοί and taxiarchs but some others as well.[90] It is important to note that when Chabrias was impeached in 366/65 following the loss of Oropus, so was his political associate, the orator Callistratus.[91] Similarly, Callistratus, who had been acquitted on this earlier occasion, was impeached in 361/60 by εἰσαγγελία, evidently for having taken bribes to propose decrees contrary to the interests of the people; he was found guilty *in absentia* and sentenced to death, and when he returned to Attica a few years later he was promptly arrested and executed.[92]

In the early 320s, in his speech defending Euxenippus, whom Polyeuctus had impeached by εἰσαγγελία for making a false report to the assembly, Hyperides complains about the debasement of εἰσαγγελία and describes it as a procedure designed for use against politicians, claiming that he himself has never impeached by εἰσαγγελία any private citizens, ἰδιῶται; consequently we may assume a political motive in the impeachment by Hyperides of both Aristophon, some time

around 350, and Diopeithes, around the same time; but there is
no reason to believe that either man held an official post at the
time of his impeachment. When Hyperides impeached by
εἰσαγγελία Philocrates, who had taken part in the three
embassies sent to Philip in 346, he charged him not with misconduct on his embassy but rather with his behavior in the
ἐκκλησία: Hyperides maintained that he had been bribed to
propose decrees contrary to the interests of the Athenian
people.[93] And shortly after the Battle of Chaeronea it was
evidently by εἰσαγγελία that Autolycus was impeached for
having sent his family away for their safety.[94] He was an
Areopagite, but this seems to have been irrelevant to the case.
Other means besides εἰσαγγελία could certainly be employed
against politicians who had displeased the δῆμος. It is worth
noting that, after the execution of the victors of Arginusae, the
Athenians were angry with several of those who had been
instrumental in bringing about the condemnation of the generals, and they imprisoned them after a προβολή. They escaped
before their cases came up for trial, but one of them, Callixeinus, was so universally detested that, according to
Xenophon, he died of starvation; and we have already seen
how Theramenes, who also played a role in the condemnation
of the generals, was rejected the next year at his δοκιμασία.[95]

The Athenians, then, had three principal weapons at their disposal with which they might discipline private citizens who
participated in politics. Ostracism they employed not only as a
safety valve in settling factional disputes but also, like more
traditional kinds of accountability trials, to resolve serious disagreements about important matters of policy. The way in
which the γραφὴ παρανόμων functioned as part of political life
is less clear, but it does not appear that this form of indictment
worked successfully to lessen the gap between unofficial rhe-
tors and those who held formal office. Εἰσαγγελίαι, however,
were often brought against those who held no office — and
the consequences of εἰσαγγελία for private citizens were
every bit as grave as for officials of the state.

IX CONCLUSION: ACCOUNTABILITY AND THE ATHENIAN DEMOCRACY

IF the interpretations which I have offered in the preceding chapters are substantially correct, then at some times the accusations against Athenian officials probably arose, at least in part, out of genuine violations of the law. Of the στρατηγοί, Miltiades was probably guilty of deceiving the people — whatever that may mean. He may not have lied, but his promises were not fulfilled, and he had made them entirely of his own volition. If Xenophon, Hestiodorus, and Phanomachus were charged with exceeding their instructions in negotiating with the surrendered Potidaeans, then they were probably guilty. The two generals who assisted the return of the Theban exiles in 378 almost certainly acted without orders from the ἐκκλησία and thus were in grave violation of the law. Timomachus doubtless broke the law by his transport of the exile Callistratus on a state trireme. Ergocles may have been guilty of κλοπή, and so may have Agyrrhius. There is no strong evidence to suggest that any of the στρατηγοί accused of προδοσία were guilty except possibly Ergocles, although, as such things do happen, probability dictates that some were — and why, after all, should evidence of such a crime have survived to this day? Some may wish to make a case for the guilt of, say, Phrynichus or Alcibiades. Among the ambassadors, Antiphon, Archeptolemus, and Onomacles seem clearly to

161

have been guilty of treason. Aeschines was guilty of disobeying instructions. Many other Athenian officials were tried on charges which are unknown to us today. Of these men it is of course impossible to assess the technical guilt or innocence.

A number of Athenian officials, moreover (especially those who were convicted at their impeachment trials), appear to have in some degree mismanaged their offices — or to have given the Athenians some reason to imagine that they had mismanaged them. On some occasions, this mismanagement amounted to incompetence. Such an accusation, I have suggested, could comprehensibly have been leveled against the ambassador Aeschines and against a good number of generals. Aeschines throughout his dealings with Philip misread and misrepresented to the Athenians Philip's true intentions. Sophocles and Eurymedon may have borne part of the responsibility for their late arrival in Sicily, and along with Pythodorus they had acquiesced without a murmur in a Sicilian peace settlement openly predicated on the assumption of Athenian aggression, present and future. Thucydides and his associate Eucles lacked the foresight to deal with Brasidas in Thrace and lost Amphipolis. The generals at Arginusae did not exercise sufficient presence of mind in a crisis which ought to have been foreseen by experienced commanders — which many of them were, particularly Thrasyllus, who was the commander-in-chief on the day of the battle. As a result, many Athenian sailors drowned, and their corpses went unburied. Dionysius and his fellow στρατηγοί in the Hellespont in 387 ignored information that Antalcidas was planning to lure them into a trap. As a direct result, the Athenians lost the Corinthian War. Callisthenes showed bad judgment in accepting the good faith of Perdiccas, and as a result the Athenians failed to regain Amphipolis. Similarly, Cephisodotus' misplaced faith in Charidemus led to the defeat of the Athenian forces in Perinthus and to a humiliating treaty. Finally, the Athenian commanders at Chaeronea allowed themselves to be forced to give battle in conditions favoring Philip's tactics, and failed to overcome them in the field.

In addition, a number of officials seem to have abused their offices in one degree or another — Miltiades, for example, who had taken an unwarranted degree of responsibility upon himself; his too was the responsibility when his scheme to take Paros fell through. In addition, the Athenians had good reason to be disappointed in Alcibiades' performance after his reinstatement on *de facto* probation, and his was the responsibility when his lavish promises of Persian aid could not be fulfilled and he was unable to redeem his position by scoring a striking military succees. His lack of judgment in selecting Antiochus for a lieutenant was confirmed in the event.

What can we infer from all this? We can infer, I think, that the charges of bribery and treason which the Athenians leveled against their highest officials were intentionally extreme. The men who brought these accusations did not necessarily believe that the defendants were guilty as charged. As Westlake has pointed out in discussing the case of Paches, "it must be remembered that the formal charge was not necessarily identical with the real cause of complaint."[1] The evidence bears out, I believe, Andrewes' contention that "the standard of ingenious villainy ascribed to the speaker's opponent" in Athenian trials "is hardly meant to be accepted literally."[2] Extreme charges against those officials with whom the δῆμος was not satisfied were intended to remind Athenian office holders of the exacting standards by which their conduct would be judged. Athenian officials must surely have entered on their offices well aware of the dangerous rules of the game. Pritchett has commented quite rightly (as regards Athens, at least) that

> the ancient strategos must have entered upon his command in the sort of frank acceptance of risk well expressed in a statement of Marshal Ferdinand Foch: "Great results in war are due to the commander. History is therefore right in making generals responsible for victories — in which case they are glorified; and for defeats — in which case they are disgraced."[3]

If the analyses of the case histories I have discussed are correct, moreover, factional strife played a role in a number of

Athenian impeachment trials. As we have seen, Miltiades' accuser Xanthippus had married into the rival Alcmaeonid family, and Aristotle distinguishes two political parties quarreling for supremacy at Athens at the time of the Parian expedition, that of the people, led by Xanthippus, and that of the aristocrats, led by Miltiades. Factional considerations seem to have played a role in the impeachment of Miltiades' son Cimon by Xanthippus' son Pericles. It seems likely that Pericles had inherited something of a family political feud with the house of Miltiades. Plutarch and Aristotle, as we have seen, both claim that combatting the popularity of Cimon was a principal concern of Pericles in his early political life; part of Pericles' motive, certainly, in accusing Cimon in connection with the Thasian expedition was to undermine the position of his rival while at the same time drawing attention to himself.

Factional considerations also appear to have played a role in the abortive attempt to call in Pericles' accounts before the outbreak of the Peloponnesian War, probably in 438. The attempt seems to have been accompanied by attacks on Pericles' associates Phidias, Anaxagoras, and Aspasia and sought to undermine Pericles' standing at Athens. I have indicated too that the year of Anytus' trial, 408, suggests that the attack on him was mounted at least in part by the radical democrats, who had been in control of Athens since the summer of 410 and had used the courts to persecute the moderates. It also seems likely that the political motives of Theramenes and his Alcibiadist associates contributed to the attack on the victors of Arginusae, as did the combination in the assembly, I have argued, between pro-Spartan oligarchs on the one hand and radical democrats like Callixeinus and Lyciscus on the other. I have argued in Chapter V that the rash of impeachments which broke out during the Corinthian War is to be traced in part to factional strife between the radical and moderate camps in cooperation against the conservatives. The impeachment of Chabrias, I have suggested, arose in part from his association with Callistratus. It may be that the same was true of the impeachment of Leosthenes, although the evidence there is shadowy and inconclusive.

In addition, we have seen that the impulse to self-preservation sometimes motivated a man in bringing an action of impeachment. Theramenes, for example, was probably motivated in his attack on the victors of Arginusae by the need to preserve his own safety, since the generals had implicated him in the disaster. Leon in his accusation against his fellow envoy Timagoras was probably anxious about his own position following Pelopidas' coup at the Persian court. Demosthenes in his accusation against his fellow envoy Aeschines feared for his own safety after the Athenians realized the implications of the Peace of Pholocrates. (If Conon indeed ever prosecuted Adeimantus for his behavior at Aegospotami, as Demosthenes suggests, it is probable that he was motivated in this accusation by a desire to consolidate his own position after that fatal battle.[4]) Considerations of self-preservation must surely have motivated Apollodorus in the impeachment of the στρατηγός Timomachus and the trierarch Callippus; Apollodorus had reason to fear that he would be implicated in the illegal transport of the exile Callistratus.

One man who appears to have understood how to use the machinery of impeachment to advance his own long career was the στρατηγός Chares. It is not a coincidence, I have argued, that we know of three military operations in which Chares was involved that led to the impeachment of one or more of his colleagues: the Oropus campaign which led to the impeachment of Chabrias; the naval battle during the Social War which led to the impeachment of Timotheus, Iphicrates, and Menestheus; and finally the battle of Chaeronea, which led to the impeachment of Lysicles. Finally, an unusual case of self-preservation arose in the case of the impeachment of the στρατηγοί who were indicted after they helped the Thebans liberate the Cadmeia from Spartan control in 379/78. Soon after the Spartans had been forced to evacuate the Cadmeia, three Spartan ambassadors were sent to Athens; they made clear, it seems, that the repudiation of the generals who had aided the Thebans would help divert from Attica the invading army of King Cleombrotus. The Athenians promptly condemned the two generals, not, by and large, out of lack of sympathy with their views, but out of fear of war with the Spartans.

I have suggested, moreover, that the kinds of political differences which led to Athenian impeachment trials were not always factional disputes of a largely personal nature. A number of impeachments arose, I think, in some part out of sincere differences among the Athenians over important issues of policy; and impeachment trials might serve too as arenas in which these might be argued out. The deposition of Pericles in 430 is probably the most striking case. Indeed, his very deposition itself served as the instrument of policy: the Athenians, I have argued, removed Pericles from office in the summer of 430 because they were disappointed in his moderate policy and wanted to explore other methods of dealing with the Spartans, some wanting to make peace, others wanting to pursue the war more aggressively. Issues of policy may have been involved as well in the accusation made by Cleon later that year against the three generals who accepted the surrender of Potidaea. The generals probably did in fact exceed their authority in negotiating with the surrendered Potidaeans, but the real source of the accusation may well have been a fundamental disagreement over the kind of policy to be employed in dealing with capitulated rebels, an issue which was soon to be debated passionately in the case of Mytilene. It appears, moreover, that the men who voted the deposition of Phrynichus and Scironides during the winter of 412/11 thought that in office they would hinder the return of Alcibiades, whose sworn enemy Phrynichus was. Thrasybulus of Steiria had pursued a particularly aggressive policy in Asia, alienating many Athenians; had he lived he would surely have been impeached. It seems all but certain that the attack on Timotheus in 373 arose from opposition to his restoration of the Zacynthian exiles, an act which arose from his pro-Theban, anti-Spartan orientation, and which led to the renewal of hostilities between Athens and Sparta. One issue in the trial of Timotheus, Iphicrates, and Menestheus during the Social War was the Athenians' conflict over the wisdom of the policy of moderation in dealing with the allies, which was represented by Timotheus and to some extent by Iphicrates, as opposed to the more aggressive approach of Chares. Finally, differences over Athenian policy towards Macedon played a large part in the trial of Aeschines in 343.

The case histories which have been analyzed in the preceding chapters, in other words, suggest a great deal about the use which the Athenians of the fifth and fourth centuries made of the laws they had framed to ensure the accountability of their officers. Sometimes the machinery of control was used to discipline those who had broken the law. On other occasions, impeached officials, though not guilty of the charges on which they stood technically accused, had genuinely given the Athenians reason to doubt whether they had discharged their offices honorably: some had given reason to suspect incompetence, and others appeared to have abused their offices. The Athenians had no hesitation about reacting swiftly and strongly to inadequacy in their officials. Rarely indeed did they wait until the regular εὔθυναι at the end of the official year to bring accusations; rather, officials suspected of malfeasance were likely to find themselves deposed pending trial during the course of their terms. But if my view of the case histories I have discussed is correct, many officials who were impeached had provoked opposition on political grounds as well — grounds which often had no connection whatever with the action of which they stood formally accused. The balance between opposing political forces at Athens was often sufficiently delicate to permit the election of a man who advocated policies unacceptable to a significant segment of the population and who might have powerful enemies among Athens' other politicians as well. It is in part to this situation, I think, that the impeachment of so many prominent Athenians can be attributed — a fact rarely appreciated by modern historians, who tend, as we have seen, to find most Athenian impeachment trials inexplicable on any rational grounds and have therefore been inclined to attribute their frequency, following Thucydides and Plutarch, to the irrational and excessive expectations of the ungrateful δῆμος.

It is not surprising that modern scholars should take this view. Their inability to comprehend the Athenians' use of accountability trials as arenas for the airing and settling of partisan or policy questions is not due solely to the influence of Thucydides or Plutarch. It must also be traced to the way in which impeachment is viewed in the modern world. In England, impeachment was used by the House of Commons with great frequency throughout the seventeenth century, and to a lesser extent during the eighteenth, to attack unpopular ministers of the king. After the impeachment of Lord Melville in 1806, however, impeachment fell into desuetude, and its place was taken by the present parliamentary system. In this system, no government which fails to represent the views of the majority can stand: disagreements over policy or factional disputes need not therefore be disguised in accusations of criminality. In the United States, however, there are no votes of confidence between regularly scheduled elections; there is machinery for impeachment, but it is not commonly used. For the founding fathers took a very un-Athenian view of impeachment, rejecting the suggestion of George Mason that "maladministration" be the catch-all term for an impeachable offense. As Charles Black of the Yale Law School has written, the rejection of this phrase and the substitution of the phrase "high Crimes and Misdemeanors" "seems absolutely to forbid the removal of a president on the grounds that Congress does not on the whole think his administration of public affairs is good. This distinction . . . tells us — and Congress — that whatever may be the grounds for impeachment and removal, dislike of a president's policy is definitely not one of them."[5] But the Athenians were willing to do what neither the British nor the Americans have done: to combine the machinery of impeachment with the function of the vote of no confidence. For this, as we have seen, they have received much censure.

A number of scholars have also censured the Athenians for another aspect of their system of accountability: the alleged limitation of this system to those who held official positions in the state, and specifically its concentration on στρατηγοί. Greenidge described politicians who held no official position as "unassailable"[6]; Hignett has complained that during the Peloponnesian War Athens' civilian politicians "could not technically be called to account for the failure of the policies they had advocated."[7] Harper describes the "so-called demagogue" of the Peloponnesian War period, the "independent orator," as "free from the restraints imposed upon responsible magistrates" and concludes that "such men are dangerous":

> Pericles as general might persuade the ekklesia . . . but all the while he knew that this ekklesia, grown impatient and swollen by refugees from the countryside, might repudiate his leadership by an impeachment — which, in fact, it did. A demagogue such as Hyperbolus, on the contrary, might as a private citizen with impunity urge the Assembly to vote reckless military adventures overseas, knowing that the penalty for possible failure would fall on the heads of the generals appointed to command.[8]

The problem of the accountability — or lack of it — of Athens' unofficial advisers was a particularly acute one during the fourth century, when so many prominent politicians did not hold the στρατηγία. Perlman in one of his studies of political life in fourth-century Athens has maintained that "in the second half of the fourth century the strategi were dependent on the politicians and were even obliged to cultivate good relations with them in order to get their support in the political assemblies of Athens," whereas the politicians, for their part, "made good use of their influence in order to defend themselves in case of accusations relating to the general conduct of the war and put all the blame on the strategi."[9]

The Athenians, however, did not lack the means to discipline those who held influence without holding office. Ostracism was the weapon used against Hyperbolus, to whom Harper has ascribed "impunity" in proposing measures to the assembly, and many other prominent Athenians, not all of whom held office. By ostracism the Athenians expelled Aristides, the opponent of Themistocles' naval policy; Cimon, whose philolaconian policy had just led the πόλις into humiliation; and Thucydides, the son of Melesias, the rival of

Pericles, who had taken up the cause of the allegedly oppressed allies.

In addition, the γραφὴ παρανόμων was available as a control precisely on the proposing of measures in the assembly, although instead the men of Athens often preferred εἰσαγγελία (and quite probably other forms of indictment as well) against private citizens who had given offense in public life. It was by εἰσαγγελία that the Athenians had finally rid themselves of the provocative Themistocles, whose unpopularity among the Spartans was causing them serious embarrassment. When Chabrias was impeached following the loss of Oropus, as we have seen, so was his associate Callistratus. Although both men were acquitted on this occasion, Callistratus was impeached in 361/60 by εἰσαγγελία for having been bribed to propose decrees in the assembly contrary to the interests of the people. Callistratus was found guilty *in absentia* and sentenced to death, and indeed when he ventured to return to Attica a few years later he was executed. A similar accusation underlay Hyperides' εἰσαγγελία against Philocrates. Those instrumental in the condemnation of the victors of Arginusae were imprisoned after a προβολή but escaped before their cases came to trial. One of them, Xenophon reports, Callixeinus, returned to the city after the amnesty of 403 but was universally detested and died of starvation. Littman has complained that during the Peloponnesian War "a general could be fined or executed on some trumped-up charge if his policy was faring badly but a demagogue in the assembly could not legally be touched if the policies which he advocated fared ill."[10] But if ever a man was tried on a "trumped-up charge," that man was Cleophon, surely one of the most notorious of the so called "demagogues" of the war, who had persuaded the Athenians to reject the Spartans' offers of peace after Aegospotami.[11] The βουλή impeached Cleophon in 404, probably by εἰσαγγελία, for alleged dereliction of military duties. Fearing that he might be acquitted, the βουλή saw to it, Lysias says, that the case was tried by a packed jury including every member of the βουλή — and by this jury Cleophon was found guilty and sentenced to death.[12] So perished one of these "unassailable" civilian politicians. Not for nothing had Diodotus (during the Mytilenean debate) contrasted irresponsible listeners with responsible advisers.

Isocrates complained that the Athenians of his day chose as generals "men whose advice no one would seek on any matter, either public or private," and Plutarch followed the tradition when he wrote that in Phocion's day "public men had distributed among themselves as if by lot the work of general and orator." [13] Some, he goes on, like Eubulus, Aristophon, Lycurgus, and Hyperides limited their activities to the assembly, while others like Diopeithes, Menestheus, Leosthenes, and Chabrias pursued military careers. (Phocion, Plutarch maintains, wanted to restore the old days of Pericles, Aristides, and Solon, in which one man moved in both spheres.) Modern scholars have carried this tradition forward. Thus Perlman writes:

> One of the characteristic developments of the fourth century was the growing differentiation between the strategi, fulfilling mainly military tasks, and the politicians, dealing with decisions on internal and external policy. Though, perhaps, at the beginning of the century there were still politicians (like Thrasybulus, Aristophon, or Kallistratos) who served as strategi, in the second half of the century, actually none of the important politicians filled the office of strategos. [14]

Jebb speaks of the "separation of military from political function" during the fourth century, and in their introductory histories of Greece, Laistner, Bury, and Botsford and Robinson are all careful to alert students to the gap that divided the politician from the general during the fourth century. [15]

The case histories I have analyzed suggest that there is a danger in exaggerating this separation of function. For political issues and political motives were involved in nearly all the impeachment trials of στρατηγοί in the fourth century just as in the fifth. Most of the generals impeached in connection with the Corinthian War owed their unpopularity, I have suggested, to their political backgrounds. The convictions of the generals who assisted the return of the Theban exiles were the direct cause of the act — enormous in its political implications — for which they were condemned. Similarly, Timotheus' first trial resulted in large part from opposition to his restoration of the Zacynthian exiles, an act which grew directly out of his fundamentally pro-Theban, anti-Spartan orientation. The trial of Chabrias arose in large part from his association with Callistratus and with the attack on Timotheus in 373; Timomachus was tried in large part for his association with Callistratus. In the trial of Timotheus, Iphicrates, and Menestheus, a principal issue, I think, was the Athenians' conflict over the wisdom of the policy of moderation in dealing with the allies which Timotheus, and to some extent Iphicrates, represented, as opposed to the more aggressive approach of Chares.

While it is certainly true, then, that many powerful leaders of the assembly — men like Callistratus, Aristophon, Eubulus, and Demosthenes — rarely held the στρατηγία, no hard and fast distinction existed in fourth-century Athens between generals on the one hand and politicians on the other. Bury is probably correct when he writes that "the art of war became every year more and more an art, and little could be accomplished except by generals who devoted their life to the military profession" — men, he goes on, like Timotheus, Chabrias, and Iphicrates.[16] But it is not true that the political influence of these men was, as Laistner claims, "either wholly negligible or else transitory."[17] Iphicrates was in fact famous for his oratory, and some historians have attributed his acquittal during the Social War to his skill in that department.[18] Aeschines mentions Leosthenes' reputation for rhetorical accomplishments.[19] On occasion, generals got into difficulty indirectly through alliance with some powerful politician; both Chabrias and Timomachus, for example, seem to have suffered as a result of the unpopularity of their associate Callistratus. But in most cases the political opinions which brought generals into court as defendants were their own.

Nor, I think, will the evidence support the notion of an antagonism between στρατηγοί and Athens' other prominent men working itself out with any regularity in the courts during the fourth century. Only about half of all the accountability trials attested between 400 and 338 — even excluding trials by γραφὴ παρανόμων — were aimed at στρατηγοί. Now it may be true that in some cases politicians cleverly attacked στρατηγοί for the failure of military expeditions which the politicians themselves had advocated. Such *may* have been the case with Aristophon's εἰσαγγελία against Leosthenes in 361, with Euthycles' εἰσαγγελία against Cephisodotus in 359, with Aristophon's attack on Iphicrates, Timotheus, and Menestheus during the Social War, or with Lycurgus' attack on Lysicles after the defeat at Chaeronea. But no clear pattern emerges, and in many cases such a view of an impeachment would clearly be a false one. The motive of Apollodorus' impeachment of the general Timomachus and the trierarch Callippus, for example, seems to have been self-defense: Apollodorus had himself been invited to aid in the illegal transport of Timomachus' relative Callistratus and doubtless he wanted to clear his name. It is important to notice that the εἰσαγγελία against Timotheus in 373 was mounted by a coalition of Callistratus *and* the famous στρατηγός Iphicrates. Callistratus himself, moreover, as we have seen, was impeached twice. Nothing could illustrate more clearly than the impeachments and execution of Callistratus the lack of impunity which pertained to Athens' unofficial advisers or the lack of a clear division between the spheres of ῥήτωρ and στρατηγός.

If it is true that the division between orators and generals in fourth-century Athens has been exaggerated, then the overlap between political and military leadership at Athens in both the fifth century and the fourth must have created special problems. Precisely because of the Athenians' concern about the accountability of their officials and the preservation of their democracy, the Athenian state was characterized by an extremely weak executive branch. There was no president or premier at Athens. The closest the Athenians came to an executive office was the στρατηγία, but they were careful to dilute the strength of this post by dividing it among ten men.[20] Nonetheless, an inherent danger lurked in the military character of the office — the danger that policy would be made not, as was intended by the careful emasculation of the executive branch, by the assembly, but rather by individual generals in the field. The case of General Douglas MacArthur's independent policy decisions in Korea provides a recent example of how grave this danger can be even in a society with an executive office as powerful as the United States Presidency; the danger would certainly seem to have existed many times over in Athens, where no higher executive existed than the military commander in the field. And what civil discord might not erupt in Athens when it had no public officers higher than the men who led its armies? A century of bloodshed in Rome was to show what could happen when the same men served as political leaders and military heroes: at Athens it was the rigorous use of the machinery of control which prevented the military character of the στρατηγία from posing a threat to the democratic constitution.

It is because the generals were Athens' highest public officers that the impeachment of στρατηγοί has been given so much space in this study in accountability. Inevitably, the military character of the στρατηγία affected the nature of the impeachments of στρατηγοί, and we should bear in mind that impeachments had often to fill the role of court-martials. As Pritchett has pointed out, the "overwhelming majority" of impeachment trials of στρατηγοί "were connected with military failure."[21] The failure in some degree of Athenian military efforts formed the backdrop for nearly three-fourths of impeachment trials of Athenian στρατηγοί attested between 490 and 338: twenty of the forty-six known impeachments of generals occurred during the Peloponnesian War; another five occurred in connection with the Corinthian War, and eight more between 362 and 359, during the struggle to hold the Hellespont.

But this connection between impeachment trials and military failure should not lead us to obscure the other, more complex factors operating in Athenian impeachment trials. Again and again we have seen policies advocated by στρατηγοί playing major parts in the attacks on them; and it is only natural that the issue of policy, which nearly always amounted to foreign policy, should have been most crucial in wartime. It is in part because conflicts over policy played such a large role in Athenian impeachments that so many impeachments took place during wartime, and it is because of the importance of questions of policy in Athenian impeachment trials that so many of Athens' most prominent men were impeached when they served as στρατηγοί even though the total proportion of impeached generals was probably less than a tenth of those who served. The impeachment of Miltiades in 489, while not an attack on his anti-Persian policy, was nonetheless a strong statement of the policy the Athenians proposed to follow in controlling their generals, even when those generals might be national heroes. The attack on Cimon in 463 was conceived as a tentative assault on his pro-Spartan policy and his conservative attitude to Athenian democracy. The attack on Pericles in 430 which Thucydides explained as an emotional outburst on the part of the δῆμος in fact aimed at opening the way to alternate modes of dealing with Sparta, whether by pressing the war forward more aggressively or by making peace. The accusation against the generals who accepted the surrender of Potidaea on lenient terms in that same year reflected, I have suggested, not the Athenians' resentment of the generals' inability to force a surrender on stiffer terms, for there is no evidence that they were unable to do so; rather the assembly, led probably by Cleon, simply disagreed with the generals' lenient policy. The deposition of Phrynichus and Scironides in 411 was designed to enable the Athenians to follow a new policy in the hopes of ending the Peloponnesian war: the adoption of a new form of government and the recall of Alcibiades.

During the fourth century, the trials of the Corinthian War reflected the Athenians' reservations about the war itself, and that of Ergocles also reflected their dissatisfaction with Thrasybulus' aggressive Asian policy. Their frightened withdrawal from a policy of aid to the Theban exiles led to the condemnation of the generals of 378; their ambivalence about how to deal with Sparta on the one hand and Thebes on the other led to the deposition and trial of Timotheus in 373. The attack on Chabrias (along with Callistratus) in 365 was probably in part the result of a partisan quarrel between the faction of Callistratus and that of Timotheus; but the Athenians may also have resented Chabrias' connection with Callistratus because of Callistratus' advocacy of the alliance with the Peloponnesian states who let them down when they called them to their assistance at Oropus. The question of how to handle the powerful mercenary leader Charidemus was one issue in the trial of Cephisodotus in 359, after he had concluded an unfavorable treaty with Charidemus. Finally, the conviction of Timotheus after the trials of Timotheus, Iphicrates, and Menestheus for treason in the Hellespont during the Social War was in part at least a vote in favor of the more aggressive policy in dealing with the allies represented by Chares and against the moderate and diplomatic approach advocated by Timotheus.

The role played by disagreements over policy in the impeachments of στρατηγοί was a substantial one, and many examples show that the system of accountability was effective in preventing a general from presenting the δῆμος with a *fait accompli* that implemented his own personal concept of the best policy for Athens. Miltiades tried to do so at Paros; he failed and was impeached. Xenophon, Hestiodorus, and Phanomachus did so in accepting the surrender of Potidaea on lenient terms; they too came under fire. Thrasybulus had pursued an extremely aggressive policy in Asia and had alienated many of the coastal cities by his financial exactions. He would surely have been impeached, I have suggested, had he lived. The generals of 378 who decided for themselves that the Theban exiles should receive Athenian aid paid for their independence, and their *fait accompli* was repudiated. For a while, Timotheus' popularity led the Athenians to accept the *fait accompli* of his unauthorized restoration of the Zacynthian exiles, as he probably suspected that it would. But his luck did not hold, for when Sparta resumed hostilities and he was unable to defend the Corcyreans against her, the Athenians decided that perhaps he should pay for having, in their view, renewed the war. Cephisodotus had evidently concluded a treaty with Charidemus on his own responsibility; the Athenians did not favor its terms and impeached him. By their rigorous use of the machinery of control, then, the Athenians made certain that decisions about matters of policy would lie where, in their view, they belonged — with the δῆμος gathered together in the ἐκκλησία.

But we must now ask whether the rigorous control which the Athenians at home in the assembly exercised over their στρατηγοί in the field did not hamper the effectiveness of the Athenian armed forces.

Beloch has argued that the frequency of impeachment trials at Athens undermined the confidence of Athenian troops in their commanders.[22] There exists not a shred of evidence to support this contention, nor indeed is there any reason why a high degree of accountability in the στρατηγία should have had that effect. Athenian soldiers were never held to account for the actions of their officers. The most compelling evidence in this regard derives from the restoration of the Theban exiles in 378. This restoration was assisted by a large number of Athenian soldiers under two Athenian στρατηγοί. One of the στρατηγοί was put to death; the other, who did not remain to stand trial, was banished; but no action at all seems to have been taken against the many soldiers who participated in this daring project. Clearly the Athenians took seriously the dictum of Deinarchus that "it is all too true that their leaders are responsible for all the citizens' good or bad fortune."[23]

Nor is there evidence to support the contention of Glotz and of Henderson that the frequency of impeachment trials undermined the quality of military leadership among the Athenians.[24] Indeed there is no reason why it should have, for although a large number of Athens' most prominent generals were impeached, our evidence at present shows that only about fifty στρατηγίαι (out of 1420 during the period under discussion) ended in impeachment, and about a third of these resulted in acquittals; this amounts to the conviction of less than three percent. Even allowing for a very large number of additional trials for which the evidence has not yet come down to us, I would guess that the odds against any individual στρατηγία ending in impeachment and conviction were very high. We know of only two instances, moreover, in which the conduct of an Athenian general in his office was affected by his fear of the δῆμος, although there must have been others. One is the case of Nicias in Sicily in 414, the other of Chabrias at Naxos in 376.

Nicias, as all our sources agree, was by nature a timid man. He had obviously been shocked by the ascendance of a man as aggressive as Cleon in the assembly. He assumed that his fellow moderates who had been impeached during the Archidamian War had been railroaded by an ungrateful δῆμος through no fault of their own, and he feared to withdraw from Sicily without direct orders from home lest the same fate befall him. Plutarch reports that Nicias' fears of the δῆμος led him to avoid onerous campaigns.[25] Clearly this is an exaggeration, for Nicias played a major role in the Peloponnesian War and did after all serve in Sicily. In view of his fears, however, Nicias would have done well to withdraw from public life. He failed to understand what the Athenians had tried to make clear already half a century before by the conviction of Miltiades — that a heavy responsibility went along with the στρατηγία, a responsibility not only to mean well but to do well. No Athenian who was not willing to accept the risks that went with the job should have stood for the generalship. Nicias did not perceive this, nor did Thucydides, but that is no reason why we should be unable to see it from a greater distance today.

Nicias' conduct, then, arose not really from the frequency of impeachment trials but from his own natural timidity and from his inability to perceive the principles by which the democracy functioned. The case of Chabrias is quite different. Diodorus records that although Chabrias could easily have pursued the fleeing enemy after his victory at Naxos, and utterly destroyed their fleet, nonetheless he

> abstained utterly from pursuit; for he recalled the battle of Arginusae, when the people in exchange for the great service performed by the victorious generals had condemned them to

death, blaming them because they had not buried those who had
perished in the sea battle, and he was afraid, since the circumstances were so similar, that he might run the same risk.
Accordingly, refraining from pursuit, he collected those citizens
who were afloat, saving those who yet lived and burying those
who were dead.[26]

Had he pursued the enemy, Diodorus repeats regretfully, he
could easily have destroyed their whole fleet.

Diodorus is implying here that Chabrias' fear for his own
safety qualified his performance as a general. He suggests that
the victors of Arginusae were altogether undeserving of their
fate, and he repeats here the obviously false contention that he
had put forward earlier in his history — that the fault of the
generals lay merely in leaving the dead unburied — although
he does notice that the rescue of the living formed part of
Chabrias' project. It is unmistakably clear from the account of
Xenophon that the victors of Arginusae were prosecuted principally because they failed to rescue the living. Diodorus gives
the impression that Chabrias' decision not to follow up his
victory at Naxos was a sad thing and exactly what the Athenians deserved for their treatment of the victors of Arginusae.

Diodorus is correct only insofar as the conduct of Chabrias
at Naxos was precisely the kind of behavior which the Athenians wished to promote by their vote of condemnation in 406
against the victors of Arginusae. That the Athenians did not
consider Chabrias' failure to pursue his victory at Naxos their
penalty for their treatment of the victors of Arginusae is made
amply clear by the extraordinary honors voted to him immediately afterwards.

The stories of Nicias and Chabrias have a great deal to tell us
about the functioning of the machinery of control at Athens.
Because the principle of accountability was so closely tied up
with that of democratic government, Nicias could not grasp
it — nor could Thucydides, despite his keen political insight.
But the system succeeded in ensuring that commanders would
follow not their own consciences, thereby instituting a kind of
representative government, but rather, like Chabrias, would

take care to follow the policy of the people, whatever it might be, thereby maintaining the democratic government which the Athenians had chosen over all other constitutions. We cannot know, of course, how many men of independent and creative minds may have been deterred from entering public life by the fear of impeachment. But the data I have assembled concerning the impeachment trials about which we know in Athens from the Persian Wars to the death of Philip strongly suggest that the Athenians were indeed able to preserve their democratic government by impeachments of στρατηγοί with whom they were dissatisfied without depriving themselves of courageous political or military leadership.

The Athenian system of control was unquestionably severe by modern standards. Why precisely this should have been so is not entirely clear — nor is it the subject of this book. It had something to do, no doubt, with the great importance which all Greek πόλεις, states as different as Athens and Sparta, placed upon civic responsibility — much greater than is customary in the larger nations of today. It had something to do, probably, with the Greeks' comparatively limited interest in the question of moral responsibility. As Adkins has written in his important study of *Merit and Responsibility* in Greece,

> the importance of building this [section of the book] round the Greek concept of moral responsibility lies precisely in the relative unimportance of that concept, as compared with the status which we should allot to it, for this radical difference of emphasis is a significant symptom for those basic differences in outlook which sometimes make Greek ethics so baffling to the modern reader.[27]

As Adkins points out, this aspect of the Greek world view leads to a very different attitude from the one which prevails in Europe and America today towards "the evaluation of success and failure." For the agent's "intentions are" in ancient Greece "unlikely to be considered: No one *intends* to fail."[28] In a shame culture like classical Athens, as Gouldner has put it, "merit and excellence are reckoned less by intentions than by results."[29] Plutarch, moreover, though he might have given a more balanced view of the Athenians' motivation in dealing with their leaders, was on to something when he spoke of the importance of envy in Athenian political life. Gouldner is probably quite right to see envy as a natural and potent side of Greek competitiveness and to conclude (while writing, as was Plutarch, in the context of the institution of ostracism) that "the Greeks did not wait patiently for divine retribution to be inflicted on the great, but energetically took justice into their own hands"; a survey of the problem of envy among the Greeks has just been provided by Walcot in his *Envy and the Greeks*.[30] I have nowhere tried to suggest that emotional factors played *no* part in Athenian accountability trials. Of course they played a part. How could the Athenians not have been influenced by any emotions whatever during the summer of 430 or at the trial of the victors of Arginusae?

But it is not my purpose in this book to explain why the Athenians held the views they did about the function of accountability trials, merely to show what those views were. The Athenians were unquestionably very exacting towards their political and military leaders; no fear of appearing weak or disunited to the world outside inhibited them from exercising their right to discipline officials with whom they were dissatisfied. As Dover has pointed out, "we tend nowadays to associate democracy with tolerance" and "to imagine that democracies are by nature lenient in punishment and reluctant to take the lives of their own citizens. If we have made this assumption," he warns, "the conduct of the classical Athenian democracy will sometimes surprise us."[31] He is right, and many people have been surprised. I have sometimes been surprised. When all is said and done, the execution of the victors of Arginusae remains deeply unsettling. It is one thing to agree with Andrewes' contention that "the standard of ingenious villainy ascribed to the speaker's opponent" in Athenian trials "is hardly meant to be accepted literally"; it is another to read without a shudder Demosthenes' singularly savage attack on Aeschines and his family in the speech on the false embassy —

a speech designed not merely to damage Aeschines' political prestige but to compass his death.[32] Yet however the system may strike us today, most men who chose to serve the Athenians as political leaders, whether in an official or an unofficial capacity, civilian or military, understood and shared the risks. Finley has described these risks with particular sensitivity in his article on "Athenian Demagogues." Athenian leaders, he writes,

> had *no* respite. Because their influence had to be earned and exerted directly and immediately . . . they had to lead in person, and they had also to bear, in person, the brunt of the opposition's attacks. More than that, they walked alone. They had their lieutenants, of course, and politicians made alliances with each other. But these were fundamentally personal links, shifting frequently . . . lacking that quality of support, that buttressing or cushioning effect, which is provided by a bureaucracy and political party, in another way by an institutionalized Establishment like the Roman Senate, or in still another way by large-scale patronage as in the Roman clientage system. The critical point is that there was no government in the modern sense. . . . A man was a leader solely as a function of his personal . . . status within the Assembly itself. . . . These were the conditions which faced all leaders in Athens, not merely those whom Thucydides and Plato dismissed as "demagogues", not merely those whom some modern historians mis-call "radical democrats", but everyone, aristocrat or commoner . . . who, in George Grote's phrase, "stood forward prominently to advise" the Athenians. No doubt the motives which moved men to stand forward varied greatly. But that does not matter in this context, for each one of them without exception, *chose* to aspire to, and actively to work and contest for, leadership, knowing just what that entailed, including the risks.[33]

REFERENCES

ABBREVIATIONS

Short titles in the notes which do not appear below will be found in the Bibliography under the author's name.

AJA	*American Journal of Archaeology*
AJP	*American Journal of Philology*
ATL	B. D. Meritt, H. T. Wade-Gery, and M. F. McGregor, *The Athenian Tribute Lists, 4 vols.*
Beloch, *AP*	K. J. Beloch, *Attische Politik seit Perikles*
Beloch, *GG*	K. J. Beloch, *Griechische Geschichte*
Bonner and Smith, *Administration*	R. Bonner and G. Smith, *The Administration of Justice from Homer to Aristotle*
Busolt, *GG*	G. Busolt, *Griechische Geschichte*
Busolt-Swoboda, *GS*	G. Busolt and H. Swoboda, *Griechische Staatskunde*
CAH	*Cambridge Ancient History*
CJ	*Classical Journal*
CP	*Classical Philology*
CQ	*Classical Quarterly*
CR	*Classical Review*
Curtius	E. Curtius, *History of Greece*
CW	*Classical World*
Daremberg-Saglio	C. Daremberg and E. Saglio, edd., *Dictionnaire des antiquités grecques et romaines*
Fornara	C. Fornara, *The Athenian Board of Generals from 501 to 404*
Glotz, *Greek City*	G. Glotz, *The Greek City and Its Institutions*
Glotz and Cohen	G. Glotz and R. Cohen, *Histoire Grecque*
Gomme, *HCT*	A. W. Gomme, with A. Andrewes and K. J.

	Dover, *A Historical Commentary on Thucydides*
GRBS	*Greek, Roman, and Byzantine Studies*
Grote	G. Grote, *History of Greece*
Hager	H. Hager, "On the *Eisangelia*," *Journal of Philology* 4 (1871) 74–111
Hansen, *Eisangelia*	M. H. Hansen, *Eisangelia, The Sovereignty of the People's Court in Athens in the Fourth Century B. C. and the Impeachment of Generals and Politicians*
Hansen, *Sovereignty*	M. H. Hansen, *The Sovereignty of the People's Court in Athens in the Fourth Century B. C. and The Public Action Against Unconstitutional Proposals*
Harrison, *Procedure*	A. R. W. Harrison, *The Law of Athens: Procedure*
Hauvette, *SA*	A. Hauvette-Besnault, *Les Stratèges Athéniens*
Hignett, *AC*	C. Hignett, *A History of the Athenian Constitution to the End of the Fifth Century B. C.*
HSCP	*Harvard Studies in Classical Philology*
Jacoby, *FGrH*	F. Jacoby, *Die Fragmente der Griechischen Historiker*
JHS	*Journal of Hellenic Studies*
Kagan, *AW*	D. Kagan, *The Archidamian War*
Kagan, *Outbreak*	D. Kagan, *The Outbreak of the Peloponnesian War*
Krause, *AS*	A. Krause, *Attische Strategenlisten bis 146 v. Chr.*
Lipsius, *AR*	J. Lipsius, *Das Attische Recht und Rechtsverfahren*
M and L, *GHI*	R. Meiggs and D. Lewis, *A Collection of Greek Historical Inscriptions*
Meyer, *GdA*	E. Meyer, *Geschichte des Altertums*
Pritchett, *Greek State*	W. K. Pritchett, *The Greek State at War*
RE	A. Pauly, G. Wissowa, and W. Kroll, edd., *Realencyclopädie der Klassischen Altertumswissenschaft*
REA	*Revue des études anciennes*
REG	*Revue des études grecques*
Rev. hist.	*Revue historique*

RhMus	*Rheinisches Museum für Philologie*
TAPA	*Transactions of the American Philological Association*
Tod, *GHI*	M. Tod, *A Selection of Greek Historical Inscriptions*, vol. 2
Westlake, *Essays*	H. Westlake, *Essays on the Greek Historians and Greek History*
Wilamowitz, *A. u. A.*	U. von Wilamowitz-Möllendorff, *Aristoteles und Athen*

NOTES

I. INTRODUCTION

1 Lenardon, *The Saga of Themistocles*, 12–15.
2 Line 324. All translations from the Greek in this book are my own.
3 Lines 212–14.
4 Herod. 3.80.
5 Aeschin. 3.22.
6 Arist. *Pol.* 2.36 (1272a).
7 Plato, *Laws*, 9 (875a–875c).
8 Vinogradoff, *Outline of Historical Jurisprudence* 2: *The Jurisprudence of the Greek City*, 167.
9 Jones, *Athenian Democracy*, 61.
10 Thuc. 3.43.4.
11 Arist. *Pol.* 4.4.26–28 (1292a).
12 Schömann has written for example that "the administration of the state was conducted without prudence, and the judicature without integrity or firmness; then arose the seditious and mercenary demagogue . . . to cajole and mislead the ignorant multitude — for such were the mass of those who frequented the assemblies and courts." The irresponsibility of the citizens, according to Schömann, manifested itself nowhere more clearly than in the use of the machinery of accountability, for accusations against officials "were eagerly received by men of ignorant minds and suspicious dispositions, who were in constant dread . . . of some infringement upon their own sacred dignity, or some attempt to dissolve their loved democracy." *A Dissertation on the Assemblies of the Athenians*, 184.
13 Cavaignac, *Histoire de l'antiquité* 2: *Athènes*, 195–200.

14 Thuc. 4.65.4.
15 Thuc. 7.48.4.
16 Plut. *Arist.* 26.1; *Nic.* 6. 1–2.
17 Cicero, *De Orat.* 2.13.56.
18 Butcher, *Demosthenes*, 23.
19 Smith, *The Ancient Greeks*, 49.
20 Beloch, *AP*, 43; Glotz, *Greek City*, 231.
21 Henderson, *The Great War between Athens and Sparta*, 275.
22 Reverdin, "Remarques sur la vie politique d'Athènes au V⁰ siè- cle," *Mus. Helv.* 2 (1945):201–12; Connor, *New Politicians*, pas- sim.
23 Connor, *New Politicians*, 7–8.

II. ATHENIAN OFFICIALS AND THE LAW

 1 Discussions of the δοκιμασία can be found in Bonner, *Aspects of Athenian Democracy*, 12–13; Bonner and Smith, *Administration* 2:243–45; Glotz, *Greek City*, 217–18; Harrison, *Procedure*, 200–203; MacDowell, *The Law in Classical Athens*, 167–69; Hig- nett, *AC*, 205–8; and Smith's *Dictionary*, s.v. "*docimasia.*" The fullest treatment appears in Lipsius, *AR*, 269–85 and Koch, "Δοκιμασία," *RE* 5:1268–73.
 2 Arist. *Ath. Pol.* 45.3 and Harp. s.v. δοκιμασθείς. The role of the βουλή in δοκιμασίαι is discussed in Rhodes, *The Athenian Boule*, 171–78.
 3 Arist. *Ath. Pol.* 55.3–4.
 4 Arist. *Ath. Pol.* 4.2; Dein. 1.71.
 5 Arist. *Ath. Pol.* 43.4 and 61.2. Ἀποχειροτονία is treated in Boer- ner, "Ἐπιχειροτονία," *RE* 6:41–42; Busolt-Swoboda, *GS*, 988 and 1007–8; Glotz, *Greek City*, 225; Hansen, *Eisangelia*, 41–45; Kahrstedt, *Untersuchungen*, 105–24; and Lipsius, *AR*, 295–96.
 6 Arist. *Ath. Pol.* 61.2.
 7 Arist. *Ath. Pol.* 59.2; Pollux 8.87–88; Harrison, *Procedure*, 13–14.
 8 Arist. *Ath. Pol.* 61.2.
 9 The best ancient sources for the εἰσαγγελία are Harp., s.v.; Pollux, 8.51–53; Hyp. 4.1–10; and Arist. *Ath. Pol.* 8.4, 29.4, 43.4, and 59.2. The most thorough treatments in secondary sources are probably those of Bonner and Smith, *Administration*, 1:294–309; Busolt-Swoboda, *GS*, 1006–8; Hager; Hansen, *Eisangelia*; Har- rison, *Procedure*, 50–59; Lipsius, *AR*, 176–211; MacDowell, *The Law in Classical Athens*, 183–86; Rhodes, *The Athenian Boule*,

162–71; and Thalheim, "Zur Eisangelie in Athen," *Hermes* 37 (1902):339–52 and *RE* 5:2138–41. These sources also treat the vexed question of the passing of a νόμος εἰσαγγελτικός prescribing trial by εἰσαγγελία for these particular offenses.

10 Harrison, *Procedure*, 57; Thalheim, "*Eisangelia*," *RE* 5:2140.

11 Arist. *Ath. Pol.* 45.2. But IG I² 110, 38–47, which deals with the impeachment of some citizens accused of taking bribes in connection with voting a citizenship decree, seems to represent, as Hansen suggests (*Eisangelia*, 115–16), an impeachment to the βουλή; Cleophon probably held no office when he was impeached, evidently by an εἰσαγγελία to the βουλή; and the impeachment of the corn dealers, which forms the subject of Lys. 22, may have been an εἰσαγγελία to the βουλή.

12 The fixing of the sentence is discussed in Hansen, *Eisangelia*, 33–36 and 53–54.

13 Dem. 24.63; Arist. *Ath. Pol.* 59.2; Thalheim, "*Eisangelia*," *RE* 5.2140; Harrison, *Procedure*, 56.

14 Hyper. 4.1–3.

15 Pollux 8.52; Hyper. 1.8 and 12; Harp. s.v. εἰσαγγελία; Hager, 109–10; Bonner and Smith, *Administration*, 1:296; Hansen, *Eisangelia*, 30–31.

16 Harrison, *Procedure*, 56.

17 The text of the heliastic oath as it stood in Demosthenes' day is given in Dem. 24.149–51.

18 The relationship between εἰσαγγελία and ἀποχειροτονία is poorly understood. As Busolt and Swoboda point out, it is quite possible that εἰσαγγελία entailed automatic dismissal from office and did not need to be accompanied by an official vote of ἀποχειροτονία (Busolt-Swoboda, *GS*, 1008). Glotz (*Greek City*, 225) suggests that the order was optional. The problem of the relationship between the two procedures is discussed in depth by Hansen (*Eisengelia*, 41–45).

Although Harrison calls ἀποχειροτονία "in effect an *eisangelia*," there were important differences between the two actions. From a conceptual standpoint, ἀποχειροτονία was preliminary to the institution of legal procedure, whereas a complaint by way of εἰσαγγελία was in fact the first step in such a procedure. A trial resulting from ἀποχειροτονία, moreover, would not be held in the assembly (unless it had become an εἰσαγγελία) and would therefore deprive the accuser of the opportunity of influencing the verdict by swaying the large crowd or even of influencing the penalty in the event of conviction, which in cases of ἀποχειροτονία was set by the dicastery. Lastly, attacks by εἰσαγγελία could be preferred against private citizens, or against officials for acts which had nothing to do with their administration, as in the notorious case of Alcibiades in 415 (an episode which I have not treated in this book, as the accusation against Alcibiades, though political in intent, did not deal with his official conduct.)

19 The εὔθυναι are discussed at length by Bonner and Smith, *Administration*, 2:34–36 and 256–69; Busolt-Swoboda, *GS*, 1033, 1060–61, 1069–70, 1074–88 and 1153; Glotz, *Greek City*, 225–28; Hansen, *Eisangelia*, 45–47; Hignett, *AC*, 203–5; Kahrstedt, *Untersuchungen*, 165–80; Lipsius, *AR*, 286–98; MacDowell, *The Law in Classical Athens*, 170–72; M. Pierart, "Les EYΘΥNOI athéniens," *L'Antiquité classique* 40 (1971):526–73; R. Sealey, "Ephialtes," *CP* 59 (1964):18–20; and Wilamowitz, *A. u. A.*, 2:243–251.

20 *Lex. Cantabr.* 664; Pollux 8.54; Harp. s.v. λογισταί.

21 Aeschin. 3.22.

22 Arist. *Ath. Pol.* 48.3–5.

23 Arist. *Ath. Pol.* 48.5 and 59.2.

24 Aeschin. 3.23.

25 Arist. *Ath. Pol.* 48.4–5.

26 Aeschin. 3.21–22.

27 Vinogradoff, *Outline of Historical Jurisprudence* 2: *The Jurisprudence of the Greek City*, 168.

28 Hansen, *Eisangelia*, 49. Pritchett takes the opposite view in *The Greek State at War*, 2:27; he alleges fourteen cases of γραφὴ προδοσίας and seven of γραφὴ δωροδοκίας, but he cannot, I think, demonstrate this.

   On the προβολή, see Arist. *Ath. Pol.* 43.5; Dem. 21, passim; Pollux, 8.46 and 87; Berneker, "προβολή," *RE* 23:43–48; Hansen, *Eisangelia*, 38–39; Harrison, *Procedure*, 59–64; and Smith's *Dictionary*, s.v. "*probole*."

29 Dem. 4.47.

30 Hansen, *Eisangelia*, 50–64. Hansen also deals in these pages with the extremely thorny question of what proportion of Athenian στρατηγοί were impeached. His guess is as good as any, I suppose: two out of every board of ten.

31 Lys. 13.10.

32 Lys. 31, passim.

33 Lys. 26.13, 21–24. As M. H. Hansen has kindly pointed out to

me, combining Lys. 26.9 and Arist. *Ath. Pol.* 55.4, we can infer that the law about δοκιμασία was changed in 403/2 and that after this time it was possible to reject a candidate on political grounds only (cf. Hansen, "Did the Athenian *Ecclesia* Legislate after 403/2?" [*GRBS* 20 (1979):36–37 with n. 18)].

34 Plut. *Lys.* 5.2 (Alcibiades); Dem. 49.9 (Timotheus); Dem. 50.12 (Autocles) and Dem. 23.167–68 (Cephisodotus).

35 Plut. *Per.* 35.4; Diod. 12.45.4; Thuc. 2.65.3 (Pericles); Thuc. 3.115.2 and 5–6 (Laches); Plut. *Alc.* 19–22; Thuc. 6.53.1 and 6.61; Nepos. *Alc.* 3–4 (Alcibiades); Thuc. 8.54.3 (Phrynichus and Scironides); Xen. *Hell.* 1.7.1; Diod. 13.101.5 (the victors of Arginusae); Arist. *Rhet.* 1380b; Dem. 23.104 (Callisthenes and Ergophilus); Diod. 16.21.4, Nep. *Tim.* 3.5 (Timotheus, Iphicrates, and Menestheus).

36 Dem. 58. 27–28.

37 Herod. 6.136 (Miltiades); Xen. *Hell.* 1.7.1–2 and Diod. 13.101–2 (the victors of Arginusae); Dem. 49.10 (Timotheus); Hyper. 4.1–2 (Timomachus, Leosthenes, Theotimus); Aeschin. 3.51–52 and Schol. (Cephisodotus).

38 Hansen, *Eisangelia*, 59.

39 Dem. 36.53 and 51. 8–9.

40 Dem. 47, passim.

41 Dem. 49.10.

42 Aeschin. 3.171; Plut. *Dem.* 4; Libanius *Dem.* 2.

43 Ant. 6.35

44 Lys. 13.19–38.

45 Ps.-Plut. *Vit. X Orat.* 833E.

46 Philoch. fr. 149a (Jacoby).

47 Dem. 19.191; Xen. *Hell.* 7.1.38.

48 Ant. 6, passim, on the first two cases; Ps.-Plut. *Vit. X. Orat.* 833d–34b (the ambassadors); Lys. 30.10–13, Lys. 13.12, Arist. *Ath. Pol.* 28.3, *Xen. Hell.* 1.7.35 (Cleophon); Lys. 30 (Nicomachus); Dem. 51.8–9 (Leosthenes' trierarchs); Dem. 47.41–4 (Theophemus); Aeschin. 1.110–112 (Timarchus).

49 For example, by Busolt-Swoboda, *GS*, 1008; Lipsius, *AR*, 184–92; Glotz, *Greek City*, 225.

50 One should, however, note what I suppose is a theoretical possibility — that each of these trials went through a first stage in the assembly and was then sent to a δικαστήριον for the official final decision but that in these cases the first stage was the crucial one so it alone appears in the sources.

51 Lipsius, *AR*, 191–92; Thalheim, *Hermes* 37:351–52; Hansen,

Eisangelia, 51–55, "How Often Did the *Ecclesia* Meet?" *GRBS* 18 (1977):68–69, and "*Ekklesia Synkletos* in Hellenistic Athens," *GRBS* 20 (1979): 149–56.

52 See below, p. 65 and nn. and pp. 46–47 and nn.

53 Plut. *Arist.* 4.3.

54 Arist. *Ath. Pol.* 27.1.

55 Dem. 19.273.

56 Schol. on *Peace* 347 (Phormio); Plut. *Nic.* 6.1–2 and *Arist.* 26.5 (Paches).

57 Lys. 20 (Polystratus) and 12 (Eratosthenes).

58 Dem. 24.127.

59 Aeschin. 1.13.

60 Dein. Fr. 25.

61 Sources for these and other possible attacks at εὔθυναι have been assembled by Hansen in *Folkedomstolen* (1979), 83, n. 463, of which Dr. Hansen has kindly furnished me a copy.

62 Twenty-four generals were clearly deposed during their terms: Pericles, Laches, Phrynichus and Scironides, Alcibiades, the victors of Arginusae, Pamphilus, the two generals of 378, Timotheus (twice), Autocles, Leosthenes, Timomachus, Theotimus, Cephisodotus, Iphicrates, and Menestheus. The same is probably true of eleven others: Miltiades, Xenophon, Phanomachus and Hestiodorus, Sophocles, Pythodorus and Eurymedon, Thucydides, Anytus, Callisthenes, and Ergophilus. Cimon and Paches, on the other hand, were probably accused at the regular εὔθυναι at the end of their terms, and Ergocles, Chabrias, and probably Agyrrhius were accused after the expiration of their terms. About seven others — Aristarchus, Thrasybulus of Collytus, Dionysius, Menon, Philon, Hegesileos, and Lysicles — we do not know.

63 For example, Swoboda, *Hermes* 28 (1893):554; Busolt-Swoboda, *GS*, 1069–70; Glotz, *Greek City*, 228; Kahrstedt, *Untersuchungen*, 117; Hignett, *AC*, 244.

64 Diod. 12.38.3.

65 Kagan, *AW*, 91.

66 Plut. *Per.* 23.1. The sources are confused; was it Pericles' accounts as ἐπιστάτης of the chryselephantine statue of Athena that were being questioned? The account of Plutarch is of course based on the works of earlier writers. See Theophrastus and Ephorus (Jacoby, *FGrH*, 3b, F193).

67 Hauvette, *SA*, 56–59.

68 Arist. *Ath. Pol.* 27.1.

69 In chronological order, Miltiades, Cimon, Pericles (twice),
Xenophon, Hestiodorus and Phanomachus, Phormio (?), Paches,
Laches, Sophocles, Pythodorus and Eurymedon, Thucydides,
Phrynichus and Scironides, Aristarchus, Anytus, Alcibiades, the
eight victors of Arginusae (Pericles the younger, Diomedon, Ar-
istocrates, Lysias, Thrasyllus, Erasinides, Protomachus, and
Aristogenes), Pamphilus, Ergocles, Thrasybulus of Collytus,
Dionysius, Agyrrhius, the anonymous pro-Theban generals of
379/78, Timotheus (twice), Chabrias, Callisthenes, Ergophilus,
Autocles, Leosthenes, Menon, Timomachus, Theotimus, Cephi-
sodotus, Iphicrates, Menestheus, Hegesileus, and Lysicles.

70 Lysias says that Aristophanes and Nicophemus died before coming to trial — ἄκριτοι ἀπέθανον (19.7). It is astonishing how little
attention these words have received from scholars. Most assume
that Nicophemus and Aristophanes were executed; although it is
possible that they simply died before their cases came up, it must
be remembered that ἀποθνήσκω served frequently as the passive
of ἀποκτείνω (throughout Plato's *Apology*, for example) and
often means "to be put to death" (see Liddell and Scott, *A
Greek-English Lexicon* [Oxford, 1890] s. v. ἀποθνήσκω).
W. R. M. Lamb in a footnote to the Loeb Library edition of
Lysias explains (421) that Nicophemus and Aristophanes were
put to death "on a summary impeachment allowed in special
cases of treason or embezzlement." I know of no such summary
impeachment at Athens. If indeed Nicophemus and Aristophanes
were executed without trial, it is likely that their deaths were
outside the law.

71 Dem. 24.136. The case for the date has been argued by Dinsmoor, "The Burning of the Opisthodomos at Athens, I, The
Date," *AJA* 36 (1932):143–72.

72 Plut. *Cim.* 15.1 (Cimon); Diod. 13.64.6 and Arist. *Ath. Pol.* 27.5
(Anytus); Thrasybulus of Collytus was probably acquitted since
the speaker who attacked Evander at his scrutiny in 383 (Lys. 26)
would surely have mentioned not only the suspicions against him
but his conviction, had he been able; Dem. 49.6–24, Diod.
15.47.3 (Timotheus); the acquittal of Chabrias is to be inferred
from Dem. 21.64, where Demosthenes speaks of Chabrias'
leniency afterwards to one of his accusers and mentions a trial
but no conviction; Isocr. 15.129 (Iphicrates and Menestheus).

73 Their acquittal, if indeed a trial took place, can be inferred from
the return of Xenophon and Phanomachus to the στρατηγία at
the elections of 429 (see Thuc. 2.70 and Chapter III below).

74 Herod. 6.136 (Miltiades); Thuc. 2.65.3, Plut. *Per.* 35.4 (Pericles); Schol. on *Peace*, 347 (Phormio); Thuc. 4.65.3 (Sophocles, Pythodorus, and Eurymedon); Thuc. 5.26.5, Marcellinus, *Life of Thuc.* A 23; B 46, Anon. *Life of Thuc.* 3 (Thucydides); Thuc. 6.61.7, Nep. *Alc.* 4.5 (Alcibiades); Lyc. 1.112–115 (Phrynichus); Xen. *Hell.* 1.7.28, Lyc. 1.115 (Aristarchus); Xen. *Hell.* 1.7.34, Diod. 13.101.7–102.5 (the victors of Arginusae); Dem. 40.20 and 22 and Schol. on *Plutus*, 174 (Pamphilus); Lys. 29.2 and Dem. 19.180 (Ergocles); Dem. 19.180 (Dionysius); Dem. 24.134–135 (Agyrrhius); Xen. *Hell.* 5.4.19 (anonymous generals of 378); Arist. *Rhet.* 1380b, Dem. 19.180, and Aeschin. 2.30 (Callisthenes and Ergophilus); Diod. 15.95.3 (Leosthenes); Aeschin. 1.56 and Schol. (Timomachus); Dem. 23.167 (Cephisodotus); Isocr. 15.129, Plut. *Mor.* 504F (Timotheus); Diod. 16.88.1–2 (Lysicles).
75 Ant. 6.35 and 49; Dem. 49.10 and 47.41–44.
76 Dem. 19.180.
77 Hansen, *Eisangelia*, 35–36.
78 Dem. 19.273.

III. POLITICS AND POLICY

1 Plut. *Per.* 35.4; Diod. 12.45.4; Thuc. 2.65.3–4; Plato *Gorgias* 516a.
   In each case history the reader is advised to consult the relevant portions of Beloch, Busolt, Grote, Glotz and Cohen, Meyer's *Geschichte des Altertums*, the *Cambridge Ancient History*, and of course the pertinent entries in Hansen's *Eisangelia* and in *RE*; I have not cited all these *loci* separately.
2 Plut. *Per.* 35.4; Diod. 12.45.4; Thuc. 2.65.3. The amount is variously reported: Diodorus, 80 talents; Plutarch refers to sources varying between 15 and 50 talents; Thucydides is silent.
3 Gomme, *HCT*, 2:182–83.
4 See above, n. 2. That conviction for κλοπή brought with it disfranchisement is stated by Andocides, 1.74.
5 Thuc. 2.65.4.
6 Miltner, "Perikles," *RE*, 37:787; Wilamowitz, *A. u. A.*, 2:247–48.
7 Diod. 12.45.4.
8 Diod. 12.38.3; cf. Plut. *Alc.* 7.2. The story certainly suggests that the charge against Pericles was financial. That Dracontides' decree was effectively foiled by the amendment of Hagnon

seems to rule out the applicability of this anecdote to the accusations of 438.

9   Plut. *Per.* 35.4.

10 That Cleon was already a leader of the war party in 430 is indicated by a fragment from Hermippus (*Moirai*, fr. 46).

11 Plutarch (*Per.* 35.3) stresses the effect of the failure of the Epidaurus campaign on Pericles' position at Athens.

12 Diod. 12.45.5.

13 Thucydides writes that concerning public affairs (δημοσίᾳ) the Athenians were won over, sent no further embassies, and became more zealous for the war; nonetheless privately (ἰδίᾳ) they were distressed at the sufferings caused by the war, and this distress finally resulted in the fining of Pericles (2.65.2–3). He goes on to say that Pericles was returned to office because the Athenians, seeing that he was invaluable to the state, became less concerned about their private sufferings (2.65.4). Thucydides clearly implies that the Athenians had no intellectual reservations about Pericles' war policy but were temporarily swept away by selfish emotions. This is Thucydides' personal opinion and I see no reason to agree with it (see Chapter VII). Consequently, if disagreement with Pericles' policy led to his deposition, the reconciliation "as regards public affairs" which Thucydides reports must have been only temporary. At some point it ceased, and the Athenians may well have then sent embassies to the Spartans once again.

14 Thuc. 2.65.4–5; Plut. *Per.* 36.1. Later on, however (*Per.* 37.1), Plutarch seems to understand the situation in political terms, for he writes that Pericles was returned to office by the Athenians "after the city had made trial of its other generals and advisers for the leadership of the war and nobody of sufficient authority or worthiness for such leadership appeared."

15 Curtius, 3:75.

16 Bury, *History of Greece*, 408–9; Laistner, History, 84.

17 Thuc. 2.70.4.

18 Thuc. 2.70.4; Kagan, *AW*, 98.

19 Gilbert, *Beiträge*, 122; Hauvette, *SA*, 112.

20 Thuc. 2.70.4; Pritchett, *Greek State*, 2:204; Kagan, *AW*, 98.

21 The data assembled by Betant in the *Lexicon Thucydideum* 1:355 s.v. ἐπαιτιᾶσθαι confirm this use of the verb.

22 *Knights*, 438.

23 Diod. 12.47.3.

24 Gilbert, *Beiträge*, 122–23.
25 Thuc. 2.70.2. It is likely that some Athenians would have wanted not merely vengeance but also the profit that would come from selling the inhabitants into slavery — a profit that would in part defray the costs of the long siege.
26 Kagan, *AW*, 98. The evidence is not absolutely conclusive, but the data assembled by Pritchett (*Greek State*, 2:47–49) certainly suggest that this was true. The prisoners taken at Mytilene (Thuc. 3.28.1), at Pylos (Thuc. 4.15ff), at Corcyra (Thuc. 4.46), at Thyrea (Thuc. 4.57, accidentally cited in Pritchett's otherwise careful work as Thuc. 4.47), at Cythera (Thuc. 4.54.2) and at Byzantium (Xen. *Hell.* 1.3.22 and Diod. 13.67.7) were all to be judged by the Athenian δῆμος.
27 Thuc. 8.54.3–4. Thucydides says merely that the two generals were deposed when Peisander accused Phrynichus of treason in connection with the loss of Iasus; it is an inference that the charge against Scironides was the same. The active role taken by Phrynichus in political life in 411, and the silence of the sources about any trial, suggests that the generals were not prosecuted after their deposition.
28 Thuc. 8.54.3.
29 Thuc. 8.27.
30 Thuc. 8.27.1.
31 Thuc. 8.27.5.
32 Towards the end of his speech, according to Thucydides, "as Phrynichus argued, so he acted" (8.27.5). Perhaps Phrynichus began to withdraw his own ships in order to leave his unpersuaded colleagues no choice but to follow suit.
33 Thuc. 8.27.6.
34 Thuc. 8.90.
35 Lys. 20.11–12 and 25.9.
36 McCoy, "Theramenes, Thrasybulus and the Athenian Moderates," 27–28. Busolt (*GG*, 3:2.1412) and Lenschau ("Phrynichos," *RE* 39:907), however, maintain that he was already an oligarch at this time.
37 Thuc. 8.50–51; Plut. *Alc.* 25.5–9. Hatzfeld (*Alcibiade*, 235–36) has argued that this correspondence was in fact an invention of Alcibiades, but his views have been refuted amply, I think, by Westlake's article "Phrynichos and Astyochos (Thuc. VIII.50–51)," (1967), 115–18. An excellent discussion of this episode is offered by Gomme, Andrewes, and Dover (Gomme, *HCT*, 5.115–21).

38 Thuc. 8.54.3.
39 Thuc. 8.27.1. See above, n. 32.
40 Thuc. 8.54.3.
41 Thuc. 8.48.
42 Thuc. 8.50.4.
43 For the enmity between Peisander and Alcibiades in 415 see McCoy, "Theramenes," 29; Meyer, *GdA*, 4:513; and Ferguson, *CAH*, 5:286.
44 Dem. 49; Xen. *Hell.* 6.2.13; Diod. 15.47.3–4. Diodorus maintains that Timotheus was reinstated in his command, but he is surely mistaken.
45 Xen. *Hell.* 6.2.11–13; Dem. 49; Diod. 15.47.2–3.
46 Xen. *Hell.* 6.2.39; Dem. 49.13–17.
47 Diod. 15.47.4; Xen. *Hell.* 6.2.14.
48 *AP*, 147, followed by Rice, "Why Sparta Failed," 157.
49 Xen. *Hell.* 6.2.16–24; 6.2.31–36; Diod. 15.47.7.
50 Dem. 49.22. The trial must have been by εἰσαγγελία, for Apollodorus' speech against Timotheus records that it took place in the assembly (Dem. 49.9).

The chronology of this period is extremely confused and has been much debated by modern scholars. I would propose the following guidelines:

winter	375/74	Athens and Sparta conclude peace
spring	374	Timotheus lands exiles on Zacynthus
autumn	374	Mnasippus becomes navarch and sails for Corcyra
April	373	Timotheus sent to Corcyra
summer	373	Timotheus recalled and deposed
fall	373	Corcyreans defeat Spartans
		Callistratus returns to Athens
November	373	Trial of Timotheus

I follow the basic outline of Xenophon, rather than that of Diodorus, who imagines that Timotheus was sent out to Corcyra before the dispatch of Mnasippus, that Timotheus was reinstated in his command and that he went on to serve with Iphicrates at Corcyra (15.47). According to Xenophon, the landing of the exiles on Zacynthus, the sending of a Spartan force to Corcyra, and the dispatch of Timotheus to Corcyra all took place in fairly rapid succession. As the trial of Timotheus did not take place until Maimacterion (Dem. 49.22), however, these events must be stretched out somewhat. A valuable clue is afforded by the navarchy of Mnasippus, who commanded the Corcyrean expedition from its inception to his death. Xenophon (6.2.4) reports that Mnasippus was sent out to Corcyra at the same time as he became navarch, and Diodorus echoes the idea, although he calls Mnasippus a στρατηγός (15.47.1). Now as the Spartan navarch took office in the fall and the office was not renewable, consequently the Corcyrean operation must have commenced in the fall of 374, rather later than Xenophon suggests. It must have been completed, moreover, by the time of Timotheus' trial in November of 373.

Alternative chronologies and discussions of some of the issues are offered in Woodhead, "Chabrias, Timotheus and the Aegean Allies, 375–373 B.C.," *Phoenix* 16 (1962):258–66; Sealey, "*IG* II² 1609 and the Transformation of the Second Athenian League," *Phoenix* 11 (1975):99–104; Cawkwell, "Notes on the Peace of 375–374," *Historia* 12 (1963):84–95; Momigliano, "Un momento di storia greca: la pace del 375 a. C. e il *Plataico* di Isocrate," *Athenaeum* 14 (1936):3–35; Beloch, *AP*, 142–43; and Grote, 7:134–35.

51 Dem. 49.

52 Demosthenes (49.16) claims that Timotheus attempted to obscure the fact that the Boeotian trierarchs, for example, were being paid by money he had secured through a personal loan.

53 Evidently Antimachus had been employed as a go-between in Timotheus' efforts to borrow money. Timotheus claimed that at least one of the debts for the campaign had been taken out in Antimachus' name (Dem. 49.44–45).

54 The precise date and indeed the very reality of Jason's enrollment in the Athenian league have been disputed, but in any event his influence counted for a good deal in November of 373. The relations between Jason and the Athenians are discussed in Fabricius, "Zur Geschichte des zweiten athenischen Bundes," *RhMus* 46 (1891):589–95; Wilcken, "Zur Iason von Pherai," *Hermes* 59 (1924):123–27; Westlake, *Thessaly in the Fourth Century B.C.*, 73–76; and Woodhead, "IG II² and Jason of Pherai," *AJA* 61 (1957):367–73. If Jason was not yet a formal member of the confederacy at the time of Timotheus' trial, the Athenians had all the more reason to placate him by Timotheus' acquittal. I regret that this work was already in proof when I heard Fordyce Mitchel's interesting suggestions about Jason's membership in the league presented at the 1981 meeting of the Classical Association of the Midwest and South at St. Louis, Missouri.

Unfortunately there is no evidence by which to assess the validity of the charge against Antimachus, and this gap in our knowledge makes it difficult to assess the role played by Jason in Timotheus' acquittal. It may be that the case against Antimachus was weak and that the Athenians convicted him so as not to be cheated of their scapegoat by their need to placate Jason; or it may be that Timotheus' acquittal was due in part to his success in persuading the Athenians that the irregularities in his accounts were the fault of Antimachus. Demosthenes (49, passim) suggests that Timotheus may have tried to pass some of the blame on to Antimachus, but it is difficult to know what to make of the tendentious remarks in this (or any other) oration.

55 Xen. *Hell.* 6.2.1 merely records the making of peace; Diodorus discusses it at greater length (15.38.2–4). I see no compelling reason to reject Diodorus' contention that the Thebans were excluded from this peace when the Athenians refused to allow Epaminondas to sign for all Boeotia. Many scholars, however, contend that Diodorus has confused this peace with the peace of 371, from which the Thebans were indeed excluded for precisely this reason: Cawkwell, for example, in "Epaminondas and Thebes," *CQ* 22 (1972):257; Ryder, *Koine Eirene*, 124; Lauffer, "Die Diodordublette XV 38–50 über die Friedensschlusse zu Sparta 374 und 371 v. Chr.," *Historia* 8 (1959):315–48; Roos, "The Peace of Sparta of 374 B.C.," *Mnemosyne*, 2 (1949):265–85. Rice, however, "Why Sparta Failed," 148), believes the story of Diodorus. The most thorough discussion of the issues appears in Hack, "The Rise of Thebes: A Study of Theban Politics and Diplomacy, 386–371 B.C.," 126–41, where the case for accepting Diodorus is persuasively argued. For the issues involved in the more precise dating of the peace, see Buckler, "Dating of the Peace of 375/4," *GRBS* 12 (1971):353–62.

56 Xen. *Hell.* 6.2.2–3; Diod. 15.45.

57 Plut. *De genio Socr.* 575e; Beloch, *AP*, 143. Cawkwell (*Historia* 12 ([1963]:94) argues that Timotheus was in fact not a member of a pro-Theban party at this time, although he acknowledges that "Timotheus may well have been the chosen instrument of those who were less distrustful of Thebes than of Sparta."

58 Rice, "Why Sparta Failed," 152.

59 Beloch, *AP*, 143; Rice, "Why Sparta Failed," 154.

60 Rice, "Why Sparta Failed," 152.

61 Woodhead, *Phoenix* 16 (1962):261.

62 Dein. 1.14 and 3.17; Isocr. 15.129; Diod. 16.21.4; Nep. *Tim.* 3.

4–5 and *Iph.* 3.3; Dion. Hal. *Dein.* 13.667–68. A discussion of the date and format of the trial appears just below, pp. 46–47.

63 Diod. 16.7.3–4; Nep. *Chab.* 4.

64 Nepos' assertion that the chief command of the war was placed in the hands of Menestheus and that Timotheus and Iphicrates were added on as advisers (*Tim.* 3.2) may be true, but it should certainly not be taken to suggest that Timotheus and Iphicrates were not στρατηγοί.

65 Polyaenus says Embata (3.9.29), and most modern scholars agree, but Diodorus (16.21.3) claims that the abortive battle was joined in the straits, and he is followed by Grote (7:656).

66 Diod. 16.21.3–4; Nep. *Tim.* 3.2–5.

67 See for example Schaefer, *Demosthenes*, 1:153–63 and Rehdantz, *Vitae Iphicratis Chabriae Timothei Atheniensium*, 233ff., where a delay before the trial is suggested, and Grote, 7:658–659 and Beloch, *AP*, 362–65, where the case for an immediate trial is argued.

68 Diod. 16.21.4; Nep. *Tim.* 3.5; Isocr. 15.129.

69 Dion. Hal. *Dein.* 13.667 and *Lys.* 12.480.

70 Diod. 16.22.1.

71 The popularity of Iphicrates is attested in Polyaen. 3.9.29.

72 Isocr. 15.101; Grote, 7:659.

73 It strains belief that Dionysius' use of the word εἰσαγγελία in reference to Iphicrates should have no bearing on the format of the trials of Timotheus and Menestheus.

74 Isocr. 15.129.

75 Dion. Hal. *Dein.* 1.14 and 3.17.

76 Beloch, *AP*, 166.

77 Diod. 15.95.3.

78 Arist. *Rhet.* 3.10.7 (1411). Concerning the reputation of Timotheus at Athens, as Frank Frost has kindly reminded me, Plutarch reports (*Moralia* 856B) that the enemies of Timotheus portrayed him as sleeping while the cities entered of their own accord into a kind of lobster-trap. The story also appears in *Moralia* 187B–C and Plutarch's *Sulla* 6.3–4.

79 Isocr. 15.130–134.

80 Polyaen. 3.9.29.

81 Grote, 7:659.

82 Dem. 10.257; Ps.-Plut. *Vit. X Orat.* 840B, Dem. 22.

83 Dem. 19.40.

84 Aeschin. 3.71.

85 Dem. 19.15, 16, 159, 178, and 290ff.; Aeschin. 2.68 and 79.
86 Dem. 19.278.
87 Aeschin. 2.103–4.
88 Dem. 19.156.
89 Dem. 19.158.
90 Aeschin. 2.102–104.
91 Dem. 19.18, 31, and 32.
92 Dem. 19.19–26, 34–41, 44–48, 68, 102, 120; Aeschin. 2.119–23.
93 Aeschin. 1.102–4 and 128.
94 Diod. 16.9.
95 Dem. 19.128.
96 Dem. 19.211.
97 Dem. 19.257.
98 Grote, 8.107–167.
99 These detractors include Grote (above, n. 98); Curtius, *History of Greece*, 5:322ff.; L. van Hook, *Greek Life and Thought*, 87; and P. Lévêque, *The Greek Adventure*, 323.
100 Cawkwell, "The Fall of Themistocles," in *Auckland Essays Presented to E. M. Blaiklock* (1970), 45.
101 Cloché, *Demosthènes* (1951), 147.

IV. FACTIONAL STRIFE

1 Sources for the trial of Cimon are Plut. *Per.* 10.5; Plut. *Cim.* 14.4–15.1; and Arist. *Ath. Pol.* 27.1.
   Demosthenes (23.205) gives another version of Cimon's trial. Listing Athenians who were punished for their misdeeds despite signal services to the state, he writes that "because Cimon had dislocated the ancestral constitution (πάτριον μετεκίνησε πολιτείαν), he escaped the death sentence by only three votes and was fined fifty talents." It is not clear of what actual event (if any) this is a rhetorical version; confusion with Miltiades seems probable, and indeed some manuscripts read, for πάτριον . . . πολιτείαν, Παριὼν . . . πολιτεάν. Whatever the significance of this passage may be, I do not believe it should be taken as evidence for the trial of 463.
2 Plut. *Cim.* 14.4.
3 Plut. *Per.* 10.5.
4 Arist. *Ath. Pol.* 27.1.
5 Lipsius, *AR*, 294.
6 Bonner and Smith, *Administration*, 2.27.

7 Busolt, *GG*, 3:1.245; Jacoby, *FGrH*, 3b (Suppl.), 2. Notes, 120.
8 Glotz, *Greek City*, 228.
9 Wilamowitz, *A. u. A.*, 2:245.
   If in fact the accusation against Cimon was first brought at Cimon's regular εὔθυναι, then we have one instance of a general who submitted to εὔθυναι between two consecutive terms, for Cimon seems to have been στρατηγός from the Thasian campaign through 462/61.
10 Plut. *Cim.* 14.3.
11 Meiggs, *Athenian Empire*, 88. It is certainly a mistake to accept Plutarch's implication that the task of prosecuting Cimon was thrust upon an unwilling Pericles in connection with his official duties as public prosecutor, as do Bonner and Smith, who write that "in the prosecution of Cimon, Pericles was an elected public advocate and played into the hands of the defense by handling the case in a perfunctory manner. . . . Pericles was influenced by the pleas of Elpinice, the sister of Cimon" (Bonner and Smith, *Administration*, 2:33). These pleas are recorded by Plutarch (*Per.* 10.4–5 and *Cim.* 14.4).
12 Wade-Gery, *Essays in Greek History*, 164 n. 3; so also Davies, *Athenian Propertied Families*, 295 and 300.
13 Plut. *Per.* 9; Arist. *Ath. Pol.*, 27.
14 Plut. *Cim.* 16.8.
15 Some recent historians, it should be noted, have cast doubt on the supposedly sweeping and democratic character of this legislation, notably E. Ruschenbusch, *Athenische Innenpolitik im 5. Jahrhundert v. Chr.*, 57–65 and R. Sealey, "Ephialtes," *CP* 59 (1964):18–20.
16 Arist. *Ath. Pol.* 25.
17 Plut. *Per.* 10.5 and *Cim.* 14.4.
18 Plut. *Per.* 31–32; Diod. 12.38–39.
19 Jacoby, *FGrH* 3b (Suppl.), 2. Notes, 484–496.
20 This view is supported by Meyer, *Forschungen zur Alten Geschichte*, 2:299–301 and 326–33; Adcock, *CAH* 5:477–80; Frost, "Pericles and Dracontides," *JHS* 84 (1964):69–72 and "Pericles, Thucydides, son of Melesias, and Athenian Politics before the War," *Historia* 13 (1964):385–99; Kagan, *Outbreak*, 194–98; and of course Jacoby, *FGrH* 3b (Suppl.), 2. Notes, 484–96 (to Philoch, 328, fr. 121). Beloch, however, in *AP*, 19–22 and *GG*, 2:1:294–98, follows Plutarch, as does Wade-Gery in *Essays in Greek History*, 259–60; and the evidence of Philochorus is

attacked by Kienast, "Der Innenpolitischen Kampf in Athens von der Rückkehr des Thukydides bis zu Perikles' Tod," *Gymnasium* 60 (1953):212; Lendle, "Philochoros über den Prozess des Pheidias," *Hermes* 83 (1955):284–303; Morgan, "Pheidon and Olympia," *Hesperia* 21 (1952):295–339; and Dinsmoor, "Attic Building Accounts: I, The Parthenon," *AJA* 17 (1913):70–71.

21 Plut. *Per.* 22.2–23.1. It is, I suppose, possible that Pericles bribed Pleistoanax to withdraw in 446. Although he had excellent terms to offer the Spartans in any event, he may have wished to seal the bargain by involving Pleistoanax in a criminal transaction which he might later threaten to reveal — a transaction which, as events were to show, would cause far more embarrassment to Pleistoanax than to Pericles.

22 Diod. 12.39.2.

23 Jacoby, *FGrH* 3b (Suppl.), 2. Notes, 484–96.

24 Plut. *Per.* 14.2.

25 Plut. *Per.* 32.1 and 3. Plutarch properly understood the purpose of these attacks, as he wrote that this decree was meant "to direct suspicion at Pericles through Anaxagoras" (32.1).

26 Thuc. 3.37–40.

27 Diod. 13.64.6; Arist. *Ath. Pol.* 27.5. Xenophon's account of the fall of Pylos fills only a sentence (*Hell.* 1.2.18) and, as Grote points out (5:466), was evidently drawn from Spartan sources.

28 Diod. 13.64.5–7.

29 Arist. *Ath. Pol.* 27.5.

30 Fornara shows no previous στρατηγία for Anytus, nor is any trierarchy attested.

31 Schol. Plat. *Apol.* 18; Isocr. 18.23.

32 Arist. *Ath. Pol.* 24.4; McCoy, "Theramenes," 176–77.

33 Andoc. 1.75–78. Soldiers who had been faithful to the Four Hundred, for example, were not permitted to speak in the assembly or to serve on the council.

34 Lys. 30.7.

35 Lys. 25.25–26.

36 Lys. 20.7.

37 McCoy, "Theramenes," 133. The plight of the moderates during the years following the restoration of 410 is discussed by McCoy, 130–33 and Busolt (*GG*, 3:2.1540–46).

38 Grote, 5:466.

39 Curtius, 4.44. The story of Anytus' bribery has won more acceptance among constitutional historians. Bonner, for example,

speaks of "the sensational exploit of Anytus" (*Aspects*, 37). The rumors concerning Anytus may have been partly responsible for the revision of the judiciary at the end of the fifth century. During the fifth century, a panel of dicasts was assigned to a particular court for a period of a year. Each panel numbered five hundred, but it might function with less. The fixed personnel of the court made bribery possible, but the size of the panel limited this option to the very wealthy. During the fourth century, however, a new and extraordinarily intricate system of selection by lot described by Aristotle (*Ath. Pol.* 63–66) assured that it would be impossible to know the identity of the jurors on any case in advance. It was always possible, however, to spread the report that a verdict of acquittal would be richly rewarded. The elaborate procedure for jury selection employed during the fourth century, discussed in detail by Gilbert (*Constitutional Antiquities*, 394–402 and 415), is parodied by Aristophanes in the *Ecclesiazusae* (676ff).

40 Henderson, *Great War*, 450.
41 Xen. *Hell.* 1.7; Diod. 13.101–2. Neither Diodorus nor Xenophon, the sources for the trial of the eight generals, uses the word εἰσαγγελία to describe it, but the serious nature of the case and, more decisively, the fact that it was tried in the assembly both suggest that the procedure was in fact εἰσαγγελία, as is assumed in Schömann, *Dissertation on the Assemblies*, 200–202; Hignett, *AC*, 234; Bonner and Smith, *Administration*, 1:307; Lipsius, *AR*, 185; Busolt, *GG*, 3:2.1600; Gilbert, *Beiträge*, 376–78; and Swoboda, "Über den Prozess des Perikles," *Hermes* 28 (1893):566 and 570. A charge of προδοσία is suggested in Thalheim, "Zur Eisangelie in Athen," *Hermes* 37 (1902):343 and Bonner and Smith, *Administration*, 1:307.

   Much of my discussion of the trial of the generals here reproduces my article "Arginusae Once Again," *CW* 71 (1977):107–11. The most valuable discussions of the Arginusae trial are the articles of Cloché, "L'Affaire des Arginuses," *Rev. hist.* 130 (1919):3–68 and, most recently, of Andrewes, "The Arginousai Trial," *Phoenix* 28 (1974):112–22.

42 Xen. *Hell.* 1.6.35; 1.7.29–32; Diod. 13.100.1–3.
43 Xen. *Hell.* 1.7.17; Diod. 13.101.2.
44 Diod. 13.101.2–3.
45 Xen. *Hell.* 1.7.2.
46 Beloch, *AP*, 86.

47 Beloch, *AP*, 85–89; McCoy, "Theramenes," 151–52; Henderson, *Great War*, 472; Cloché, *Rev. hist.* 130 (1919):39–40.
48 Beloch, *AP*, 89, followed by McCoy, "Theramenes," 151.
49 McCoy, "*Theramenes*," 146.
50 Cloché has argued for the authenticity of the pretext on the grounds that because of his antipathy towards Theramenes, Xenophon would have been sure to say so had Theramenes been the moving force behind the adjournment. Perhaps; but it may be that Xenophon did not realize what was actually happening, and quite possibly the instigators of the adjournment were other enemies of the generals (*Rev. hist.* 130 [1919]:46).
51 *Hell.* 1.7.35. Xenophon's account of the machinations of Theramenes at the Apaturia is attacked by Grote (5:521, 523); Cloché (*Rev. hist.* 130 [1919], 48–49) suggests that Theramenes may simply have prevailed on the bereaved to display their sentiments as publicly as possible.
52 Xen. *Hell.* 1.7.9–10.
53 Xen. *Hell.* 1.7.12, 20–23. The origins and provisions of the psephism of Cannonus are discussed by Bonner and Smith, *Administration*, 1:205–8; Busolt-Swoboda, *GS*, 884 n. 1; Hignett, *AC*, 304–5; and most recently by MacDowell, *The Law in Classical Athens*, 88–9.

In my article in *CW* 71 (1977):10, I stressed that Euryptolemus was a relative of Pericles and a friend of Diomedon. Too much, however, should not be made of this, since, as Erich Gruen has kindly reminded me, Euryptolemus was also, of course, the cousin of Alcibiades.
54 Xen. *Hell.* 1.7.13–14.
55 Xen. *Hell.* 1.7.14–15; Cloché, *Rev. hist.* 130 (1919):49–51.
56 Xen. *Hell.* 1.7.34–35.
57 See above, n. 53.
58 Dem. 21.64; Arist. *Rhet.* 1.7 (1364). All the ancient sources and many conflicting modern interpretations of the Oropus affair have been assembled by Rehdantz, *Vitae*, 109–14.
59 Histories of Oropus are offered in Grote, 7:251 and Schaefer, *Demosthenes*, 1:92–94.
60 Isocr. 14.22–40.
61 Grote, 7:251.
62 Xen. *Hell.* 7.4.1; Diod. 15.76.
63 Xen. *Hell.* 7.4.1.
64 Arist. *Rhet.* 1.7.19 (1364) and 3.10.6 (1411).

65 Krause (*AS*, 18 and 52) attributes a στρατηγία to Callistratus in 367/66, but there is no evidence for this, as Swoboda points out ("Kallistratos," *RE* 10:1733).

66 Xen. *Hell.* 7.1.33–36; Dem. 19.137.

67 Plut. *Pelop.* 30; Xen. *Hell.* 7.1.38; Dem. 19.137. Leon accused Timagoras of being in league with Pelopidas, and Demosthenes alleged that Timagoras had accepted bribes from Artaxerxes.

68 Xen. *Hell.* 7.1.40.

69 Rehdantz (*Vitae*, 112) maintains that Chabrias was actually a member of the pro-Theban party, but I find this difficult to believe, both in view of his acquittal and because his accuser Leodamas was a pro-Theban (Aeschin. 3.138). A more judicious view of Chabrias' Theban connections is taken by Schaefer (*Demosthenes*, 1:95).

70 Xen. *Hell.* 7.4–5.

71 Diog. Laert. 3.23–24. The date of the return of Plato and of the trials of Chabrias and Callistratus are discussed and debated in Schaefer, *Demosthenes*, 1:97–98; Sealey, "Callistratus of Aphidna and His Contemporaries," *Historia* 5 (1956); and Cawkwell, "The Common Peace of 366/5 B.C.," *CQ*, N.S. 11 (1961):84 n. 2.

72 See p. 41 above.

73 Dem. 15.9; Sealey, *Historia* 5 (1956):180 and 194.

74 The campaigns of Timotheus and Iphicrates during this period are analyzed by Grote (7:323–24) and Sealey (*Historia* 5 [1956]:196).

75 Dem. 23.130 and 149.

76 Cloché in "La politique de l'athénien Callistratos," *REA* 25 (1923):28, denies any connection between the rising fortunes of Timotheus and the attack on Callistratus and Chabrias on the grounds that no independent evidence exists for friction between Callistratus and Timotheus around this time, but his caution strikes me as excessive. Grote (7:265) stresses the shift from Iphicrates to Timotheus but does not connect it with the trial of Callistratus and Chabrias. Beloch, however, perceives the connection and writes that the trial of 365 "was the answer to the trial of Timotheus in the fall of 373" (*AP*, 154).

77 Aeschin. 3.138–39.

78 Schaefer (*Demosthenes*, 1:95) sees the plight of the pro-Thebans as a major factor in the trials of Callistratus and Chabrias. For the curious frequency with which Chares was involved in military

operations which led to the impeachment of someone else, see below pp. 77–78.

79 Schaefer, *Demosthenes*, 1:95.

80 Diog. Laert. 3.23–24; Beloch, *AP*, 154; Cloché, *REA* 25 (1923):27–28.

81 The complexity of the case is stressed by Beloch, *AP*, 154–155.

82 Dem. 51.9; Diod. 15.95.3; Aeschin. 2.21 and 124; Hyper. 4.1. Diodorus claims that the attack on Peparethus took place in 361/ 60, i.e., during the archonship of Nicophemus (15.95.1), and this date is accepted by Glotz and Cohen (3:185) and by Geyer ("Leosthenes," *RE* 24:2060). I doubt, however, that Diodorus is correct, for Demosthenes gives the precise date of the decree sending the fleet out as the 24th of Metageitnion, in the archonship of Molon, i.e., August, 362/61 (50.4). I would agree with Beloch, therefore (*AP*, 297), in placing the only known στρατηγία of Leosthenes in the year 362/61, when he went out with Autocles. It is, of course, possible that he was also στρατηγός in 361/60, but as Peparethus was already under siege in August of 362 (Dem. 50.5), I find it difficult to believe that Alexander's attack on Leosthenes did not take place until nearly a year later.

83 Xen. *Hell.* 7.5.4; Dem. 50.5.

84 Dem. 50.4–6.

85 Diod. 15.95.2–3.

86 Polyaen. 6.2.2.

87 Such is the most likely interpretation of Hyper. 4.1. Hyperides gives a list of five men who did not appear at their εἰσαγγελίαι: Timomachus, Leosthenes, Callistratus, Philon of Anaea, and Theotimus. One of these, he says, was an orator impeached for his bad advice. Timomachus, Leosthenes, and Theotimus, as we shall see, were all impeached for their conduct as στρατηγοί. The orator, then, would have to be Callistratus or Philon. We know nothing of Philon; Pritchett (*Greek State*, 2:10) and Hager (84) are probably correct, however, in assuming that he was a στρατηγός. The point of Hyperides' argument is that in earlier days trial by εἰσαγγελία was reserved for men in prominent positions. Had Philon been a prominent orator, surely we would have heard of him. Callistratus, then, who was indeed impeached in the late 360s, must have been the orator in question.

88 Cloché, *REA* 25 (1923):29–32.

89 Cloché, *REA* 25 (1923):22–32.

90 Aeschin. 2.138. This statement of Aeschines is accepted by Glotz and Cohen (3:186) and Schaefer (*Demosthenes*, 1:132–133).
91 Dem. 51.8 and 16.
92 Apollodorus, for example, accused three of the generals under whom he had served as trierarch.
93 Plut. *Pelop.* 30; Xen. *Hell.* 7.1.38; Dem. 19.137.
94 Dem. 19.191. Hansen believes in the actuality of this impeachment, although he is uncertain as to the format and suggests either εἰσαγγελία or a γραφὴ προδοσίας. As Hansen points out, it is likely that if such a trial ever took place it must have been in 393/92, the only time Conon was in Athens after the end of the Peloponnesian War.
95 Dem. 36.53; Dem. 50.52.
96 Hansen, *Eisangelia*, 97.
97 Other factors may have contributed to the impeachment of Callippus. It is possible that 360 witnessed a great purge as far as the party of Callistratus was concerned. Hegesander, Timomachus' ταμίας, was an associate of Leodamas, who had impeached both Chabrias and Callistratus in 366 in the matter of the loss of Oropus; he was also the brother of Hegesippus, the democratic leader who had attempted to dissuade Plato from speaking in defense of Chabrias in 365, and the two brothers were close (Aeschin. 1.56, 69–71). Now Aeschines maintains that it was the embezzlement of Hegesander that was chiefly responsible for the ruin of Timomachus. But it would be unwise, I think, to read too much into the words of Aeschines, who writes: καὶ τρόπον τινὰ οὐχ ἥκιστα αἴτιος ἐγένετο Τιμομάχῳ τῆς συμφορᾶς (1.56). Hegesander, according to Aeschines, was said to have taken advantage of the simple-mindedness of Timomachus and embezzled eighty minae of silver. But none of this places Hegesander squarely in the camp of Timomachus' accusers; and besides, Aeschines in this passage is reviving the old accusation against Timarchus for prostitution and embezzlement of public funds, in which accusations Hegesander, he maintains, was unofficially named as an unindicted co-conspirator of sorts. Aeschines has every motive in this passage for blackening the name of Hegesander, and his accusations are not, I think, to be taken too seriously.
    The accusation against Callippus may or may not have been connected with the attack around the same time on Philon of the same deme; Callippus' father bore that name and may have been the Philon whom Hyperides lists as a victim of εἰσαγγελία (4.1).

(The genealogy of Callippus is discussed in Davies, *Athenian Propertied Families* 274–76. He does not seem to be the same man named in a lawsuit by Apollodorus [Dem. 51] at an earlier time.) After the attack on him, Callippus transferred his political activities to Sicily, where he became the lieutenant, murderer and finally the successor of Dion.

98 Lyc. frr. 75, 77, 105; Diod. 16.88.1–2.

99 Polyaen. 4.2.8.

100 Polyaen. 4.2.14.

101 Cavaignac, *Histoire de l'antiquité*, 2:201.

102 For modern views of the complex political constellations of this era, see Frost, "Themistocles' Place in Athenian Politics," *California Studies in Classical Antiquity* 1 (1968):105–24 and *Plutarch's Themistocles*; Gomme, "Athenian Notes. 1. Athenian Politics 510–483 B.C.," *AJP* 65 (1944):321–31; Karavites, "Realities and Appearances, 490–480 B.C.," *Historia* 26 (1977):129–47; Robinson, "The Struggle for Power at Athens in the Early Fifth Century," *AJP* 60 (1939):234–37; MacGregor, "The Pro-Persian Party at Athens from 510 to 480 B.C.," *HSCP*, Suppl. 1 (1940):71–95; and Walker and Munro, *CAH*, 4.138, 170, 231–32, 252–53, 265–66.

103 Herod. 6.132–136; Ephorus fr. 64 (Jacoby); Nep. *Milt.* 7–8; Plut. *Cim.* 4. The episode is discussed in Kinzl, "Miltiades Paros-expedition in der Geschichtsschreibung," *Hermes* 104 (1976):280–307; Berve, *Miltiades: Studien zur Geschichte des Mannes und seiner Zeit*, *Hermes* Suppl. 2, 1937; Ehrenberg, *Aspects of the Ancient World*, 116–43; How, "Cornelius Nepos on Marathon and Paros," *JHS* 39 (1919):48–61; Macan in his commentary on Herodotus, *The Fourth, Fifth and Sixth Books*, 1:387 and 2:254; and MacGregor, *HSCP* Suppl. 1, 1940. The question of Nepos' sources is discussed most fully in Kinzl.

According to Plato, the ἐκκλησία considered putting Miltiades to death by casting him into the barathron but was dissuaded by the βουλή and settled on the fine instead (*Gorgias*, 516a).

104 Nep. *Milt.* 7–8.

105 Nep. *Milt.* 8.4.

106 Nep. *Milt.* 7. This last detail is difficult to believe.

107 Nep. *Milt.* 8.4.

108 Nep. *Milt.* 7.1–2.

109 Grote (3:311–324) in particular seems to accept Herodotus' account in all its colorful detail and indeed expands it to heighten the dramatic potential of the situation.

110 Macan (above, n. 103) suggests that Miltiades and his political associates may have circulated the report that the object of the proposed expedition was Thasos.
111 Xen. *Hell.* 5.4.19; Plut. *Pelop.* 14.1.
112 Xen. *Hell.* 5.2.25–35.
113 Xen. *Hell.* 5.4.2–8.
114 Xen. *Hell.* 5.4.9–10.
115 Xen. *Hell.* 5.4.11–14.
116 Xen. *Hell.* 5.4.19.
117 Diod. 15.25–26.
118 The word is that of Rehdantz (*Vitae*, 44). The view of Rehdantz is shared by Fabricius, "Die Befreiung Thebens," *RhMus* 48 (1893):448–471 and by Judeich, "Athens und Theben vom Königsfrieden bis zur Schlacht bei Leuctra," *RhMus* 76 (1922):171–97.
119 Burnett, "Thebes and the Expansion of the Second Athenian Confederacy: *IG* II² 40 and *IG* II² 43," *Historia* 11 (1962):16. Cf., however, the criticism of Burnett in Cawkwell, "The Foundation of the Second Athenian Confederacy," *CQ* 23 (1973):57–58.
120 Grote, 7:80–86. It has also been argued by Grote and others that Athenian assistance would have violated the principle of autonomy prescribed by the Peace of Antalcidas. Why? Aid to the exiles, while certainly a provocative act, did not infringe any polis' autonomy.
121 Whether or not the pro-Spartan faction at Athens was led at this time by Callistratus is an open question. Rice ("Why Sparta Failed," 99–100) maintains that it was, but Cloché sees no reason to think so (*REA* 25 [1923]:13), and Sealey in his article on Callistratus and his contemporaries (*Historia* 5 [1956]) avoids the issue.

Beloch (*AP*, 138) maintains that the landed aristocracy formed the core of the opposition to the generals because the urban masses were least threatened by an invasion. But many poor farmers lived in the country, surely. It is more likely, I think, that the fear of war with the Spartans was shared in some degree by members of all social, political and economic groups.

V. THE IMPEACHMENT TRIALS OF THE CORINTHIAN WAR

1 Meyer, *GdA*, 5:260–61 and 264–65; Glotz and Cohen, 3.96.
2 Xen. *Hell.* 3.1–2.
3 *Hell. Ox.* 2.1.

4 The slow growth of Athens to a position of sufficient strength to challenge Sparta is argued convincingly by Kagan in "The Economic Origins of the Corinthian War (395–387 B.C.)," *Parola del Passato* 16 (1961):323–28. I fail to see, however, why the lack of Athenian protest over the actions of Pharax should, as Kagan (324) argues, be taken as a sign of "the obedience of the Athenians" since, after all, it was the Athenians who had sent the ambassadors to Persia in the first place; rather, I should think it must signify either ambivalence or deep internal division.

5 *Hell. Ox.* 1.1–3.

6 In equating οἱ γνώριμοι καὶ χαρίεντες with οἱ ἐπιεικεῖς καὶ τὰς οὐσίας ἔχοντες, I differ from the approach which I presented in "The Athenian Conservatives and the Impeachment Trials of the Corinthian War," *Hermes* 108 (1980):100–114. Most of this chapter, however, presents the same material as that article. Seager in "Thrasybulus, Conon and Athenian Imperialism, 396–386 B.C.," *JHS* 87 (1967):95–96 questions whether these two groups were in fact identical.

7 *Hell. Ox.* 2.2.

8 Perlman, "The Causes and the Outbreak of the Corinthian War," *CQ*, N.S. 14 (1964):66–67; Cloché, "Les conflits politiques et sociaux à Athens pendant la guerre de Corinthe, *REA* 21 (1919):163; Kagan, *Parola del Passato* 16 (1961):325–27; Bruce, "Athenian Foreign Policy, 396–395 B.C.," *CJ* 58 (1963):290; Hamilton, *Sparta's Bitter Victories*.

The political issues involved in the impeachment trials of the Corinthian War, and in particular the role of the conservatives in these trials, has been studied by Cloché, *REA* 21 (1919):167–192, and I am greatly indebted to his work, though I differ from him in seeing the hand of the conservatives in the impeachment of the ambassadors in 391. For my study of politics at Athens during the Corinthian War I am also indebted to Sealey, who discusses the political alignments of this period in "Callistratus of Athens and His Contemporaries," *Historia* 5 (1956):178–203; to the prosopographical data collected by Davies in *Athenian Propertied Families*; and in particular to Hamilton's fine and full study. I have also profited from the work of Longo, *"Eterie" e gruppi politici nell-Atene del IV sec. a. C.* and Mossé, "Les procès politiques et la crise de la démocratie athénienne," *Dialogues d'histoire ancienne* 1 (1974): 207–36.

9 Xen. *Hell.* 3.2.21–31; Diod. 14.17, 34, and 38.

10 Xen. *Hell.* 3.5.8–15.

11 Pausanias 3.9–11.

12 Xenophon's account of the Theban alliance appears in *Hell.* 3.5.3–16. It is commonly assumed that Thrasybulus proposed the motion to ally with Thebes, but all Xenophon says is that it was Thrasybulus who delivered the decision of the Athenians to the Theban envoys (3.5.16).

13 Xen. *Hell.* 3.5.1–2.

14 The causes of the outbreak of the Corinthian War are discussed in detail in Accame, *Ricerche intorno alla guerra corinzia*; Kagan, *Parola del Passato* 16 (1961); Bruce, "Internal Politics and the Outbreak of the Corinthian War," *Emerita*, 28 (1960):75–86 and *CJ* 58 (1963):289–97; Perlman, *CQ*, N.S. 14 (1964) and "Athenian Democracy and the Revival of Imperialistic Expansion at the beginning of the Fourth Century B.C.," *CP* 63 (1968):257–67; and Hamilton, *Sparta's Bitter Victories*, 25–208.

15 The nature and chronology of these attempts have been the subject of lively debate. See in particular Judeich, "Die Zeit der Friedensrede des Andokides," *Philologus* 81 (1927):141ff.; Wilcken, "Über Entstehung und Zweck des Königsfriedens," *Abhandlungen der Preuss. Akademie, Phil-hist. Klasse*, 1941, No. 16; Martin, "Sur une interpretation nouvelle de la 'Paix du Roi,'" *Museum Helveticum* 6 (1949):127–39; Beloch, *GG*, 3:1.80ff.; Cary, *CAH*, 6:50.ff.; Bruce, "Athenian Embassies in the Early Fourth Century," *Historia* 15 (1966):272–81; Ryder, *Koine Eirene*, Ch. 2; and Hamilton, *Sparta's Bitter Victories*, Ch. 8.

16 Xen. *Hell.* 4.8.13–15.

17 Cary, Beloch, Martin, and Hamilton all envision first a three-way conference at Sardis in which the abandonment of the Ionians was considered, followed by a conference at Sparta: Cary, *CAH*, 6:50ff.; Beloch, *GG*, 3:1.80ff.; Martin, *Museum Helveticum* 6 (1949):130ff.; Hamilton, 189–203. Judeich and Wilcken place the conference at Sparta first and the one at Sardis second: Judeich, *Philologus* 81 (1927):141ff.; Wilcken, *Abhandlungen der Preuss. Akademie*, 1941, No. 16, 6–11, where he also envisions a conference at Sparta in which the abandonment of the Ionians was discussed as preparatory to Antalcidas' attempt to interest the king in a common peace.

18 Didym., in *Demosth.* 10.34 in Jacoby, *FGrH* 3b, 328 (Philochorus) fr. 149a.

19 Jacoby, *FGrH* 3b, 328 (Philochorus) fr. 149b.
20 Dem. 19.278–79.
21 Clearly Aristides imagined that the impeachment of the ambassadors was to be associated with the peace of Antalcidas, for he writes that the Athenians agreed only grudgingly to the peace and indicted the ambassadors who had persuaded them to assent to it (203 [Oliver]; [Dindorf] 1:283). The view of Aristides is shared by Bruce, *Historia* 15 (1966):272–81 and Hamilton, *Sparta's Bitter Victories*, 236–39, 318–22.
22 Cloché, "La Politique de l'athénien Callistratos," *REA* 25 (1923):8; Accame, *Ricerche intorno alla guerra corinzia* 128; Jacoby, *FGrH* 3b, Suppl., 519; Sealey, *Historia* 5 (1956):184–85.
23 Xen. *Hell.* 4.4.7–13.
24 Xen. *Hell.* 4.8.10–11.
25 Xen. *Hell.* 4.8.16.
26 On the composition of Athenian embassies, see Mosley, *Envoys and Diplomacy in Ancient Greece, Historia*, Suppl. 22, Ch. 10, "The Composition of Athenian Embassies" and Adcock and Mosley, *Diplomacy in Ancient Greece*, passim.
27 Andoc. 1, passim.
28 Xen. *Hell.* 4.8.17.
29 Καλλιστράτου γράψαντος (see above, n. 18).
30 Andoc. 3.33.
31 Plut. *De genio Socr.* 597d; Diod. 15.38.3; Xen. *Hell.* 6.3.3 and 6.3.10–17.
32 Dem. 24.134–35.
33 Xen. *Hell.* 5.1.1–5.
34 Dem. 40.20 and 22; Schol. Aristoph. *Plut.* 174; Xen. *Hell.* 5.1. Pamphilus must have been tried before he had served out his term; a reference to his misfortunes at the hands of Plutus which seems to point to his trial for κλοπή occurs in Aristophanes' *Plutus*, which can have been produced no later than the Great Dionysia in March, 388.
35 Schol. Aristoph. *Plut.* 174.
36 Kirchner, *Prosographia Attica*, 2898–2900. The date of the birth of these descendants is not clear; see the genealogy and discussion in Schaefer, *Demosthenes*, 3:213–215.
37 See esp. Rice, "Why Sparta Failed," 26.
38 On the εἰσφοραί of the Corinthian War see esp. Thomsen, *Eisphora*, 180–81.
39 Lys. 19.7.
40 See above, pp. 64–69.

41 Lys. 19.35; Diod. 14.81.4.
42 Xen. *Hell.* 4.8.8; Lys. 19.12–13; Lys. 19.36.
43 Lys. 19.19–20.
44 Lys. 19.21–27.
45 An inference from Xen. *Hell.* 5.1.6.
46 See below, p. 102.
47 Seager, however, in "Thrasybulus, Conon and Athenian Imperialism, 396–386 B.C.," *JHS* 87 (1967):114, denies that any hostility to Conon was implied in the impeachment of Aristophanes and Nicophemus.
48 Xen. *Hell.* 4.8.25.
49 Lys. 28.12.
50 Lys. 28 and 29. Ergocles was probably a fellow στρατηγός of Thrasybulus.
51 Xen. *Hell.* 4.8.25–30.
52 Tod, *GHI*, no. 114; Cloché, *REA* 21 (1919):184.
53 Xen. *Hell.* 4.8.30.
54 Lys. 28.5.
55 Lys. 28.5.
56 Xen. *Hell.* 4.8.30.
57 Lys. 28 and 29.
58 Lys. 28.
59 It is not clear whom precisely Lysias has in mind; we do not know the names of the other στρατηγοί who were associated with Thrasybulus and Ergocles in Asia. Around the same time as Ergocles' trial, Philocrates, who had served as trierarch on the expedition, was tried (see below, p. 102).
60 Xen. *Hell.* 4.8.30.
61 Grote, 6.513; Bury, *History of Greece*, 550.
62 On the financial condition of Athens during the Corinthian War, see below, p. 100.
63 Sealey, *Historia* 5 (1956):184; Perlman, *CP* 63 (1968):265–66.
64 Lys. 28.5–6.
65 Accame, *Ricerche*, 138.
66 Thuc. 3.98.5. Characteristically, Thucydides suggests that it was a terrible thing that Demosthenes should have had to live with such a fear. In fact, as the evidence of Thucydides himself clearly shows, the Athenians had good reason to be angry. Demosthenes might well be afraid.
67 Xen. *Hell.* 3.5.16; Tod, *GHI*, no. 101.
68 Lys. 30.21–22.

69 Lys. 19; 27; 28; 29; 30.
70 Xen. *Hell.* 5.1.6.
71 Curtius, 4:280.
72 The conservative element in the opposition to Thrasybulus is stressed by Cloché, *REA* 21 (1919):185–191.
73 Lys. 28.11.
74 Schol. Aristoph. *Plut.* 550.
75 Lys. 29.
76 Xen. *Hell.* 4.8.24.
77 Dem. 19.180.
78 Lys. 26.23; Dem. 24.134.
79 The project of Antalcidas in the Hellespont is analyzed by Graefe, "Die Operationen des Antalkidas im Hellespont," *Klio* 28 (1935): 262–270 and Hamilton, *Sparta's Bitter Victories*, 309–10. My reconstruction of his campaign owes much to their careful work.
80 Xen. *Hell.* 4.8.34 and 5.1.25–28.
81 Tod, *GHI*, no. 116; Sealey, *Historia* 5 (1956):185–86.
82 Xen. *Hell.* 2.1.25–26; Plut. *Alc.* 36.5–37.2.
83 Dem. 24.134.
84 See above, n. 64.
85 Arist. *Ath. Pol.* 41.3; Harp, s.v. θεωρικά; Schol. Aristoph. *Eccles.* 102.
86 The democratic background of Agyrrhius is treated most fully by Beloch, *AP*, 119–20.
87 Dem. 24.134.

VI. GUILT AND INADEQUACY

1 Ps.-Plut. *Vit. X Orat.* 834; Lys. 12.67.
2 Ps.-Plut. *Vit. X Orat.* 834.
3 Ps.-Plut. *Vit. X. Orat.* 834; the law concerning convicted traitors also appears in Xen. *Hell.* 1.7.22.
4 Xen. *Hell.* 2.3.2. Hansen thinks he is the same person (*Eisangelia*, 115).
5 Thuc. 8.89.2–3.
6 Thuc. 8.86.9.
7 Thuc. 8.90.2; Ps.-Plut. *Vit. X Orat.* 834.
8 Thuc. 8.91.1.
9 Thuc. 8.91.2–3.
10 Thuc. 8.68.1.

11 Thuc. 8.92.2.
12 Thuc. 8.93–95.
13 Thuc. 8.92.1–2; Arist. *Ath. Pol.* 33.
14 Thuc. 8.98; Xen. *Hell.* 1.7.28.
15 Thuc. 8.68.2 maintains that Antiphon gave at his trial the best defense on a capital charge he had ever heard in his life.
16 Harpocrat. s.v. *Andron.*
17 According to Xenophon (*Hell.* 1.6.28), at some point Aristarchus, who had betrayed Oenoe to the Thebans, was impeached, although whether he returned to stand trial is unclear. Aristarchus, if tried, may have been prosecuted either by the Five Thousand or by the restored democracy; but as Ferguson has pointed out, the impeachment of Antiphon and Archeptolemus must have taken place under the Five Thousand, if for no other reason than that Theramenes left town in March of 410 not to return for some years ("The Condemnation of Antiphon," *Mélanges Glotz,* 349–66).

A delightfully detailed account of this year in Athenian history is offered in Grote.
18 Dem. 19.180; Aeschin. 1.56; Hyper. 4.1.
19 Dem. 50.17.
20 Dem. 23.115.
21 Dem. 50.
22 Bonner, *Lawyers and Litigants,* 130–31.
23 Xen. *Hell.* 7.1.41.
24 Timomachus was not, as far as we know, forcibly removed from this earlier command or tried on any charge. Sealey is probably right in imagining that Athenian dissatisfaction with him was indicated by the transfer of his command at the end of the official year 367/66 to Chares, a close associate of Aristophon, who seems to have belonged to a different political group ("Callistratus of Aphidna and His Contemporaries," *Historia* 5 [1956]:194; Schol. Aesch. 1.64).
25 Dem. 50.
26 Dem. 19.158; Aeschin. 2.102–4.
27 Aeschin. 2.30; Dem. 23.104 and 19.180; Arist. *Rhet.* 2.3.13 (1380). Aristotle says that the Athenians' ἀφεῖσαν Ergophilus, but he probably means by this word to contrast Ergophilus' fate with that of Callisthenes, for Demosthenes includes Ergophilus in a list of generals who were either executed or heavily fined.
28 Aeschin. 2.30; Grote, 7:325–26; Glotz and Cohen, 3.181.

29 Dem. 19.180; 23.167.
30 Dem. 23.157–69.
31 Dem. 23.167.
32 The family connections are mentioned in Aeschin. 3.52.
33 It is not clear whether a political motive also lay behind the attack on Cephisodotus, although Demosthenes (23.156) alleges that Cephisodotus and Iphicrates were enemies. Aeschines claims (3.51–52) that Demosthenes was among Cephisodotus' accusers at his εἰσαγγελία, but this is probably a misunderstanding or a distortion of the fact that no doubt Demosthenes was summoned by the prosecutor to give testimony at the trial since he had served as Cephisodotus' trierarch. Demosthenes had carried Cephisodotus on his own ship in part because of strong ties of friendship between their families, and only months after Cephisodotus' impeachment, Cephisodotus appears as Demosthenes' supporter in the trial concerning the trierarchic crown (Aeschin. 3.52; Dem. 51.1; Mittelhaus, "Kephisodotos," *RE* 21:231). I would consider it extremely unlikely, therefore, that Demosthenes' was among Cephisodotus' accusers.
34 Thuc. 4.65.3.
35 Thuc. 3.115.1. In the winter of 426/25, it seems, the στρατηγός Laches was recalled from Sicily and accused by Cleon of peculation. Cleon's accusations may have culminated in a formal trial for κλοπή. If so, Laches was probably acquitted, for he went on after Cleon's death to take a prominent part in negotiating the peace of Nicias. That Laches was accused by Cleon and tried for κλοπή has been inferred by some scholars from the clear parody of such a trial in Aristophanes' *Wasps*, since the *Wasps* contains a trial of the dog Labes (an evident pun on both Laches and λαμβάνω) in which one Kuon (of the same deme as Cleon) serves as the prosecutor. These scholars include Busolt (*GG*, 3:2.1083), Wilamowitz (*A. u. A.*, 2:245), Beloch (*AP*, 337f.), and Swoboda ("Laches," *RE* 23:337). Some, like Mastromarco and Mac-Dowell, have argued that the play *preceded* the trial (Mastromarco, *Storia di una commedia di Atene*, 62; MacDowell, ed., *Wasps*, 164.) Others have found the evidence insufficient to warrant belief in an actual trial and have concluded that the only reality underlying Aristophanes' "trial of Labes" was Cleon's constant vituperation of Laches in the assembly (Gomme, *HCT*, 2:431; Cloché, "Les Procès de stratèges athéniens," *REA* 27 [1925]:103; Jacoby, *FGrH* 3b [Suppl.], 2. Notes, 405–6). It is

probable, I think, that Laches was tried and acquitted. Except for the case of Phrynichus (which was, as I shall argue, a special one), Athenian στρατηγοί who were recalled and deposed by ἀποχειροτονία were tried. ᾿Αποχειροτονία, after all, consisted only of temporary deposition from office pending trial.

36 Thuc. 4.1 and 4.24–25.

37 Thuc. 4.2.3.

38 Thuc. 4.3.2. Kagan (*AW*, 269–270) rightly calls attention both to the mediocre performance of Pythodorus and to Sophocles' and Eurymedon's responsibility for their late arrival.

39 It is hard to see how Westlake (*Essays*, 105) can insist that Thucydides "is not . . . manipulating the evidence" here.

40 Thuc. 4.60.1; 4.63.1.

41 Thuc. 7.16.2.

42 Beloch, *AP*, 35; Busolt, *GG*, 3:2.1019; Kagan, *AW*, 169; Jacoby, *FGrH* 3b (Text), 553–54.

43 Westlake (*Essays*, 120–21), Busolt (*GG*, 3:2.1133), and Kagan (*AW*, 269) all suggest that the generals may have laid themselves open to this charge by accepting some gifts.

Westlake maintains that "few even of their most severe critics can have seriously believed that their approval of the settlement . . . was gained by bribes." It should be pointed out, however, that it is likely that the returning soldiers accused the generals of precisely this. A decade later Nicias was to express the anxiety — reported by Thucydides himself — that if he were to withdraw from Sicily without orders from home then the same soldiers who were begging to be taken home would accuse him at Athens of having withdrawn as a result of bribery (Thuc. 7.48.4). It is a logical inference (though not, of course, necessary) that Nicias was extrapolating from the complaints of the soldiers who returned from Sicily on this earlier occasion.

44 Thuc. 5.26.5. The charge of προδοσία is given by Marcellinus (*Life of Thuc.* A 23; B 46) and in the Anonymous *Life of Thuc.* (3); a reference in Aristophanes' *Wasps* (288–90), produced in 422, to treachery in Thrace suggests that the ancient biographers are correct. They also name Cleon as Thucydides' accuser, but this of course may be a conjecture based on the implacable hatred for Cleon which is evident in Thucydides' work. It is not possible in my opinion to determine whether or not Eucles was tried along with Thucydides. Kagan (*AW*, 301) argues that the silence of all the sources suggests that Eucles was not tried. Ordinarily I find

the silence of Thucydides strong evidence against the historicity of any impeachment. In this case, however, as Westlake has amply demonstrated (*Essays*, 123–37), Thucydides' manipulation of the evidence is subtle in the extreme, and I find it not impossible that he has omitted the condemnation of Eucles for some reason — perhaps to throw his own fate more sharply into relief. The silence of the other sources may be easily enough explained: Eucles' fate might surely have been overshadowed by that of his famous colleague.

Thucydides' language ξυνέβη μοι φεύγειν certainly "admits the view that" the historian "withdrew by voluntary exile," as Pritchett points out (*Greek State*, 2:10), and in view of the punishments meted out to Sophocles, Pythodorus, and Eurymedon only a few months before, Thucydides may have considered it imprudent to return to Athens to stand his trial. Most scholars agree that, whatever the charge, the penalty was surely exile, but Grundy argues that Thucydides was condemned to death (*Thucydides and the History of his Age* [1911], 35). I see no reason to believe, as has sometimes been suggested, that Thucydides was recalled by special decree rather than by the general amnesty at the end of the war. The data concerning this possibility are collected by Andrewes (Gomme, *HCT*, 4:14–15).

45 Diod. 12.68.1–3.

46 Thuc. 4.103.3–104.3.

47 Thucydides says that the message was sent by the enemies of the traitors acting μετὰ Εὐκλέους τοῦ στρατηγοῦ (4.104.4). This is the only mention of Eucles by name in the entire narrative, and it certainly does not show Eucles taking any initiative. It is hard to know what to make of Thucydides' portrait of Eucles' weakness, particularly as we are ignorant of Eucles' fate and of the transcript of Thucydides' trial. The signal must have gone by semaphore (Gomme, *HCT*, 3:579; R. Bauman, "A Message for Amphipolis," *Acta Classica* 11 [1968]:179).

48 Thuc. 4.105.1–107.2.

49 Grote, 4:503–5. Busolt's remarks appear at *GG*, 3:2.1154–55.

50 Bauman (above, n. 47), 170–81; Kagan, *AW*, 300–302. A more positive view is taken by Finley, *Thucydides*, 200 and by Delbrück, *Die Strategie des Perikles*, 177–78.

51 Thuc. 5.26.5.

52 He may, for example, have been using his Thracian connections to recruit reinforcements; he may have chosen to station himself

at Thasos because of its harbor (far superior in winter to that of Eion, as Delbrück points out [*Strategie*, 185–86]). It is never stated by Thucydides that he was "stationed" at Thasos, as many historians assume. He is simply described as ὄντα περὶ Θάσον (4.104.4).) He may have had word of disturbances in Thrace. That Eucles knew where Thucydides could be found certainly suggests that the decision for him to go to Thasos was taken jointly, which argues against any personal motive (perhaps connected with his own holdings among the Thracian gold mines) Thucydides may have had for going there; besides the best way to protect Thrace against Brasidas, who had no ships, was clearly to hold the line of the Strymon. (Schmid's allegation of a personal motive of this kind in Schmid-Stahlin, *Geschichte der Griechischen Literatur*, 5:2.12) is attacked on precisely these grounds by Gomme [*HCT*, 3:585].)

53 By Meyer, for example (*Forschungen*, 2:343) and Westlake (*Essays*, 124).

54 Thuc. 4.104.5.

55 That Eucles knew where Thucydides could be found suggests that probably the decision for Thucydides to go to Thasos was taken jointly.

56 De Romilly, *Histoire et raison chez Thucydide* (1956), 174–79.

57 Thucydides' failure to explain his absence at Thasos is discussed at some length in Chapter VII.

58 Thuc. 4.103.5–104.2. If Eucles had only a handful of men at his disposal, this difficulty would certainly lend credence to the idea of a recruiting expedition on Thucydides' part. At this time, of course, the chief Athenian effort was in Boeotia, and preparations there could easily have ciphoned off resources from Thrace.

59 Thuc. 3.65.4.

60 It is possible too, of course, that political animosities may have contributed to the attack on Thucydides. It may be that by the winter of 424/23 Thucydides had already made clear his lack of sympathy with the rising politicians of Cleon's stamp — that distrust of a democracy led by the so-called demagogues, men who were not like the historian himself and the hero of his story, Pericles, which marks his history of the war. Regarding the political views of Thucydides, I consider decisive the ideas put forward in MacGregor, "The Politics of the Historian Thucydides," *Phoenix* 10 (1956):93–102 and Kagan, *The Great Dialogue*, 96–112. Perhaps too the vote for conviction was a vote against

Thucydides as a Periclean and arose from the bitterness about the war that followed the disaster at Delium; and of course Thucydides' obvious hatred for Cleon may have been mutual — may have preceded rather than followed the historian's impeachment. (Emotional factors too may have played a part in the conviction of Thucydides, though it is hard to see how, after Delium, Thucydides could have been "the victim of the people's exorbitant hopes" in precisely the same way that Sophocles, Pythodorus, and Eurymedon had been after Pylos, as Finley claims that he was [*Thucydides*, 200]). It is not impossible that Thucydides' intellectual gifts and inclinations, the keen insight that so often (though not always) enabled him to view both sides of a question dispassionately, cost him dear at his trial; his objectivity may have been cited to impugn his patriotism, and it may be that the attack on the intellect which Cleon had employed to incite the assembly in the case of Mytilene made a subsequent appearance at Thucydides' trial.

61 Henderson, *Great War*, 450.
62 Xen. *Hell.* 1.5.11–18; Diod. 13.71 and 74; Plut. *Alc.* 36 and *Lys.* 5; Lys. 21.7; Nepos, *Alc.* 7; for the indictment of Cleophon, Himerius 36.16 (Phot. *Bibl.* 377). I follow once again the basic chronology of Ferguson, although I see no reason to fix the date of the battle as he does in March; it could just as well have been January or February. But it was not, I think, fought in the early months of 407, as some have suggested (e.g., Busolt, *GG*, 3:2.1529–1532 and Henderson, *Great War*, 448), for the board of generals chosen at the elections which followed the battle were those who commanded at Arginusae in the late summer of 406, and a reelection of the entire slate such as Henderson suggests (*Great War*, 448) is most improbable.

Whether the generals were deposed by ἀποχειροτονία or simply failed of reelection has been the subject of considerable debate. Most agree that the men were in fact deposed (Busolt, *GG*, 3:2.1578; Meyer, *GdA*, 4:635; Gilbert, *Beiträge*, 365; Curtius, 3:528; Grote, 5:491); some are cautiously noncommittal (Bloedow, *Alcibiades Re-examined*, 77; Bury, *History of Greece*, 500; McCoy, "Theramenes," 143), and at least one (Beloch, *AP*, 85 and "Zur Chronologie der letzten Jahre des peloponnesischen Krieges." *Philologus* 43 [1884]:269) maintains that Alcibiades was not deposed but only rejected at the polls. The language of most of the ancient sources is vague; Xenophon, Diodorus, and Plutarch (in his life of Alcibiades) report only that the Athenians chose new generals. But in fact the evidence for ἀποχειροτονία is decisive. The term is used by Plutarch in his life of Lysander (*Lys*. 5), where he writes that the Athenian people ἀποχειροτόνησε Alcibiades, and we have no reason to suppose that Plutarch was mistaken.

More important, the sending of Phanosthenes to replace Conon, who had been sent to take over from Alcibiades, makes clear that Alcibiades was out of office before the end of the official year 407/6, for Phanosthenes did not serve again during 406/5 (Xen. *Hell*. 1.5.16; Diod. 13.74.1). It is not credible, moreover, that the Athenians would have permitted Alcibiades to remain in office through the summer. I see no reason, however, to imagine a special election for the new generals; I assume they were chosen at the regular elections in March.

63 Xen. *Hell*. 1.4.22–1.5.18; Plut. *Alc*. 35; Diod. 13.69.
64 Xen. *Hell*. 1.5.8.
65 Diod. 1.71.1.
66 Diod. 13.71.1; Xen. *Hell*. 1.5.11; Plut. *Alc*. 35.4.
67 Diod. 13.73.3–6; Nepos, *Alc*. 7. Only Diodorus and Nepos tell the story of Alcibiades at Cyme. But is the Cymean Ephorus really the source for both accounts? The tales they tell are entirely different. According to Diodorus, Alcibiades was accused of maltreating Cyme, whereas Nepos claims that the Athenians were angry that his attack on it was not more successful. Possibly Cyme was in revolt, but the evidence is inconclusive (although Henderson calls it "clear" and claims that Cyme's rebellion was a "fact" [*Great War*, 449–50]).
68 Diod. 13.71.1; Xen. *Hell*. 1.5.11; Plut. *Alc*. 35.4–5.
69 Diod. 13.71.2–4; Xen. *Hell*. 1.5.12–14; Plut. *Alc*. 35. 5–6.
70 Diod. 13.71.4; Xen. *Hell*. 1.5.15; Plut. *Alc*. 35.6.
71 Diod. 13.74.1.
72 Not to be confused with Thrasybulus of Steiria, the son of Lycus.
73 Plut. *Alc*. 36.1–2.
74 Diod. 13.73.6; Plut. *Alc*. 36.2.
75 Bury, *History of Greece*, 500.
76 Grote alleges that Alcibiades acted "against all Athenian precedent, putting the pilot, a paid officer of the ship, over the heads of the trierarchs who paid their pilots, and served at their own cost" (5:488), while Henderson maintains indignantly that "Alcibiades

had no colleague of higher rank with him at Notium" (*Great War*, 446). The evidence is not at all clear, but it is probable that Alcibiades had with him not only trierarchs but his colleagues Aristocrates and Adeimantus as well.

77 Henderson, *Great War*, 450.

78 A rather emotional but thorough debunking of the legend of Alcibiades' military abilities is offered in Bloedow, *Alcibiades*.

79 Cloché, "L'Affaire des Arginuses," *Rev. hist.* 130 (1919):10–11.

VII. THUCYDIDES, PLUTARCH, AND ATHENS' GENERALS

1 Thuc. 4.65.4.

2 Grote, 5:122; Finley, *Thucydides*, 200. An important examination of Thucydides' studied presentation of material appears in Hunter, *Thucydides: The Artful Reporter*.

3 Thuc. 2.60–64.

4 Thuc. 2.65.1.

5 Thuc. 2.65.4.

6 Thuc. 2.70.2–4.

7 Grundy, *Thucydides and the History of his Age*, 1:30.

8 Meyer, *Forschungen*, 2:343; Gomme, *HCT*, 3:584. Elsewhere, however (3:578), Gomme comments on 4.104.5, where Thucydides writes of his speedy trip to rescue Eion, that these "are almost the only words written by Thucydides in self-defense."

9 Thirlwall, *History of Greece*, 1:383; Classen, *Thucydides*, 4 (1900), notes to 102–7; Delbrück, *Die Strategie des Perikles*, 177–78; Adcock, *CAH*, 5:245; Finley, *Thucydides*, 200.

10 Busolt, *GG*, 3:2.1154–55; Schmid in Schmid-Stählin, *Geschichte der Griechischen Literatur*, 5:2 and 12; Grote, 4:503–5; Gomme, *HCT*, 3:585–87; Bauman, "A Message for Amphipolis," *Acta Classica* 11 (1968):170–81; Kagan, *AW*, 300–302.

11 Thuc. 5.26.5.

12 Holm, *History of Greece*, 2:395.

13 Westlake, *Essays*, 123.

14 Westlake, *Essays*, 132–33.

15 Gomme, *HCT*, 3:586–87.

16 Meyer, *Forschungen*, 2:343.

17 Cornford, *Thucydides Mythistoricus* 250.

18 Busolt, *GG*, 3:2.1158; Finley, *Thucydides*, 200.

19 Thuc. 8.54.3.

20 Thuc. 8.54.3.
21 Plut. *Arist.* 26.3.
22 Plut. *Arist.* 27.1–2.
23 Plut. *Per.* 34.3.
24 Plut. *Per.* 35.4.
25 Plut. *Per.* 36.1.
26 Plut. *Per.* 37.1–2.
27 Curtius, 3:75.
28 Plut. *Nic.* 6.1–2.
29 Plut. *Them.* 2.6.
30 Plut. *Arist.* 26.3.
31 Beloch, *AP*, 33; Busolt, *GG*, 3:2.1034; Kagan, *AW*, 167–68; *Anth. Pal.* 7.614.
32 Diod. 12.55.10.
33 Westlake, "Paches," *Phoenix* 29 (1975):116.
34 Busolt, *GG* 3:2.1034; Lenschau, "Paches," *RE* 18.1:2068.
35 Meiggs, *The Athenian Empire*, 313.
36 Thuc. 3.33.3; Westlake, *Phoenix* 29 (1975):111.
37 Westlake, *Phoenix* 29 (1975):112.
38 Hansen, *Eisangelia*, 65.
39 Cawkwell, "Demosthenes' Policy after the Peace of Philocrates, II," in Perlman, ed., *Philip and Athens*, 169.
40 Hansen, *Eisangelia*, 65.

VIII. THE ACCOUNTABILITY OF PRIVATE CITIZENS

1 Modern works discussing this strange institution include Hignett, *AC*, 159–66; Busolt-Swoboda, *GS*, 884–86; Bonner and Smith, *Administration*, 1:193–95; Martin, "Ostrakismos," Daremberg-Saglio, 4:1.259–62; Reinmuth, "Ὀστρακισμός," *RE* 18:1.1674–85; Podlecki, *Life of Themistocles*, 185–94; and, most prominently, Carcopino, *L'Ostracisme athénien* and Vanderpool, *Ostracism at Athens*.
2 The question of the quorum is discussed at some length by Carcopino, *L'Ostracisme*, 89–104 and Bonner, "The Minimum Vote in Ostracism," *CP* 8 (1913):223–25.
3 Bonner and Smith, *Administration*, 1:194.
4 Carcopino, *L'Ostracisme*, 114–42. Carcopino's "ostracisés imaginaires" are Cleisthenes, Hippocrates, a Callias, Miltiades (the son of Cimon), Cleippides, and Damon.
5 Arist. *Ath. Pol.* 22.3–7; Plut. *Them.* 2.2.

6 The ostracism of Alcibiades the elder, mentioned at Lys. 14.30 and Ps.-Andoc. 4.34 is credited by Carcopino (145–48), although others are skeptical.

7 Plut. *Them.* 22.3; Nepos *Them.* 8.1.2; Thuc. 1.135.3; Plato *Gorg.* 516D.

8 Andoc. 3.3 and Plut. *Per.* 9.4; *Cim.* 15 and 17 (Cimon); Plut. *Per.* 14 (Thucydides).

9 Plut. *Alc.* 13, *Arist.* 7.3, *Nic.* 11.6; Thuc. 8.73.3.

10 Arist. *Ath. Pol.* 22.1–4; Philochorus in Jacoby, *FGrH*, 3B, 108; Aelian, *Var. hist.* 13.24; Diod. 13.55.

11 *Ath. Pol.* 22.1 and 3–4; Androtion 374 F 6 (Jacoby). Plutarch attributes the institution of ostracism to the Athenians' naturally jealous nature (*Arist.* 7.2, *Nic.* 11.1, *Alc.* 13.4).

12 The origins of ostracism are discussed by Hignett, *AC*, 159–64; Carcopino, *L'Ostracisme*, 5–36; Raubitschek, "The Origin of Ostracism," *AJA* 55 (1951):221–29; Robinson, "Cleisthenes and Ostracism," *AJA* 56 (1956):23–26; Hands, "Ostraka and the Law of Ostracism: Some Possibilities and Assumptions," *JHS* 79 (1959):69–79; Kagan, "The Origin and Purposes of Ostracism," *Hesperia* 30 (1961):393–401; Keaney, "The Text of Androtion, F 6 and the Origin of Ostracism," *Historia* 19 (1970):1–11; Stanton, "The Introduction of Ostracism and Alcemeonid Propaganda," *JHS* 90 (1970):180–83; and most recently in Thomsen, "The Origin of Ostracism. A Synthesis," *Humanitas* 4 (1972, Copenhagen).

13 As Kagan, for example, points out (*Hesperia* 30 [1961]:393–401).

14 Robinson, "The Struggle for Power at Athens in the Early Fifth Century," *AJP* 66 (1945):244–45. The political constellations of this period are also treated in MacGregor, "The Pro-Persian Party at Athens from 510 to 480 B.C." in *HSCP*, Supl. 1 (Cambridge, Mass.: 1940), 71–95; Gomme, "Athenian Notes. 1. Athenian Politics, 510–483 B.C.," *AJP* 65 (1944):321–31; Frost, *Plutarch's Themistocles*, Chapter 3; and in the works cited in n. 12 above.

15 Kagan, *Hesperia* 30 (1961):398.

16 Hands, *JHS* 79 (1959):69–79.

17 Arist. *Ath. Pol.* 22:5–6.

18 Lenardon, *The Saga of Themistocles*, 46.

19 Arist. *Ath. Pol.* 27.7.

20 Plut. *Arist.* 4.3 (prosecution at the εὔθυναι).

21 Plut. *Arist.* 2.1.

22 The many sources for Themistocles' downfall, besides those

cited in n. 7 above, are cited by Hansen, *Eisangelia*, 70 and discussed at some length in Podlecki, *Life of Themistocles*, 34–40 and Lenardon, *Saga of Themistocles*, 98–125. The fall of Themistocles is also discussed in P. J. Bicknell, *Studies in Athenian Politics and Genealogy, Historia*, Suppl. 19 (1972):54–63; G. L. Cawkwell, "The Fall of Themistocles" in *Auckland Classical Essays Presented to E. M. Blaiklock*, ed. Harris (1970), 39–58; and Connor, "Lycomedes against Themistocles? A Note on Intragenos Rivalry," *Historia* 21 (1972):569–74.

23 Diod. 11.54.

24 The chronology is discussed in Gomme, *HCT* 1:389–413; Podlecki, *Life of Themistocles*, 197–99; Lenardon, "The Chronology of Themistokles' Ostracism and Exile," *Historia* 8 (1959):23–48; and White, "Some Agiad Dates: Pausanias and his Sons," *JHS* 84 (1964):140–52.

25 Lenardon, *The Saga of Themistocles*, 117–18.

26 Kagan, *Outbreak*, 59; Meiggs, *The Athenian Empire*, 87.

27 Lenardon, *Saga of Themistocles*, 121–25.

28 The bad feeling between Timocreon and Themistocles is discussed by Podlecki, *Life of Themistocles*, 51–54.

29 Glotz and Cohen, 2:122; Busolt, *GG*, 3:1.110–111. This interpretation of Themistocles' downfall is also rejected by Kagan, *Outbreak*, 59.

30 Plut. *Cim.* 16.8.

31 Ion, apud Plut. *Cim.* 16.8.

32 Thuc. 1.102.3; Plut. *Cim.* 17.2; Diod. 11.63.2.

33 Kagan, *Outbreak*, 146.

34 Plut. *Per.* 11.

35 Plut. *Per.* 12.2.

36 Some Athenians doubtless would have felt that Pericles' reasoning was on the same plane as that of the city gentleman who salted his sidewalk to keep away alligators. "Alligators?" exclaimed his neighbor incredulously. "There aren't any alligators in this neighborhood!" The gentleman smiled triumphantly and beamed at his salted sidewalk. "Precisely," he said.

37 Plut. *Per.* 12.3–14.2.

38 See the discussions of Woodhead, "IG i² 95 and the Ostracism of Hyperbolus," *Hesperia* 18 (1949):78–83; Fuqua, "Possible Implications of the Ostracism of Hyperbolus," *TAPA* 96 (1965):165–79; and Raubitschek, 'The Case against Alcibiades (Andocides IV)," *TAPA* 79 (1948):191–210. The arguments of Fuqua are, I think, by far the most persuasive.

The traditional date of 417 for the ostracism of Hyperbolus must be discarded, I think, on the basis of Woodhead's reconstruction of *IG* I² 95, which seems to show that Hyperbolus proposed an amendment to a decree in the tenth prytany of 418/17, i.e., *after* the opportunity for an ostracism which arose every April. The ostracism, consequently, must be placed either in 416, as, for example, Fuqua (p. 173) would have it, or, following the arguments of Raubitschek, in 415. The question of the date is a particularly intriguing one since Raubitschek's date of 415 is based quite specifically on one argument, namely, the authenticity of Andocides IV. The speech purports to have been delivered at a meeting of the assembly in which an ostracism was discussed, and it seems to have been written, in actual fact or purportedly, for Phaeax; its purpose is to incite the Athenians against Alcibiades. A number of factual errors, combined with the fact that we have no evidence to suggest that such *ad hominem* orations were delivered when the Athenians decided whether or not to hold an ostracism, have led a majority of scholars to attack the authenticity of the speech and to place it among the Alcibiades literature of the early fourth century (See Fuqua, *ibid.*). Since clearly the political contest between Nicias, Alcibiades, and Phaeax which ended in Hyperbolus' exile took place prior to the departure of the fleet from Sicily, then we have a choice of two dates, spring 416 or spring 415, the earlier date seeming distinctly the more likely.

39 Plut. *Arist.* 7, *Nic.* 11, *Alc.* 13.
40 Plut. *Nic.* 11.3–4.
41 Plut. *Nic.* 11.7.
42 Plut. *Alc.* 13.4–5.
43 Connor, *New Politicians*, 81–82; Baldwin, "Notes of Hyperbolus," *Acta Classica* 14 (1971):151–56; and a series of articles by Camon: "Figura e ambiente di Iperbolo," *Rivista di studi classici*, 4 (1961):182–97; "La demagogia di Iperbolo," *Giornale italiano di filologia* 15 (1962):364–74; "Le Cariche pubbliche di Iperbolo," and "L'Ostracismo di Iperbolo," *Giornale italiano di filologia* 16 (1963): 46–59 and 142–62.
44 Plut. *Alc.* 13.4; see previous note, in particular the table in Connor, *New Politicians*, 81–82.
45 Carcopino, *L'Ostracisme* 236–39 and 249; Hatzfeld, *Alcibiade*, 144.
46 Thuc. 8.73.3; Connor, *New Politicians*, 82–83.
47 Fuqua, *TAPA* 96 (1965):177–78.

48 Fuqua, *TAPA* 96 (1965):165.

49 Plut. *Nic.* 11.6. The passage is also cited at *Alc.* 13.5.

50 Plut. *Arist.* 7.4 (κατέλυσεν); Arist. *Ath. Pol.* 43.5.

51 See above, n. 45.

52 Discussions of the γραφὴ παρανόμων appear in Bonner and Smith, *Administration* 1:264ff. and 2:296–97; Busolt-Swoboda, *GS*, 1014–15; Cloché, "Remarques sur l'emploi de la graphê paranomôn," *REA* 38 (1936):401–12; Glotz, "Paranomôn graphê," in Daremberg-Saglio 4:1.327–28; Gerner, παρανόμων γραφή, *RE* 36:3.1281–93; Hignett, *AC*, 209–13; Lipsius, *AR*, 382–96; and MacDowell, *The Law in Classical Athens*, 50–52. By far the fullest treatment appears in Hansen, *Sovereignty*, and my short study of the γραφὴ παρανόμων would have been impossible without Hansen's hard work in collecting the known cases. I have not yet been able to consult Wolff, *Normenkontrolle und Gesetzbegriff in der attischen Demokratie, Sitzungsberichte der Heidelberger Akademie der Wissenschaften Phil. Hist. Klasse*, 2.

53 Aeschin. 3.210 (ἀγὼν τιμητός); Dem. 22.69 and 23.62 (penalty of death).

54 Bonner and Smith, *Administration*, 1:264; Glotz, "Paranomôn graphê," in Daremberg-Saglio, 4:1.327; Cloché, *REA* 38 (1936):401.

55 Wilamowitz, *A. u. A.*, 2:193–94; Kahrstedt, *Studien zum öffentlichen Recht Athens*, 1, 128.

56 Andoc. 1.17 and 22.

57 Antiphon. Frr. 3 and 13.

58 Diod. 18.18.

59 Aeschin. 3.194.

60 See above, n. 57.

61 Lys. fr. 143.

62 Dem. 21.182.

63 Dem. 58, passim.

64 Dem. 58.1, 30–34.

65 Dem. 58.35.

66 See above, n. 56.

67 Xen. *Hell.* 1.7.12–35.

68 Arist. *Ath. Pol.* 40.2; Ps.-Plut. *Vit. X Orat.* 835F–836A; Aeschin. 3.195.

69 Stroud, "Greek Inscriptions: Theozotides and the Athenian Orphans," *Hesperia* 40 (1971):280–301; Hansen, *Sovereignty*, 30 and 44–48.

70 Dem. 20.146, 23.198, and 24.180.
71 Hansen, *Sovereignty*, 30–31. Hansen extrapolates the attack on the decree for Timotheus largely from Aeschines' association of it (3.243) with the attacks on the decrees for Iphicrates and Chabrias, and he is probably correct to do so. I think he is stretching a point, however, when he adduces as evidence that the decree for Timotheus must have been challenged in the courts the fact that Aeschines says to the jurors that *they* have conferred honors on Timotheus. Aeschines' remarks may not carry this implication at all. Though all ecclesiasts were not jurors, all jurors were, after all, ecclesiasts and would have had the opportunity to vote on all decrees.
72 Dem. 7.42–43 and Hypoth. 3–4.
73 Dion. Hal. *ad Amn.* 4, Dem. 22; Dem. 24.9, 11–15, 117, and hypoth. 1–3.
74 Dem. 23.
75 Dem. 59.91.
76 Dem. 59.3–8.
77 Aeschin. 2.13–15, 20, 109; 3.62.
78 Dem. 18.102–107.
79 Ps.-Plut. *Vit. X Orat.* 848F; Dem. 18.222–226; Hyper. fr. 18.111–112.
80 Hansen, *Sovereignty*, 36–37.
81 Hyper. fr. 13.
    It is possible that we should add to this list, as does Cloché (*REA* 38 [1936]:404), Demosthenes' attack in 355/54 on the law of Leptines to which Dem. 20 is devoted. I am inclined, however, to agree with Hansen in classifying this case as a γραφὴ νόμον μὴ ἐπιτήδειον θεῖναι (*Sovereignty*, 47; see above, n. 52).
82 The assembly had already passed the decree of Thrasybulus of Steiria, the decrees conferring citizenship on Apollonides of Olynthus and Peitholaus of Pherae, and the decree of Apollodorus concerning the proper disposition of the surplus of the budget.
83 Hansen, *Sovereignty*, 63.
84 Diod. 18.18.2.
85 In his speech on the crown, Aeschines dwells at great length on the value of the γραφὴ παρανόμων as the safeguard of democracy (3.1–12, 16, 23, 31, 190–200, 250–251). But both Cloché (*REA* 38 [1936]:401–12) and Hansen (*Sovereignty*, 62) are dubious about its success. Cloché has sought to show that, so far from being used in defense of democracy, the γραφὴ παρανόμων was

more frequently the tool of antidemocratic and pro-Macedonian statesmen, but, as Hansen has pointed out (*Sovereignty*, 57), his case is not a strong one. Hansen takes a more positive view when he writes that the fact that proposals attacked by γραφὴ παρανόμων were in effect treated twice "made a more well-founded decision possible." Two hearings, he suggests, "meant time gained and constituted a safeguard against the effect of mass psychosis which a clever rhetor was able to whip up in a critical situation" (*Sovereignty*, 50). But a glance at the known cases of γραφὴ παρανόμων suggests that few of them dealt with topics that were likely to whip even the most volatile of men to the point of psychosis.

86 The many sources for the εἰσαγγελίαι which arose as a result of the profanation of the Mysteries are collected in Hansen, *Eisangelia*, 74–82.

87 We know of the impeachment of Hipparchus from Lyc. 1.117–18. The sources for the impeachment of Themistocles are wide and various: they include Thuc. 1.135.2 and 128.6; Diod. 11.54–55; Aelian *Var. hist.* 10.17; Nepos *Them.* 8.2–3; Plut. *Them.* 23; Dem. 23.205; Schol. on *Knights*, 84.

88 Xen. *Hell.* 1.7.35; Arist. *Ath. Pol.* 28.3; Lys. 30.9–11.

89 IG i² 110.38–47; Hansen, *Eisangelia*, 115–116.

90 Lys. 13.19–38.

91 Plut. *Dem.* 5; Aristotle, *Rhet.* 1365a; Dem. 21.64.

92 Lyc. 1.93.

93 Hyper. 4.28–30.

94 Lyc. 1.53; Ps.-Plut. *Vit. X Orat.* 843D.

95 Xen. *Hell.* 1.7.35.

IX. CONCLUSION: ACCOUNTABILITY AND THE ATHENIAN DEMOCRACY

1 Westlake, "Paches," *Phoenix* 29 (1975):109. Westlake goes on to claim that "the latter [the real cause] is historically of much greater interest and importance than the former [the formal charge]." This is certainly a judgment call, but clearly I have found the real cause — the ἀληθεστάτη πρόφασις — of Athenian accountability trials to be a worthy subject of a book. *Si canimus silvas, silvae sint consule dignae.*

2 Andrewes, *The Greeks*, 228.

3 Pritchett, *Greek State*, 2:20.

4 Dem. 19.191.
5 Black, *Impeachment: A Handbook*, 30. The best discussion of impeachment in England and the United States is probably Berger, *Impeachment: The Constitutional Problems* (1973).
6 Greenidge, *A Handbook of Greek Constitutional History*, 188.
7 Hignett, *AC*, 263.
8 Harper, "Democracy at Athens," in *The Greek Political Experience*, 39–40.
9 Perlman, "Politicians in the Athenian Democracy of the Fourth Century B.C.," *Athenaeum* 41 (1963):348.
10 Littman, *The Greek Experiment*, 161.
11 His career and reputation are discussed in the lively article of Baldwin, "Notes on Cleophon," *Acta Classica* 17 (1974):35–47.
12 Arist. *Ath. Pol.* 28.3; Xen. *Xell.* 1.7.35; Lys. 30.10–13, 13.12. The scholiast to Aristophanes' *Frogs* (679) claims that Cleophon was στρατηγός, but most scholars have been skeptical of this allegation.
13 Isocr. 8.54–55; Plut. *Phoc.* 7.3. The division between politicians and generals in the fourth century is discussed at some length in Perlman's fine article "Political Leadership in Athens in the Fourth Century." *Parola del Passato* 22 (1967):161–176.
14 Perlman, *Athenaeum* 41 (1963):347.
15 Laistner, 358; Bury, *History of Greece*, 589–590; Botsford and Robinson, *Hellenic History*, 276.
16 Bury, *History of Greece*, 590.
17 Laistner, *History*, 358.
18 Thalheim, "Iphikrates," *RE* 9:2021; Grote, 7:658.
19 Aeschin. 2.124.
20 It is interesting to notice that during the Watergate crisis Barbara Tuchman suggested that the United States substitute for the presidency "a directorate of six to be nominated as a slate by each party and elected as a slate for a single six-year term with a rotating chairman," rather as in Switzerland ("Should We Abolish the Presidency?" *New York Times*, 13 Feb 1973).
21 Pritchett, *Greek State*, 2:24.
22 Beloch, *AP*, 43.
23 Dein. 1.74.
24 Glotz, *Greek City*, 231; Henderson, *Great War*, 275.
25 Plut. *Nic.* 6.1–2.
26 Diod. 15.35.1.
27 Adkins, *Merit and Responsibility*, 2.

28 Adkins, *Merit and Responsibility*, 167.
29 Gouldner, *Enter Plato*, 82.
30 Gouldner, *Enter Plato*, 57; Walcot, *Envy and the Greeks, passim*.
31 Dover, *Greek Popular Morality*, 289.
32 Andrewes, *The Greeks*, 228.
33 Finley, "Athenian Demagogues," *Past and Present* 21 (1962):15–16.

BIBLIOGRAPHY

TO accommodate the varying perspectives of readers, this bibliography is divided into two parts — law on the one hand and history and politics on the other. Some of the distinctions I have made are, perforce, fairly arbitrary. Works which I had not yet been able to consult at the time of writing are marked with an asterisk.

I. LAW

Black, C. *Impeachment: A Handbook*. New Haven, 1974.

Bonner, R. *Lawyers and Litigants in Ancient Athens: The Genesis of the Legal Profession*. Chicago, 1927.

Bonner, R. "The Minimum Vote in Ostracism." *CP* 8 (1913):223–225.

Bonner, R. and Smith, G. *The Administration of Justice from Homer to Aristotle*. 2 vols. Chicago, 1930–38.

*Borowski, F. S., "Dokimasia. A Study in Athenian Constitutional Law." Ph.D. dissertation, University of Cincinnati, 1976.

Briant, P., "La Boulé et l'élection des ambassadeurs à Athènes au IVᵉ siècle." *REA* 70 (1968):7–31.

Busolt, G., and Swoboda, H. *Griechische Staatskunde*. Munich, 1920–26.

Calhoun, G. *The Growth of Criminal Law in Ancient Greece*. Berkeley, 1927.

Carcopino, J. *L'Ostracisme athénien*. Paris, 1935.

Cloché, P. "Les Procès de stratèges athéniens." *REA* 27 (1925):97–118.

Cloché, P. "Remarques sur l'emploi de la *graphê paranomôn*." *REA* 38 (1936):401–12.

Connor, W. R. "The Athenian Council: Method and Focus in some Recent Scholarship." *CJ* 70 (1974):32–40.

Costa, E. "Evagoras I and the Persians, ca. 411 to 391 B.C." *Historia* 23 (1974):40–56.

Crawley, L. "Graphe Sycophantias." In *Auckland Essays Presented to E. M. Blaiklock*. Edited by B. F. Harris. Auckland and Oxford, 1970.

Day, J. and Chambers, M. *Aristotle's History of Athenian Democracy*. Berkeley and Los Angeles, 1962.

Dombrowski, H. *Die politischen Prozesse in Athen vom Archontat des Eukleides bis zum Ausgang des Bundesgenossenkrieges*. Greifswald, 1934.

Gilbert, G. *The Constitutional Antiquities of Sparta and Athens*. Translated by E. J. Brooks and N. Nicklin. Chicago, 1968.

Glotz, G. *The Greek City and Its Institutions*. Translated by N. Mallinson. London and New York, 1929.

Greenidge, A. *A Handbook of Greek Constitutional History*. London, 1896.

Hager, H. "On the Eisangelia." *Journal of Philology* 4 (1871):74–112.

Hands, A. R. "Ostraka and the Law of Ostracism: Some Possibilities and Assumptions." *JHS* 79 (1959):69–79.

Hansen, M. H. "*Demos, Ecclesia* and *Dicasterion* in Classical Athens." *GRBS* 19 (1978):127–46.

Hansen, M. H. "Did the Athenian *Ecclesia* Legislate after 403/2 B.C.?" *GRBS* 20 (1979):27–53.

Hansen, M. H. "The Duration of a Meeting of the Athenian *Ecclesia*." *CP* 74 (1979):40–49.

Hansen, M. H. *Eisangelia: The Sovereignty of the People's Court in Athens in the Fourth Century B.C. and the Impeachment of Generals and Politicians*. Odense University Classical Studies 6: Odense, 1975.

Hansen, M. H. "How Many Athenians Attended the *Ecclesia*?" *GRBS* 17 (1976):115–34.

Hansen, M. H. "How Often Did the Athenian *Dicasteria* Meet?" *GRBS* 20 (1979):243–46.

Hansen, M. H. "How Often Did the *Ecclesia* Meet?" *GRBS* 18 (1977):43–70.

Hansen, M. H. "*Nomos* and *Psephisma* in Fourth-Century Athens." *GRBS* 19 (1978):315–30.

Hansen, M. H. *The Sovereignty of the People's Court in Athens in the*

Fourth Century B.C. and the Public Action against Unconstitutional Proposals. Odense University Classical Studies 4: Odense, 1974.

Harrison, A. R. W. *The Law of Athens: Procedure.* Oxford, 1971.

Harrison, A. R. W. "Law-making at Athens at the End of the Fifth Century B.C." *JHS* 75 (1955):26–35.

Headlam, J. W. *Election by Lot at Athens.* 2d ed. Revised by D. MacGregor. Cambridge, 1933.

Hignett, C. *A History of the Athenian Constitution to the End of the Fifth Century B.C.* Oxford, 1952.

Jones, J. W. *The Law and Legal Theory of the Greeks: An Introduction.* Oxford, 1956.

Jordan, B. *The Athenian Navy in the Classical Period. A Study of Athenian Naval Administration and Military Organization in the Fifth and Fourth Centuries B.C.* Berkeley and Los Angeles, 1975.

Just, M. "Die *Apodokimasia* der athenischen *boulê* und ihre Anfechtung." *Historia* 19 (1970):132–40.

Kagan, D. "The Origin and Purposes of Ostracism." *Hesperia* 30 (1961):393–401.

Kahrstedt, U. *Studien zum öffentlichen Recht Athens.* Stuttgart and Berlin, 1934–36.

Karavites, P. "Cleisthenes and Ostracism Again." *Athenaeum* 52 (1974):326–36.

Keaney, J. J. "The Text of Androtion F 6 and the Origin of Ostracism." *Historia* 19 (1970):1–11.

Kienast, D. "*Presbeia.*" *RE* Suppl. 13, cols. 501–628. Munich, 1974.

Laix, R. de. *Probouleusis at Athens. A Study of Decision-Making.* University of California Publication in History 83: Berkeley, 1973.

Levi, M. A. *Commento storico alla Respublica Atheniensium di Aristotele.* 2 vols. Milan and Varese, 1968.

Lind, R. "Athenian *euthynai* and the Spanish Residencia." *CW* 27 (1934):86–87.

Lipsius, J. *Das Attische Recht und Rechtsverfahren.* Leipzig, 1915.

MacDowell, D. *The Law in Classical Athens.* Ithaca, 1978.

Meier, M. and Schömann, G. F. *Der Attische Prozess.* Halle, 1824.

Mosley, D. J. *Envoys and Diplomacy in Ancient Greece, Historia* Suppl. 22. Wiesbaden, 1973.

Mosley, D. J. "Voting procedure and the election of Athenian envoys." *Wiener Studien* 6 (1972):140–44.

Paoli, U. E. "La Sauvegarde de la legalité dans la démocratie athénienne." In *Festschrift für Hans Lewald*, 133–141. Basel, 1953.

Pierart, M. "Les *Euthynoi* athéniens." *L'Antiquité classique* 40 (1971):526–73.

Raubitschek, A. E. "Athenian Ostracism." *CJ* 48 (1952–53):113–22.

Raubitschek, A. E. "The Origin of Ostracism." *AJA* 55 (1961):221–29.

Robinson, C. A. "Cleisthenes and Ostracism." *AJA* 56 (1952):23–26.

Sandys, J. *Aristotle's Constitution of Athens*. London, 1912.

Schömann, G. F. *A Dissertation on the Assemblies of the Athenians*. Cambridge, England, 1838.

Sealey, R. "Ephialtes." *CP* 59 (1964):11–21.

Sealey, R. "Probouleusis and the Sovereign Assembly." *California Studies in Classical Antiquity* 2 (1969):247–69.

Stanton, G. R. "The Introduction of Ostracism and Alcmaeonid Propaganda." *JHS* 90 (1970):180–83.

Thalheim, T. "Zur Eisangelie in Athen." *Hermes*, 39 (1902):337–52.

Vanderpool, E. *Ostracism at Athens: Lectures in Memory of Louise Taft Semple*. Cincinnati, 1970.

Vinogradoff, P. *Outlines of Historical Jurisprudence*. Vol. 2. *The Jurisprudence of the Greek City*. London, 1922.

Westermann, W. "The Ephodia of Greek Ambassadors." *CP* 5 (1910):203–16.

Wilamowitz-Möllendorff, U. von. *Aristoteles und Athen*. 2 vols. Berlin, 1893.

II. HISTORY AND POLITICS

Accame, S. *L'Imperialismo ateniese all'inizio del secolo IV a.c. e la crisi della polis*. Naples, 1966.

Accame, S. *La Lega ateniese del secolo IV a.c.* Roma, 1941.

Accame, S. *Ricerche intorno alla guerra corinzia*. Naples, 1951.

Adcock, F. E. and Mosley, D. J. *Diplomacy in Ancient Greece*. London, 1975.

Adkins, A. W. H. *Merit and Responsibility*. Oxford, 1960.

*Alfieri, T. "Sulla proposta di Trasibulo per la concessione della cittadinanza ateniese." *Rendiconti Istituto Lombardo* 104 (1970):154–61.

*Alfieri, T. "L'Ultima fase della carriera politica di Trasibulo." *Rendiconti Istituto Lombardo* 106 (1972):122–48.

Amit, M. *Athens and the Sea: A Study in Athenian Sea Power*. Brussels, 1965.

Andrewes, A. "The Arginousai Trial." *Phoenix* 28 (1974):112–22.

Andrewes, A. "The Generals in the Hellespont, 410–407 B.C." *JHS* 73 (1953):2–9.

Andrewes, A. *The Greeks.* London, 1967.

Arnheim, M. T. W. *Aristocracy in Greek Society.* London, 1977.

*Aucello, E. "La Genesi della pace di Antalcida." *Helikon* 5 (1965):340–380.

Aurenche, O. *Les Groupes d'Alcibiade, de Leogoras et de Teucros. Remarques sur la vie politique athénienne en 415 avant J.C.* Paris, 1974.

Balcer, J. "Separatism and anti-Separatism in the Athenian Empire (478–433 B.C.)." *Historia* 23 (1974):21–39.

Baldwin, B. "Notes on Cleophon." *Acta Classica* 17 (1974):35–47.

Baldwin, B. "Notes on Hyperbolus." *Acta Classica* 14 (1971):151–56.

Banderet, A. *Untersuchungen zur Xenophons Hellenika.* Berlin, 1919.

Barbieri, G. *Conone.* Rome, 1955.

Barker, E. *Greek Political Theory: Plato and His Predecessors.* London, 1918.

Barrett, John F. "The Downfall of Themistocles." *GRBS* 18 (1977): 291–305.

Bauman, R. E. "A Message for Amphipolis." *Acta Classica* 11 (1968):170–81.

Beloch, K. J. *Die Attische Politik seit Perikles.* Leipzig, 1884.

Beloch, K. J. "Zur Chronologie der letzten Jahre des peloponnesischen Krieges." *Philologus* 43 (1884):261–96.

Beloch, K. J. *Griechische Geschichte.* 2d ed. in 3 vols. Berlin and Leipzig, 1924–27.

Berve, H. *Griechische Geschichte.* 2 vols. Freiburg, 1931–33.

Berve, H. *Miltiades: Studien zur Geschichte des Mannes und seiner Zeit.* Hermes Suppl. 2, 1937.

Betant, E. *Lexicon Thucydideum.* 2 vols. 1843; reprint Hildesheim, 1961.

Bicknell, P. J. *Studies in Athenian Politics and Genealogy. Historia* Suppl. 19. Wiesbaden, 1972.

Bicknell, P. J. "Was Megakles Hippokratous Alopekethen Ostracized Twice?" *L'Antiquité classique* 44 (1975):172–75.

Blass, F. *Die Attische Beredsamkeit.* 4 vols. Leipzig, 1880–93.

Bloedow, E. *Alcibiades Re-examined. Historia* Suppl. 21. Wiesbaden, 1973.

Bonner, R. J. *Aspects of Athenian Democracy.* Berkeley, 1933.

Botsford, G. W. and Robinson, C. A. *Hellenic History*. 5th ed. Revised by D. Kagan. London, 1969.

Breitenbach, H. R. "Die Seeschlacht bei Notion 407/6." *Historia* 20 (1971):152–71.

Brown, D. *Das Geschäft mit dem Staat: Die Überschneidung des politischen und des privaten im Corpus Demosthenicum*. Hildesheim and New York, 1974.

Bruce, I. A. F. "Athenian Embassies in the Early Fourth Century." *Historia* 15 (1966):272–81.

Bruce, I. A. F. "Athenian Foreign Policy in 396–395 B.C." *CJ* 58 (1963):289–95.

Bruce, I. A. F. *An Historical Commentary on the Hellenica Oxyrhynchia*. London, 1967.

Bruce, I. A. F. "Internal Politics and the Outbreak of the Corinthian War." *Emerita* 28 (1960):75–86.

Buckler, J. "Dating of the Peace of 375/4 B.C." *GRBS* 12 (1971):353–61.

Buckler, J. "Plutarch and the Fate of Antalkidas." *GRBS* 18 (1977):139–45.

Buckler, J. *The Theban Hegemony, 371–362 B.C.* London and Cambridge, Mass., 1980.

Burnett, A. P. "Thebes and the Expansion of the Second Athenian Confederacy: IG II² 40 and IG II² 43." *Historia* 11 (1962):1–17.

Bury, J. B. *A History of Greece*. 3d ed. Revised by R. Meiggs. London and New York, 1967.

Bury, J. B.; Cook, S. A.; and Adcock, F.; edd. *Cambridge Ancient History*. Vols. 4–6. New York, 1926–27.

Busolt, G. *Griechische Geschichte*. 3 vols. Gotha, 1893–1904.

Butcher, S. *Demosthenes*. London, 1891.

Calhoun, G. *Athenian Clubs in Politics and Litigation*. Austin, 1913.

Camon, F. "La Cariche pubbliche di Iperbolo." *Giornale italiano di filologia* 16 (1963):46–59.

Camon, F. "La demagogia di Iperbolo." *Gionale italiano de filologia*, 15 (1962):364–74.

Camon, F. "Figura e ambiente di Iperbolo." *Rivista di studi classici* 4 (1961):182–97.

Camon, F. "L'ostracismo di Iperbolo." *Giornale italiano de filologia* 16 (1963): 142–62.

Cary, M. "When Was Themistocles Ostracized?" *CR* 36 (1922): 161–62.

Cavaignac, E. *Histoire de l'antiquité*. Vol. 2. *Athènes*. Paris, 1913.

Cawkwell, G. L. "Aeschines and the Peace of Philocrates." *REG* 73 (1960):416–38.

Cawkwell, G. L. "The common peace of 366–365 B.C." *CQ* 11 (1961):80–86.

Cawkwell, G. L. "Demosthenes' Policy after the Peace of Philocrates." *CQ* 56 (1963):120–38 and 200–213.

Cawkwell, G. L. "Epaminondas and Thebes." *CQ* 22 (1972):254–78.

Cawkwell, G. L. "The Fall of Themistocles." In *Auckland Essays Presented to E. M. Blaiklock*, 38–59. Edited by B. F. Harris. Auckland and Oxford, 1970.

Cawkwell, G. L. "The Foundation of the Second Athenian Confederacy." *CQ* 23 (1973):47–60.

Cawkwell, G. L. "The Imperialism of Thrasybulus." *CQ* 26 (1970):62–84.

Cawkwell, G. L. "Notes on the Peace of 375–374." *Historia* 12 (1963):84–95.

Cawkwell, G. L. "Notes on the Social War." *Classica et Mediaevalia* 23 (1962):34–49.

Chambers, M. "Thucydides and Pericles." *HSCP* 62 (1957):79–92.

Chroust, A. H. "Treason and Patriotism in Ancient Greece." *Journal of the History of Ideas* 15 (1954):280–88.

Cloché, P. "L'Affaire des Arginuses." *Rev. hist.* 130 (1919):3–68.

Cloché, P. "Les Conflits politiques et sociaux à Athènes pendant la guerre de Corinthe." *REA* 21 (1919):157–92.

Cloché, P. *La Démocratie athénienne.* Paris, 1951.

Cloché, P. *Démosthènes.* Paris, 1951.

Cloché, P. "Les Hommes politiques et la justice populaire dans l'Athènes du ivᵉ siècle." *Historia* 9 (1960):80–95.

Cloché, P. "La Politique de l'athénien Callistratos." *REA* 25 (1923):5–32.

Cloché, P. "La Politique des Alcméonides de 507 à 482 av. J.-C." *REA* 30 (1928):269–79.

Cloché, P. *La politique etrangère d'Athènes de 404 a 338 av. J.-C.* Paris, 1934.

Connor, W. R. "Lycomedes against Themistocles? A Note on Intragenos Rivalry." *Historia* 21 (1972):569–74.

Connor, W. R. *The New Politicians of Fifth Century Athens.* Cambridge, Mass., 1968.

Connor, W. R. *Theopompus and Fifth Century Athens.* Washington, D.C., 1968.

Cornford, F. *Thucydides Mythistoricus.* London, 1965.

Croiset, M. *Political Parties in Aristophanes*. Translated by J. Loeb. London, 1909.

Curtius, E., *The History of Greece*, 5 vols. Translated by A. W. Ward. New York, 1874.

Daremberg, C. and E. Saglio, *Dictionnaire des antiquités grecques et romaines*. Paris, 1877–1919; reprint Graz, 1962–63.

Davies, J. K. *Athenian Propertied Families*. Oxford, 1971.

Davies, J. K. "The Date of IG ii² 1609." *Historia* 18 (1969):309–333.

Davies, J. K. *Democracy and Classical Greece*. Sussex, England and Atlantic Highlands, N.J., 1978.

Delbrück, H. *Die Strategie des Perikles*. Berlin, 1890.

Develin, R. "Miltiades and the Parian Expedition." *Antiquité classique* 46 (1977):571–577.

Dinsmoor, W. B., "Attic Building Accounts, I: The Parthenon." *AJA* 17 (1913):53–80.

Dinsmoor, W. B. "The Burning of the Opisthodomos at Athens." *AJA* 36 (1932):143–72 and 307–26.

Dover, K. J. *Aristophanic Comedy*. Berkeley and Los Angeles, 1972.

Dover, K. J. *Greek Popular Morality in the Time of Plato and Aristotle*. Berkeley and Los Angeles, 1974.

Droysen, H. *Athen und der Westen vor der Sicilischen Expedition*. Berlin, 1882.

Duncker, M. *Geschichte des Altertums*. 5th ed. in 9 vols. Leipzig, 1878–86.

Eddy, S. K. "On the Peace of Callias." *CP* 65 (1970):8–14.

Ehrenberg, V. *Aspects of the Ancient World*. New York, 1946.

Ehrenberg, V. *From Solon to Socrates. Greek History and Civilisation during the Sixth and Fifth Centuries B.C.* London, 1968.

Ehrenberg, V. *The Greek State*. Oxford, 1960.

Ehrenberg, V. *The People of Aristophanes*. New York, 1962.

Ehrenberg, V. *Sophocles and Pericles*. Oxford, 1954.

Ellis, J. R. *Philip II and Macedonian Imperialism*. London, 1976.

Fabricius, E. "Die Befreiung Thebens." *RhMus* 48 (1893):448–71.

Fabricius, E. "Zur Geschichte des zweiten athenischen Bundes." *RhMus* 46 (1891):589–98.

Fabrizio, G. *Contributo storiografico-storico allo studio della guerra deceleica*. Milan, 1944.

Ferguson, W. S. "The Condemnation of Antiphon." *Mélanges Glotz*, 1:349–366. Paris, 1932.

Ferguson, W. S. *The Treasurers of Athena*. Cambridge, Mass., 1932.

Finley, J. *Thucydides*. 1947; reprint Ann Arbor and Toronto, 1963.

Finley, M. I. "The Athenian Demagogues." *Past and Present* 21 (1962):3–24.

Fornara, C. W. *The Athenian Board of Generals from 501 to 404*. *Historia* Suppl. 16. Wiesbaden, 1961.

Forrest, W. G. *The Emergence of Greek Democracy, 800–400 B.C.* New York and Toronto, 1966.

Freeman, E. *History of Sicily*. 4 vols. Oxford, 1891–94.

Frost, F. J. *Democracy and the Athenians: Aspects of Ancient Politics*. New York, 1969.

Frost, F. J. *Greek Society*. Lexington, Mass., 1971.

Frost, F. J. "Pericles and Dracontides." *JHS* 84 (1964):69–72.

Frost, F. J. "Pericles, Thucydides, son of Melesias, and Athenian Politics before the War." *Historia* 13 (1964):385–99.

Frost, F. J. *Plutarch's Themistocles*. Princeton. 1980.

Frost, F. J. "Themistocles' Place in Athenian Politics." *California Studies in Classical Antiquity* 1 (1968):105–24.

Fuks, A. *The Ancestral Constitution. Four Studies in Athenian Party Politics at the End of the Fifth Century B.C.* London, 1953.

Fuqua, C. "Possible Implications of the Ostracism of Hyperbolus." *TAPA* 96 (1965):165–79.

Gilbert, G. *Beiträge zur innern Geschichte Athens (im Zeitalter des peloponnesischen Krieges)*. Leipzig, 1871.

Glotz, G. and Cohen, R. *Histoire grecque*. 4 vols. Paris, 1925–38.

Glover, T. R. *Democracy in the Ancient World*. 1927; reprint New York, 1966.

Gomme, A. W. "Athenian Notes. 1. Athenian Politics 510–483 B.C." *AJP* 65 (1944):321–31.

Gomme, A. W., with Andrewes, A. and Dover, K. J. *A Historical Commentary on Thucydides*. 5 vols. Oxford, 1945–1981.

Gouldner, A. *Enter Plato: Classical Greece and the Origens of Social Theory*. New York and London, 1965.

Graefe, F. "Die Operationen des Antalkidas im Hellespont." *Klio*, 28 (1935):262–70.

Grote, G. *History of Greece*. New ed. in 8 vols. London, 1862.

Grundy, G. *Thucydides and the History of his Age*. 1911. Second ed., Oxford, 1948.

Hack, H. "The Rise of Thebes: A Study of Theban Politics and Diplomacy, 386–371 B.C." Ph.D. dissertation. Yale University, 1975.

Hack, H. "Thebes and the Spartan Hegemony, 386–382 B.C." *AJP* 96 (1978):210–27.

Hamilton, C. *Sparta's Bitter Victories: Politics and Diplomacy in the Corinthian War.* Ithaca and London, 1979.

Hammond, N. G. L. *A History of Greece to 322 B.C.* 2d ed. Oxford, 1967.

Hands, A. R. "In Favour of a Peace of Kallias." *Mnemosyne* 28 (1975):193–95.

Harding, P. "Androtion's Political Career." *Historia* 25 (1976):186–200.

Harper, G. M. "Democracy at Athens." In *The Greek Political Experience: Studies in Honor of William Kelly Prentice.* Princeton, 1941.

Hatzfeld, J. *Alcibiade.* Paris, 1940.

Hatzfeld, J. "Alcibiade et les élections des stratèges athéniens en 406." *REA* 33 (1931):109–16.

Hatzfeld, J. *History of the Ancient Greeks.* Revised by A. Aymard; translated by A. C. Harrison; edited by E. H. Goddard. Edinburgh and London, 1966.

Hauvette-Besnault, A. *Les stratèges athéniens.* Paris, 1885.

Henderson, B. W. *The Great War between Athens and Sparta.* London, 1927.

Herbst, L. *Die Schlacht bei den Arginusen.* Hamburg, 1855.

Holm, A. *History of Greece.* 4 vols. London, 1902–7.

Homo, L. *Periclès, une expérience de démocratie dirigée.* Paris, 1954.

Hook, L. van. *Greek Life and Thought.* New York, 1930.

How, W. W. "Cornelius Nepos on Marathon and Paros." *JHS* 39 (1919):48–61.

Hunter, V. J. *Thucydides: The Artful Reporter.* Toronto, 1973.

Jacoby, F. *Die Fragmente der griechischen Historiker.* 3 vols. Leyden, 1950–64.

Jebb, R. *Attic Orators from Antiphon to Isaeus.* 3 vols. London, 1876.

Jones, A. H. M. *Athenian Democracy.* Oxford, 1957.

Judeich, W. "Athens und Theben vom Königsfrieden bis zur Schlacht bei Leuctra." *RhMus* 76 (1922):171–97.

Judeich, W. "Die Zeit der Friedensrede des Andokides." *Philologus* 81 (1927):141ff.

Kagan, D. *The Archidamian War.* Ithaca, 1974.

Kagan, D. "The Economic Origins of the Corinthian War (395–387 B.C.)." *Parola del Passato* 16 (1961):321–41.

Kagan, D. *The Great Dialogue: A History of Greek Political Thought from Homer to Polybius.* New York and London. 1965.

Kagan, D. *The Outbreak of the Peloponnesian War.* Ithaca, 1969.

Karavites, P. "Realities and Appearances, 490–480 B.C." *Historia* 26 (1977):129–47.

Kienast, D. "Der innenpolitische Kampf in Athens von der Rückkehr des Thukydides bis zu Perikles' Tod." *Gymnasium* 60 (1953):210–29.

Kinzl, K. "Miltiades-Forschungen." Ph.D. dissertation, University of Vienna, 1968.

Kinzl, K. "Miltiades Parosexpedition in der Geschichtsschreibung." *Hermes* 104 (1976):280–307.

Kirchner, J. *Prosopographia Attica.* Berlin, 1901–3.

Knight, D. W. *Some Studies in Athenian Politics in the Fifth Century B.C. Historia* Suppl. 13. Wiesbaden, 1970.

Kock, T., ed. *Comicorum Atticorum Fragmenta.* 3 vols. Leipzig, 1880–88.

Kounas, D. "Prelude to Hegemony: Studies in Athenian Political Parties from 403 to 379 B.C. Pertaining to the Revival of Athenian Influence in Greece." Ph.D. dissertation. University of Illinois, 1969.

Kraft, K. "Bemerkungen zu der Perserkriegen." *Hermes* 92 (1964):158–71.

Krause, A. *Attische Strategenlisten bis 146 v. Chr.* Weimar, 1914.

Laistner, M. *A History of the Greek World from 479 to 323 B.C.* New York, 1936.

*Lanzilotta, E. "La Battaglia di Nozio." *Miscellanea greca e romana*, 4 (1975):135–61.

*Larsen, J. A. O. "The Judgment of Antiquity on Democracy." *CP* 49 (1954):1–14.

Lateiner, D. "The Speech of Teutiaplus (Thuc. 3.30)." *GRBS* 16 (1975) 175–84.

Lauffer, S. "Die Diodordublette XV 38 50 über die Friedensschlüsse zu Sparta 374 und 371 v. Chr." *Historia* 8 (1959):315–48.

Lenardon, R. J. "The Chronology of Themistocles' Ostracism and Exile." *Historia* 8(1959):23–48.

Lenardon, R. J. *The Saga of Themistocles.* London 1978.

Lendle, O. "Philochoros über den Prozess des Phidias." *Hermes* 83 (1955):284–303.

Leóni, A. *Quelques aspects de la vie de Phrynichos d'après les auteurs anciens.* Aix-en-Provence, 1967.

Lévêque, P. *The Greek Adventure*. Translated by M. Kochan. London, 1968.

Liddell, H. G. and Scott, R. *Greek-English Lexicon*. Revised by H. S. Jones. Oxford, 1940.

Littman, R. J. *The Greek Experiment: Imperialism and Social Conflict 800–400 B.C.* London, 1974.

Littman, R. J. "The Strategy of the Battle of Cyzicus." *TAPA* 99 (1968):265–72.

Longo, C. P. *"Eterie" e gruppi politici nell'Atene del IV sec. a. c.* Florence, 1971.

Losado, L. A. *The Fifth Column in the Peloponnesian War*. Leiden, 1972.

Macan, R., ed. *Herodotus: The Fourth, Fifth and Sixth Books*. 2 vols. London and New York, 1895.

McCoy, J. "Theramenes, Thrasybulus and the Athenian Moderates." Ph.D. dissertation, Yale University, 1970.

McCoy, J. "Thrasyllus." *AJP* 98 (1977):264–89.

MacDowell, D. *Andocides on the Mysteries*. Oxford, 1962.

MacGregor, M. F. "The Genius of Alkibiades." *Phoenix* 19 (1965):27–46.

MacGregor, M. F. "The Politics of the Historian Thucydides." *Phoenix* 10 (1956):93–102.

MacGregor, M. F. "The Pro-Persian Party at Athens from 510 to 480 B.C." *HSCP*, Suppl. 1 (1940):71–95.

MacKendrick, P. *The Athenian Aristocracy, 399–31 B.C.* Cambridge, Mass., 1969.

Mahaffy, J. *What Have the Greeks Done for Modern Civilization?* New York, 1909.

Markle, M. M. "The Strategy of Philip in 346 B.C." *CQ* 24 (1974):253–68.

Martin, V. "Sur une interprétation nouvelle de la 'Paix du Roi.'" *Museum Helveticum* 6 (1949):127–39.

Mastromarco, G. *Storia di una commedia de Atene*. Florence, 1974.

Mattingly, H. "The Peace of Callias." *Historia* 14 (1965):273–81.

Meiggs, R. *The Athenian Empire*. Oxford, 1972.

Meiggs, R. and Lewis, D. M. *A Selection of Greek Historical Inscriptions to the End of the Fifth Century*. Oxford, 1969.

Meritt, B. D.; Wade-Gery, H. T.; and MacGregor, M. F. *The Athenian Tribute Lists*. 4 vols. Vol. 1, Cambridge, Mass., 1939; vols. 2–4, Princeton, 1949–1953.

Meyer, E. *Forschungen zur alten Geschichte*, Vol. 2. Halle, 1899; reprint Hildesheim, 1966.

Meyer, E. *Geschichte des Altertums*. 5 vols. Stuttgart and Berlin, 1884–1902.

Meyer, H. D. "Thukydides Melesiou und die oligarische Opposition gegen Perikles." *Historia* 16 (1967):141–54.

Momigliano, A. "Un Momento di storia greca: la pace del 375 a. C. e il *Plataico* di Isocrate." *Athenaeum* 14 (1936):3–35.

Morgan, C. "Pheidon and Olympia." *Hesperia* 21 (1952):295–339.

Mosley, D. J. "Callias' Fine." *Mnemosyne* 26 (1973):57–58.

Mossé, C. *Athens in Decline, 404–86 B.C.* Translated by J. Stewart. London, 1973.

Mossé, C. *La fin de la démocratie athénienne*. Paris, 1962.

Mossé, C. *Histoire d'une démocratie, Athènes, des origines à la conquête macédonienne*. Paris, 1971.

Mossé, C. "Les Procès politiques et la crise de la démocratie athénienne." *Dialogues d'histoire ancienne* 1 (1974):207–236.

Murison, C. L. "The Peace of Callias: Its historical context." *Phoenix* 25 (1971):12–31.

Nesselhauf, H. *Untersuchungen zur Geschichte der delisch-attischen Symmachie. Klio* Suppl. 30 (1933):11ff.

Oliver, J. H. "The Peace of Callias and the Pontic Expedition of Pericles." *Historia* 6 (1957):254–55.

Oost, S. I. "Two Notes on Aristophon of Azenia." *CP* 72 (1977):238–42.

Ostwald, M. "Athenian Legislation against Tyranny and Subversion." *TAPA* 86 (1955):103–28.

Pauly, A.; Wissowa, G.; and Kroll, W.; edd. *Realencyklopädie der klassischen Altertumswissenschaft*. Stuttgart, 1894–.

*Pearson, L. "Party Politics and Free Speech in Democratic Athens." *Greece and Rome* 7 (1937):41–50.

Pearson, L. *Popular Ethics in Ancient Greece*. Stanford, 1962.

Pečirka, J. "The Crisis of the Athenian Polis in the Fourth Century B.C." *Eirene* 14 (1976):5–29.

Perlman, S. "Athenian Democracy and the Revival of Imperialistic Expansion at the Beginning of the Fourth Century B.C." *CP* 63 (1968):257–67.

Perlman, S. "On Bribing Athenian Ambassadors." *GRBS* 17 (1976): 223–33.

Perlman, S. "The Causes and the Outbreak of the Corinthian War." *CQ* 14 (1964) 64–81.

Perlman, S., ed. *Philip and Athens*. Cambridge, England, and New York, 1973.

Perlman, S. "Political Leadership in Athens in the Fourth Century." *Parola del Passato* 22 (1967):161–76.

Perlman, S. "The Politicians in the Athenian Democracy of the Fourth Century B.C." *Athenaeum* 41 (1963):327–55.

Pickard-Cambridge, A. W. *Demosthenes*. New York and London, 1914.

Podlecki, A. *The Life of Themistocles: A Critical Survey of the Literary and Archaeological Evidence*. Montreal and London, 1975.

Prickard, A. O. *The Return of the Theban Exiles, 379–378 B.C.: The Story Arranged as Told by Plutarch and Xenophon*. Oxford, 1926.

Pritchett, W. K. *The Greek State at War*. 2 vols. Berkeley and Los Angeles, 1971–74.

*Ramming, G. "Die politischen Ziele und Wege des Aeschines." Ph.D. dissertation. Erlangen, 1965.

Raubitschek, A. E. "The Case against Alcibiades (Andocides IV)." *TAPA* 79 (1948):191–210.

Raubitschek, A. E. "Menon, Son of Menekleides."

Raubitschek, A. E. "The Ostracism of Xanthippus." *AJA* 51 (1947): 257–62.

Raubitschek, A. E. "The Peace Policy of Pericles." *AJA* 70 (1976):37–41.

Raubitschek, A. E. "Theopompos on Hyperbolos." *Phoenix* 9 (1955):126.

Raubitschek, A. E. "Theopompos on Thucydides the Son of Melesias." *Phoenix* 14 (1960):81–95.

Rehdantz, C. *Vitae Iphicratis Chabriae Timothei Atheniensium*. Berlin, 1845.

Reverdin, O. "Remarques sur la vie politique d'Athènes au Vᵉ siècle." *Museum Helveticum* (1945):201–12.

Rhodes, P. *The Athenian Boule*. Oxford, 1972.

Rice, D. "Why Sparta Failed: A Study of Politics and Policy from the Peace of Antalcidas to the Battle of Leuctra, 387–371 B.C." Ph.D. dissertation. Yale University, 1971.

Roberts, J. "Arginusae Once Again." *CW* 71 (1977):107–111.

Roberts, J. "The Athenian Conservatives and the Impeachment Trials of the Corinthian War." *Hermes* 108 (1980):100–114.

Robinson, C. A. "The Struggle for Power at Athens in the Early Fifth Century." *AJP* 60 (1939):234–37.

Romilly, J. de. *Histoire et raison chez Thucydide.* Paris, 1956.

Romilly, J. de. *Problèmes de démocratie grecque.* Paris, 1975.

Roos, A. J. "The Peace of Sparta of 374 B.C." *Mnemosyne* 2 (1949): 265–85.

Ruschenbusch, E. *Athenische Innenpolitik im S. Jahrhundert v. Chr.* Bamberg, 1979.

Ryder, T. T. B. "Athenian Foreign Policy and the Peace Conference at Sparta in 371 B.C." *CQ* 13 (1963):237–41.

Ryder, T. T. B. *Koine Eirene: General Peace and Local Independence in Ancient Greece.* Oxford, 1965.

Ryder, T. T. B. "The Supposed Common Peace of 366/5." *CQ* (1957):199–205.

Sanctis, G. De. *Pericle.* Milan, 1944.

Sanctis, G. De. *Storia della republica ateniese.* 2d ed. Turin, 1912.

Ste. Croix, G. E. M. de. "The Alleged Secret Pact between Athens and Philip II concerning Amphipolis and Pydna." *CQ* 13 (1963):110–19.

Ste. Croix, G. E. M. de. *The Origins of the Peloponnesian War.* Ithaca, 1972.

Schaefer, A. *Demosthenes und seine Zeit.* 3 vols. Leipzig, 1856–58.

Schmid, W. and O. Stählin, *Geschichte der griechischen Literatur.* Munich, 1948.

*Schrader, *La paz de Calias. Testimonios e interpretaciòn.* Barcelona, 1976.

Seager, R. "Alcibiades and the Charge of Aiming at Tyranny." *Historia* 16 (1967):6–18.

Seager, R. "The King's Peace and the Balance of Power in Greece, 386–362 B.C." *Athenaeum* 52 (1974):36–63.

Seager, R. "Lysias against the Corndealers." *Historia* 15 (1966): 172–84.

Seager, R. "Thrasybulus, Conon and Athenian Imperialism, 396–386 B.C." *JHS* 87 (1967):95–115.

Sealey, R. "Athens after the Social War." *JHS* 75 (1955):74–81.

Sealey, R. "Callistratus of Aphidna and His Contemporaries." *Historia* 5 (1956):178–203.

Sealey, R. "The Entry of Pericles into History." *Hermes* 84 (1956): 234–247.

Sealey, R. *Essays in Greek Politics.* New York, 1967.

Sealey, R. *A History of the Greek City-States, 700–338 B.C.* Berkeley and Los Angeles, 1976.

Sealey, R. "IG II^2 1609 and the Transformation of the Second Athenian League." *Phoenix* 11 (1957):95–111.

Sealey, R. "The Peace of Callias Once More." *Historia* 3 (1954–1955):325–33.

Sealey, R. "Proxenos and the Peace of Philocrates." *Wiener Studien* 68 (1955):145–52.

Seyffert, O. *A Dictionary of Classical Antiquities.* Revised by H. Nettleship and J. Sandys. London and New York, 1891.

Sinclair, T. A. *A History of Greek Political Thought.* Cleveland, 1867.

Singh, K. L. "The Impact of Family Relationships on Athenian Politics, 594–322 B.C." Ph.D. dissertation. University of Wisconsin, 1971.

Smith, M. *The Ancient Greeks.* Ithaca, 1960.

Smith, W., ed. *Smith's Dictionary of Greek and Roman Antiquities.* 2d ed. Boston, 1870.

Stockton, D. "The Peace of Callias." *Historia* 8 (1959):61–79.

Stroud, R. S. "Greek Inscriptions. Theozotides and the Athenian Orphans." *Hesperia* 40 (1971):280–301.

Swoboda, H. "Über den Prozess des Perikles." *Hermes* 28 (1893): 536–98.

Thirlwall, C. *A History of Greece.* 2 vols. New York, 1860.

Thompson, W. E. "Notes on the Peace of Callias." *CP* 66 (1971):29–30.

Thomsen, R. *Eisphora: A Study of Direct Taxation in Athens.* Copenhagen, 1964.

*Thomsen, R. *The Origin of Ostracism: A Synthesis.* Copenhagen, 1972.

Tod, M. N. *A Selection of Greek Historical Inscriptions.* 2 vols. Oxford, 1948.

Toeppfer, J. *Attische Genealogie.* Berlin, 1889.

Treu, M. "Der Stratege Demosthenes." *Historia* 5 (1956):420–47.

Vanderpool, E. "The Ostracism of the Elder Alkibiades." *Hesperia* 21 (1952):1–8.

Vernant, J.-P., ed. *Problèmes de la guerre en Grèce ancienne.* Paris, 1968.

Wade-Gery, H. T. *Essays in Greek History.* Oxford, 1958.

Walcot, P. *Envy and the Greeks: A Study of Human Behaviour.* Warminster, 1978.

Webster, T. B. L. *Athenian Culture and Society.* London, 1973.

Webster, T. B. L. *Potter and Patron in Classical Athens.* London, 1973.

*Wedel, W. von. "Die politischen Prozesse im Athen des 5. Jahrhunderts. Ein Beitrag zur Entwicklung der attischen Demokratie zum Rechtstaat.'' *Bolletino dell'Istituto di Diritto romano* 74 (1971):107–88.

Wentker, H. *Sizilien und Athen: Die Begegnung der attischen Macht mit den Westgriechen.* Heidelberg, 1956.

Westlake, H. D. *Essays on the Greek Historians and Greek History.* New York, 1969.

Westlake, H. D. *Individuals in Thucydides.* Cambridge, 1968.

Westlake, H. D. "Paches." *Phoenix* 29 (1975):107–16.

Westlake, H. D. "Phrynichos and Astyochos (Thuc. VIII 50–51)." *JHS* 76 (1956):99–104.

Westlake, H. D. *Thessaly in the Fourth Century B.C.* 1935; reprint Groningen, 1969.

Whibley, L. *Political Parties in Athens during the Peloponnesian War.* Cambridge, 1889.

White, M. "Some Agiad Dates. Pausanias and His Sons." *JHS* 84 (1964):140–52.

Wilcken, U. "Über Entstehung und Zweck des Königsfriedens." *Abhandlungen der Preuss. Akademie, Phil.-hist. Klasse,* 1941, No. 16.

Wilcken, U. "Zur Iason von Pherai." *Hermes* 59 (1924):123–27.

Williams, B. H. G. "The Political Mission of Gorgias to Athens in 427 B.C." *CQ* 25 (1931):55–56.

*Williams, G. W. "The curse of the Alkmaionidai, III: Themistokles, Perikles and Alkibiades." *Hermathena* 80 (1952):58–71.

Wilson, C. H. "Athenian Military Finances 378–377 to the Peace of 375." *Athenaeum* 48 (1970):302–26.

*Wolff, H. J. *Normenkontrolle und Gesetzbegriff in der attischen Demokratie. Undersuchungen zur graphê paranomôn.* Heidelberg, 1970.

Woodhead, A. G. "Chabrias, Timotheus, and the Aegean Allies, 375–373 B.C." *Phoenix* 16 (1962):258–66.

Woodhead, A.G. "IG i² 95 and the Ostracism of Hyperbolus." *Hesperia* 18 (1949):78–83.

Woodhead, A. G. "IG II² 43 and Jason of Pherae." *AJA* 61 (1957): 367–73.

*Wüst, F. *Philipp II. von Makedonien und Griechenland in den Jahren 346 bis 338.* Munich, 1938.

INDEX

Principal references to case histories of accountability trials appear in boldface type. References to nineteen- and twentieth-century scholars are to the text only (pp. 3–182) and do not include either the preface or the footnotes.

Abydos, 103, 104
Acarnania, 99, 100
Accame, S., 99
Adcock, F. E., 128
Adeimantus, general, 75, 165, 225n76
Adkins, A. W. H., 180
Aegean Sea, 46, 88, 103, 122
Aegina, 86, 93, 94
Aegospotami, 46, 86, 99
  Adeimantus at, 75, 165
  Alcibiades' advice at, 104
  Conon's escape from, 76
  Spartan offers of peace after, 170
Aelian, 143
Aenis, 155
Aeschines, 27, 28, 30, 167, 219n33, 231n71
  on Aristophon, 74, 75, 154, 157
  on the audit, 5
  disobeyed instructions, 107, 112, 162
  on γραφὴ παρανόμων, 231n85
  on Leosthenes, 75, 172
  prosecuted by Demosthenes, 24, 49–54, 75, 76, 165, 181–82
  on Timomachus, 210n97
  1.64, scholiast on, 156

Aeschylus
  Persians, 5, 147
  Prometheus Bound, 5
Aesimus, 85, 86, 101
Aetolia, 100
Agathias, 137
Agesilaus, 93
Agis, 85
Agora, the Athenian, 142
Agyrrhius, 29, 93, 99, 161
  Andocides accused by, 90
  democrat, 105, 106
  impeachment, 27, 28, 104–5, 194n62, 195n69
Alcetas, of Molossia, 41, 43
Alcibiades, the elder, 143
Alcibiades, the younger, 9, 21, 101, 161, 195n69, 207n53
  advice at Aegospotami, 104
  advice to Pericles, 31–32
  deposition, 27, 64, 120–22, 194n62, 223n62, 224nn67, 76
  Hyperbolus and, 150–51, 229n38
  multilation of Hermae, 35, 159, 192n18
  Persian aid promised by, 109, 121, 122, 163

Alcibiades (*continued*)
　Phrynicus and, 36–40, 62, 198*n37*
　Plutarch's *Life of*, 150, 224*n62*
　recall expected, 66, 133, 166, 175
Alcidas, 138
Alcmaeon, 57
Alcmaeonids, 145, 146, 147, 164
Alexander I, of Macedon, 55
Alexander III, of Macedon, 11
Alexander, of Pherae, 73, 74, 113,
　209*n82*
Alopeconnesus, 114
Alyzia, 155
Amadocus, 114
Amnesty of 403, at Athens 20, 76, 170
Amorgos, 39
Ampelinus, 22, 27, 28
Amphictyonic Council, 51
Amphipolis
　Athenian claims to, 71
　autonomy asserted, 70
　colony sent to, 61
　defended by Perdiccas, 113–14, 162
　fall, 117–20, 125, 128–32 *passim*,
　162
Amphissa, 78
Anaxagoras, 59, 62, 164, 205*n25*
Andocides, orator, 22, 63, 88–93,
　100, 106, 159
　IV, authenticity of, 229*n38*
Andrewes, A., 163, 181
Andron, politician, 108, 111
Andros, 121, 122, 147
Androtion, 144, 156, 158
Antalcidas, 88, 95, 100, 102–3, 162,
　214*n17*
　Peace of, 43, 212*n120*, 215*n21*
Antimachus, treasurer of Timotheus,
　21, 23, 27, 40, 42, 200*n53*, 201*n54*
Antimedon, 155
Antiochus, pilot of Alcibiades, 121,
　163
Antipater, 78
Antiphon, orator, 22, 23, 27, 107–11,
　154, 161, 218*nn15, 17*
Antonius, Marcus, praetor, 10

Anytus, 9, 28, 205*n30*
　bribery, 62, 63, 64, 205*n39*
　impeachment, 26, 62–64, 164,
　194*n62*, 195*n69*
　moderates led by, 63, 85, 86, 101,
　164
Apaturia, festival of, 67, 207*n51*
Apollodorus, of Megara, 159
Apollodorus, son of Pasion, 42, 76,
　112, 156, 165, 173, 199*n50*,
　210*n92*, 211*n97*, 231*n82*
Apollonides, of Olynthus, 156,
　231*n82*
Apollo Patröos, cult of, 14
Arcadia, 70
Archebius, trierarch, 158
Archedemus, 65, 66
Archeptolemus, 22, 23, 27, 107–9,
　111, 161, 218*n71*
Archidamian War, 178. *See also*
　Peloponnesian War
Archinus, 155
Areopagus, 58, 148
Argilus, 118
Arginusae, battle of, 17, 64, 65, 178
Arginusae, Victors of, 95, 139, 162,
　178, 181, 195*n69*
　Callixeinus and, 67–68, 155, 160,
　164, 170
　impeachment, 17, 21, 23, 27,
　64–69, 74, 122, 179, 194*n62*,
　223*n62*
　Theramenes and, 20, 65–67, 68, 75,
　160, 164, 165
　See also Aristocrates, general;
　Diomedon; Pericles, the younger
Argolid, expedition to. *See* Epidau-
　rus, campaign against
Argos
　Iasus campaign, 37, 133
　Sparta and, 86, 87, 148
Ariobarzanes, 71
Aristarchus, general, 27, 110, 194*n62*,
　195*n69*, 218*n17*
Aristides, statesman, 10, 24, 171
　attack on Themistocles, 146, 147

ostracism, 135, 143, **145–46**, 151, 169
Plutarch's *Life of*, 136, 137, 139, 150, 162
Aristides, Aelius, orator, 216*n21*
Aristion, 21, 22, 27, 28
Aristocrates, general, 64, 109, 195*n69*, 225*n76*. *See also* Arginusae, Victors of
Aristocrates, fourth-century Athenian, 156
Aristogeiton, politician, 156
Aristogenes, 65, 195*n69*. *See also* Arginusae, Victors of Aristophanes, dramatist
on bribery (?) of Cleon, 35
Ecclesiazusae, 206*n39*
Frogs, scholiast on, 233*n12*
on μισθὸς ἐκκλησιαστικός, 105
Peace, 24, 59
Plutus, 94, 102, 215*n34*
Wasps, 7, 57, 219*n35*, 220*n44*
Aristophanes, son of Nicophemus, 26, **95–96**, 106, 195*n69*
Aristophon, 171, 172, 218*n24*
acquittals, 154, 157
indicted, 156, 158, 159
Leosthenes attacked by, 75, 173
Timotheus *et al.* accused by, 45, 48, 173
trierarchs of Leosthenes accused by, 22, 74–75
Aristotle, 5, 24, 206*n39*
on Anytus' trial, 63
Athenaiôn Politeia, 13
on Cimon, εὔθυναι of, 25, 56
Ephialtes' attack on Aeropagus, 58
on Ergophilus, 218*n27*
on Miltiades and Xanthippus, 79, 164
on ostracism, 143, 144, 145
rivalry of Pericles and Cimon, 56, 57, 164
tyrannical nature of radical democracy, 8
Artabazus, 114, 115

Artaxerxes II, 70, 71, 72, 87, 91, 95, 100, 101, 102, 208*n67*, 214*n17*
Asia, 85, 88, 95, 120, 122
Agyrrhius in, 105
Thrasybulus and, 96–102 *passim*, 166, 175, 176, 216*n59*
Aspasia, 59, 61, 164
Aspendus, 97, 98
Assembly, the Athenian, 15, 182
accountability of, 7–8, 168–71
advantage of addressing, 17, 191*n18*
extraordinary, 23
γραφὴ παρανόμων and, 157, 170
the military and, 169, 171–73
pay for attending, 105
policy decisions to lie with, 174
trials before, 16, 22, 23, 193*n50*
See also ekklesia; ἐκκλησία
Astyochus, Spartan admiral, 38, 39, 133
Athena, statue of, 59, 60, 194*n66*
Athenian confederacy, first, 9, 44
Athenian confederacy, second, 24, 43, 46, 155, 200*n54*
Athenian envoys, put to death, 85
Attica, 41, 69, 82
audit, 5, 17–18. *See also* εὔθυναι
Autocles, general, 21, 74, 194*n62*, 195*n69*, 209*n82*
Autolycus, 160

Baldwin, B., 151
Bauman, R. E., 119, 128
Beloch, K. J., 10, 42, 43, 48, 66, 137, 177
Berisades, Thracian chieftain, 114
Black, Charles, 168
Black Sea, 97, 103, 104, 111
Boeotia, 69, 110, 222*n58*
Corcyrean expedition and, 41, 201*n55*
Philip attacks, 78
Theban hegemony over, 91
Boeotus, son of Pamphilus, 94
Bonner, R., 56, 111, 143, 153

Bosporus, 103, 104
Botsford, G. W., 171
Brasidas, 118, 119, 120, 129–30, 131, 162, 222*n52*
bribery, 15, 19, 22, 123, 140
  alleged, 9, 10, 24, 48, 52, 55, 60, 62–63, 64, 79, 80, 89, 102, 116, 170, 205*nn21, 39*, 220*n43*
  penalties for, 18, 27
Bruce, I. A. F., 86
Burnett, A. P., 82
Bury, J. B., 33, 98, 121, 171, 172
Busolt, G., 56, 118, 128, 132, 137, 138, 147
Butcher, S., 10
Byzantium, 46, 97, 99, 103, 198*n26*

Cadmeia, 44, 81, 107, 108
Caecilius, rhetorician, 107–8
Calauria, 41, 42
Callias, of Alopece, 145
Callias, ambassador, 24, 28, 29
Callippus, of Aexone, trierarch, 21, 76–77, 165, 173, 210*n97*
Callippus, of Paiania, 156
Callisthenes, general, 21, 23, 27, 113–14, 162, 194*n62*, 195*n69*, 219*n27*
Callistratus, orator, 93, 171, 212*n121*
  advocate of Peloponnesian alliances, 71, 72, 176
  associates of, jeopardized, 73, 164, 172
  envoys indicted by, 22, 88, 91, 92
  exiled for bad advice, 74, 112, 159, 170, 209*n87*
  influence, 73, 112
  Oropus affair and trial, 69–73, 77, 157, 159, 170, 208*nn76, 78*, 210*n97*
  Timotheus indicted by, 41–45 *passim*, 71, 173
  transport of, 76–77, 111, 161, 165, 173

Callixeinus, politician, 65, 67, **68**, 155, 160, 164, 170
Camarina, 116
Camon, F., 151
Cannonus, psephism of, 67, 68
Carcopino, J., 12, 143, 151, 152
Cardia, 156
Carystus, 147
Cavaignac, E., 8, 78
Cawkwell, G. L., 52, 140
Cenchreae, 112
Ceos, 156, 158
Cephallenia, 86
Cephalus, radical democrat, 86, 92
Cephisodotus, 21, 27, 28, 29, 113, 114–15, 162, 173, 176, 194*n62*, 195*n69*, 219*n33*
Cersobleptes, 114, 115
Chabrias, 9, 28, 46, 171, 195*n69*
  acquittal, 26, 73, 195*n72*
  association with Callistratus, 73, 159, 164, 170, 172, 176
  decree in honor of, 155, 157, 231*n71*
  at Naxos, 178–79
  Oropus affair and trial, **69–73**, 77, 159, 165, 170, 194*n62*, 208*n76*, 210*n97*
  pro-Theban (?), 72, 208*nn69, 78*
  Timotheus replaced by, 41, 71, 73, 208*n76*
Chaeronea, battle of, 9, 11, 19, 77, **78**, 156, 162, 165, 173
Chalcedon, 103
Chalcidice, 71, 126
Chares, 75, 155, 218*n24*
  aggressive policy of, 48, 167, 172, 176
  at Chaeronea, 77–78
  Oropus affair, 69–72 *passim*, 77
  self-preservation, 77, 78, 165, 208*n78*
  Timotheus *et al.* accused by (356), 45–49 *passim*
Charidemus, of Acharnae, mercenary, 114–15, 156, 162, 176, 177

Charidemus, son of Ischomachus, 155
Charinus, 154
Chersonese, 71, 113, 114
Chios, 46, 48
chronology of events (375–373), 199*n50*
Cicero
De oratore, 10
Cimon, 9, 28, 79, 164, 195*n69*
attack on Themistocles, 146, 147
εὔθυναι of, 24, 25, 56–57, 194*n62*, 204*n9*
ostracism, 143, 148, 151, 169
Plutarch's *Life of*, 56
trial, 55–59, 175, 203*n1*, 204*n11*
Cinesias, 154
civic requirements, 14
Classen, J., 128
Cleandridas, 60
Cleidemus, 143
Cleisthenes, statesman, 143–46 *passim*
Cleisthenes, late fifth-century democrat, 63
Cleombrotus, 82, 83, 165
Cleon, 138, 178
Laches accused by, 57, 219*n35*
Mytilene and, 62, 137
Pericles and, 32
Potidaea and, 34, 35, 127, 166, 175
Thucydides and, 117, 220*n44*, 222*n60*
war party led by, 32, 34, 61, 126, 197*n10*
Cleophon, 22, 23, 66, 120, 159, 170, 191*n11*, 233*n12*
Cloché, P., 12, 53, 68, 69, 74, 86, 122, 154
Cnidus, battle of, 76, 95
Cohen, R., 84, 106, 147
Congress (U.S.), 4, 168
Connor, W. R., 13, 151
Conon, admiral, 26, 85, 88, 96, 99, 106, 224*n62*

Adeimantus prosecuted by (?), 75–76, 165, 210*n94*
besieged at Mytilene, 65
Cnidus, victory at, 76, 95
imprisoned by Tiribazus, 90
Conon, son of Timotheus, 28, 46
Corcyra, 100, 116, 198*n26*
Athenian relief of (373), 40–42, 43, 45, 48, 71, 73, 176, 199*n50*
Chares and, 48
Corinth, 69, 70, 112
attacked by Athens, 71
Long Walls of, 90
Spartan ally, 85
war against Sparta, 86, 87 (*see also* Corinthian War)
Corinth, Gulf of, 78, 90
Corinthiad, the, 90
Corinthian War, 162
accountability trials during, 11, 22, 24, 26, 69, 84, 88–106 *passim*, 164, 171, 174, 175, 213*n8*, 215*n38*
beginnings of, 86–87
peace negotiations (392/91), 22, 88–93, 94, 100
corn dealers, impeachment of, 191*n11*
Cornford, F., 131
Cos, 46
Cotys, 71, 111, 114
Craterus, 10, 135
Cratinus, envoy, 22, 88, 91, 106
Crithote, 71
Crommyum, 90
Curtius, E., 33, 64, 101, 136
Cyclades, 74
Cyme, 121, 122, 224*n67*
Cyprus, 95
Cyrus II, 121
Cythera, 63, 95, 198*n26*

Decelea, 68, 108
Decelean War, 97, 117. See also Peloponnesian War
Deinarchus, 48, 177

Delbrück, H., 128
Delian confederacy, 146, 147
Delium, 132, 223n60
Delphi, treasures of, plundered, 51
Demades, politician, 154, 157, 158
Demaenetus, general, 85, 86, 103, 104
Demeter, sanctuary of, 80
Demomeles, 156
Demonicus, of Alopece, 108
Demophanes, radical democrat, 63
Demosthenes, general, 99–100, 116,
    127–28, 154, 216n66
Demosthenes, orator, 12–13, 27, 42,
    73, 88, 157, 172, 209n82, 231n81
  Aeschines prosecuted by, 24,
    49–51, 53, 75, 165, 181
  Against Aristocrates, 114
  Against Meidias, 154
  on Agyrrhius, 93, 104, 105
  on ambassadors of 387/86, 89
  on Callias, 24, 28
  Cephisodotus and, 114–15, 219n33
  on Chabrias, 195n72
  on Cimon, 203n1
  on Conon, 76, 165
  on death penalty for illegal propos-
    al, 153, 158
  decrees in honor of, 156
  For Phormio, 76
  indicted, 155, 156
  on prosecution of generals, 19–20
  on Timagoras, 208n67
  on Timotheus, 200n52, 201n54
de Romilly, J., 119
dicasteries, 7, 17, 157
  δοκιμασίαι held before, 14
  penalty set by, 192n18
  trial before, 15, **16**, 153
dicasts, panel of, 206n39
Didymus, 88
Dinsmoor, W. B., 26
Diocleides, informer, 159
Diodorus Siculus, 3, 46, 48, 199n44,
    202n65, 224n62
  on Alcibiades, 122, 224n62

Amphipolis, loss of, 117
Anytus' trial, 62
  on Chabrias, 178–79
  Demades' loss of civic rights, 154,
    158
  events of 375–373, 199n50, 201n55
  on ostracism, 143
  on Paches, 137, 140
  Peparethus, attack on, 74, 209n82
  on Pericles, 25, 31, 32, 33, 59,
    196n2
  Theban uprising, 82
Diodotus, politician, 7, 36, 171
Diogenes Laertius, 71, 73
Diomedon, 39, 64, 65, 67, 195n69,
    207n53. *See also* Arginusae, Vic-
    tors of
Dion, of Syracuse, 211n97
Diondas, 156
Dionysius, general, 27, **102–4**, 162,
    194n62, 195n69
Dionysius I, of Syracuse, 95, 102, 103
Dionysius, of Halicarnassus, 24,
    46–47, 202n73
Diopeithes, 160, 171
Diotimus, archonship of, 47
disfranchisement, 196n4. *See also*
    ἀτιμία; ἄτιμος
Dover, K. J., 181
Dracontides, politician, 59, 61, 196n8

Eëtioneia, 109
Eion, 118, 119, 130, 132, 222n52,
    225n8
eisangelia, 21, 140. *See also*
    εἰσαγγελία
ekklesia, 169. *See also* Assembly, the
    Athenian; ἐκκλησία
Eleutherae, 82
Elis, 70, 86
Elpinice, sister of Cimon, 58, 204n11
Embata, 46, 202n65
embezzlement, 19, 195n70
  alleged, 22, 24, 27, 30, 42, 76,
    104–5, 210n97, 219n35

penalties for, 18, 27
See also κλοπή
Epaminondas, 71, 73, 112, 201*n55*
Ephialtes, politician, 28, 58, 59, 148,
149, 151, 154
Ephorus, historian, 79, 140, 143,
224*n67*
Epichares' father, 155, 157
Epicrates, democrat, 22, 24, 86, 88,
90–92, 106
Epidaurus, campaign against, 31, 32,
33, 136, 197*n11*
Epieicea, 90
Epigenes, radical democrat, 63
Erasinides, general, 64, 65, 66,
195*n69*. *See also* Arginusae, Vic-
tors of
Eratosthenes, Athenian oligarch, 24
Eretria, 24, 69
Ergocles, general, 102, 161, 195*n69*,
216*nn50, 59*
democrat, 96, 105, 106
impeachment, 23, 27, 96–100, 175,
194*n62*
Ergophilus, general, 21, 23, 27, 28,
113, 194*n62*, 195*n69*, 218*n27*
Erythrae, 46
Eteonicus, Spartan admiral, 93
Euboea, 109, 110
Eubulides, envoy, 22, 88, 91, 106
Eubulus, politician, 50, 53, 171, 172
Eucleides, archonship of, 154
Eucles, general, 117–20 *passim*, 130,
134, 162, **220n44**, 221*n47*,
222*nn52, 58*
Euctemon, 156, 158
Eurymedon, general, 139, 195*n69*,
221*n44*
fined, 28, 116, 117
impeached, 26, **115–17**, 120, 124,
127–28, 134, 194*n62*
responsible for delay, 116, 127,
162, 220*n38*
Thucydides on, 9, 120, 124, 129,
132, 134, 135, 223*n60*

Euryptolemus, 67, 68, 155, 207*n53*
Euthycles, 156, 173
Euthycrates, of Olynthus, 157
Euxenippus, 159
Euxine, 97, 103, 104, 111
Evagoras, of Salamis, 26, 95, 96, 102
Evander, 20, 195*n72*
executive branch, 9–10, 173–74
exile
as a common fate, 10
as alternative to death, 27–28

Finley, John, 125, 128, 132
Finley, M. I., 182
Five Thousand, the, 109, 110, 218*n17*
Foch, Ferinand, Marshal, 163
Four Hundred, the, 22, 63, 109, 110,
111, 205*n33*
Frost, F. J., 59
Fuqua, C., 152

Generals of 379/78, 27, 78, **81–83**,
107, 161, 165, 171, 175, 176, 177,
194*n62*, 195*n69*
Gilbert, G., 34, 35
Glaucetes, envoy, 156, 158
Glotz, G., 10, 56, 84, 106, 147, 154,
177
Gomme, A. W., 31, 128, 131
Gorgopas, Spartan, 93
Gouldner, A., 180, 181
Graea, Athenian deme, 69
grain dealers, impeachment of,
191*n11*
Greenidge, A., 168
Grote, G., 47, 49, 52, 64, 69, 82, 98,
118, 124, 128, 182
Grundy, G., 128
Gylon, 21

Hager, H., 12
Hagnon, 59, 61, 196*n8*
Halus, 50
Hamilton, C., 86
Hands, A. R., 144

Hansen, M. H., 12, 19, 20, 21, 23, 28, 76, 140, 157
Harmodius, son of Proxenus, 156
Harper, G. M., 169
Harpocration, lexicon of, 13, 16, 110
Harrison, A. R. W., 20
Hatzfeld, J., 151, 152
Hauvette-Besnault, A., 12, 25, 34
Hegesander, treasurer of Timotheus, 210*n97*
Hegesileus, general, 194*n62*, 195*n69*
Hegesippus, democrat, 73, 156, 210*n97*
heliastic oath, 17, 191*n17*
Hellanicus, Atthidographer, 143
Helenic league, 148
Hellespont, 62, 174
    Antalcidas in (387), 95, 102–3, 162
    Autocles in (362), 74
    battle in (356), 45, **46**, 77, 176
    Ergophilus in (363), 113
Helot revolt (462), 28, 58, 148
Henderson, B. W., 10, 64, 120, 122, 177
Heracleides Ponticus, 32
Heraclia, Trachinian, 86
Herippidas, Spartan, 90
Hermae, mutilation of 12, 35, 158
Hermes, in Aristophanes' *Peace*, 59
Hermocrates, of Syracuse, 117, 128
Herodotus, 5, 79, 80, 81
Hestiodorus, general, 26, **34–36**, 107, 126, 129, 134, 138, 161, 176, 194*n62*, 195*n69*. *See also* Potidaea, Athenian generals at
Hignett, C., 168
Hipparchus, son of Charmus, 143, 144, 159
Hippias, son of Peisistratus, 144
Holm, L., 169
House of Commons (U.K.), 168
Hyperbolus, politician, 143, **150–53**, 169, 229*n38*
Hyperides, orator, 16, 156, 157, 159, 160, 170, 171, 209*n87*, 210*n97*

Iasus, **36–37**, 38, 39, 40, 133, 198*n27*
Idomeneus, biographer, 32
Imbros, 46, 91
impeachment, summary, 195*n70*
in absentia. *See* trial *in absentia*
Ionia, 91, 103, 138, 214*n17*
Iphicrates, general, 9, 42, 103, 194*n62*, 195*n69*, 219*n33*
    decree for, 156, 231n71
    popularity, 48, 49, 202*n71*
    replaced by Timotheus, 72, 208*n76*
    Timotheus opposed by (373), 41, 71, 73, 173, 199*n50*
    trial (ca. 355), 21, 24, 25, 26, **45–49**, 77, 165, 166–67, 172, 173, 176, 202*nn64, 73*
Isagoras, archon, 144
Ismenias, Spartan envoy, 70
Isocrates, 46, 47, 49, 171
Isodice, 57
Ithome, Mt., 148

Jacoby, F., 56
Jason, of Pherae, 41, 43, 200*n54*
Jebb, R., 171
Jones, A. H. M., 7
jury selection, 206*n39*

Kagan, 25, 34, 35, 86, 116, 119, 126, 128, 137, 144, 146, 148
Kahrstedt, U., 154
Kennedy, John F., 3, 4
Kerykes, 147

Laches, general, 21, 57, 116, 194*n62*, 195*n69*, **219*n35***
Lacratidas, 32
Laistner, M., 33, 171, 172
Lamb, W. R. M., 195*n70*
Laurium, 145
Lechaeum, 90
Lemnos, 91
Lenardon, Robert, 4, 145, 146, 147
Lenschau, T., 138

Leodamas, the elder, 20
Leodamas, of Acharnae, 69, 72, 155, 157, 208*n69*, 210*n97*
Leogoras, 154, 155, 157
Leon, general, 39
Leon, Athenian envoy, 22, 70, 75, 165, 208*n67*
Leontiades, Theban, 81, 82, 93
Leontichus, general, 103, 104
Leosthenes, general, 48, 171, 172, 195*n69*, 209*n82*
  impeachment, 21, 27, 73–75, 164, 173, 194*n62*, 209*n87*
  trierarchs of, 21, 22, 23, 74–75
Leptines, law of, 231*n81*
Lesbos, 97, 137, 138
Lipsius, J., 23, 56
Littman, R. J., 170
Locris, Western, 87
Lycinus, 156
Lyciscus, 67, 68, 164
Lycoleon, 73
Lycurgus, Athenian orator, 77, 171, 173
Lydia, 90, 96
Lysander, Spartan general, 76, 121
  Plutarch's *Life of*, 224*n62*
Lysias, general, 64, 195*n69*. *See also* Arginusae, Victors of
Lysias, orator, 12–13, 24, 100, 110
  Cleophon's trial, 170
  on δοκιμασία, 20
  logographer for Phanias, 154
  on Nicophemus and Aristophanes, 95, 195*n70*
  on Phrynichus, 37
  on radical democracy, 63, 64
  on Thrasybulus and Ergocles, 97, 98, 99, 102
Lysicles, general, 27, 77, 78, 162, 165, 173, 194*n62*, 195*n69*
Lysitheides, trierarch, 158

MacArthur, Douglas, 174
McCoy, J., 37, 63, 66

Macedonia, 71
  Aeschines and, 49, 50, 53, 167
  Cimon and, 55, 57, 148
  Timotheus' trip to, 41
Malea, Cape, 62
Mantinea, 73
Marathon, 9, 57, 79, 80, 81
Marmara, Sea of, 103
Mason, George, 168
Mausolus, of Caria, 46, 158
Megacles, 143, 145
Megara, decree against, 44, 59
Meiggs, R., 57, 138, 147
Melanopus, ambassador, 24, 156, 158
Melon, of Thebes, 81, 82
Melville, Lord, 168
Menecles, 68, 155
Menestheus, general, 171, 194*n62*, 195*n69*
  as chief commander, 202*n64*
  impeachment, 21, 24, 25, 26, 45–48, 77, 165, 166, 172, 173, 202*n73*
Menon, general, 111, 194*n62*, 195*n69*
Messene, 62, 70, 86, 100
Messina, 116
Methone, 76
Meyer, Eduard, 84, 128, 131
Miletus, Athenian withdrawal from, 36–37, 38, 39, 133
Milon, harmost of Aegina, 86
Miltiades, the elder, 57
Miltiades, general, 9, 137, 175, 176, 178, 195*n69*, 203*n1*, 212*n110*
  fined, 28, 29, 79, 211*n103*
  guilt, 80, 161, 163
  impeachment, 21, 23, 26, 78–81, 194*n62*
  political feud, 57, 164
Miltner, F., 31
Mnasippus, Spartan navarch, 199*n50*
monarchy, lack of accountability under, 5
Mysteries, profanation of, 11, 91, 154, 155, 159, 232*n86*

Mytilene, 198*n26*
  Conon besieged at, 65
  debate over, 7, 36, 166, 177, 223*n60*
  Paches and, 24, 137–38

Naupactus, 78, 86, 100
Nausicles, general, 112
Naxos, 72, 155, 178, 179
Neocles, 137
Nepos, Cornelius, 46, 202*n64*
  on Alcibiades, 122, 224*n67*
  on Miltiades, 79, 80, 81
Nicias, general, 9–10, **178**, 179, 220*n43*
  Hyperbolus and, 150–51, 229*n38*
  Peace of, 150, 219*n35*
  Plutarch's *Life of*, 136, 139, 150, 152
Nicomachus, registrar of decrees, 22, 23, 26
Nicophemus, general, 26, **95–96**, 106, 195*n69*
Nixon, Richard M., 3, 4
Notium, 120, **121**, 122, 225*n76*
Nymphaeum, garrison at, 21

oath, heliastic, 17
Oenoe, 110, 218*n17*
"Old Oligarch", 7
oligarchy, lack ˅of accountability under, 5
Oneum, 112
Onomacles, envoy, 22, 23, 36, 39, **107–9**, 161
Opisthodomos, the, 26
Oropus, 69–73 *passim*, 77, 157, 159, 165, 170, 176, 210*n97*
ostracism, 61, 135, **142–53**, 160, 169, 181, 227*n11*
ostrakophoria, 152
Otanes, 5
Oxyrhynchus historian, the, 85, 86, 101

Paches, general, 24, **136–40**, 163, 194*n62*, 195*n69*

Pamphilus, general, 27, 28, 29, **93–94**, 106, 194*n62*, 195*n69*, 215*n34*
Paralos, state trireme, 41, 109
Parapotamii, pass of, 78
Paros, 147
  Miltiades' expedition against, 57, 78–81 *passim*, 163, 164, 176
Patmos, 138
Pausanias, geographer, 86
peace negotiations of 392/91, 22, **88–93**, 94, 100
Peisander, politician, 36, 38–39, 109, 133, 198*n27*
Peisias, of Argos, 112
Peisistratids, 143, 144, 145
Peisistratus, 149
Peitholaus, of Pherae, 156, 231*n82*
Pella, 49, 50
Pelopidas, Theban statesman, 70, 71, 81, 165, 208*n67*
Peloponnesian ambassadors, murder of, 36
Peloponnesian league, 85
Peloponnesian War, 10, 30, 88, 134, 164, 175, 178, 210*n94*
  Athens after, 101
  civil strife at end of, 155
  impeachments during, 174
  politicians unassailable (?) during, 168–69, 170
  Sparta after, 94
  See also Decelean War
Peparethus, 74, 75, 209*n82*
Percote, 103
Perdiccas, son of Amyntas, Macedonian king, 113–14, 162
Pericles, statesman, 9, 137, 147, 169, 170, 171, 207*n53*, 222*n60*
  attacked through Anaxagoras, 61–62, 164, 205*n25*
  Cimon attacked by, 55–59, 148, 164, 204*n11*
  decree against Megara, 44
  deposition, 21, 26, 28, **30–34**, 55, 125, 129, 134, 135–36, 166, 175, 194*n62*, 195*n69*, 197*n13*

Epidaurus campaign, 197*n11*
εὔθυναι, 25, **60**, 164, 194*n66*, 196*n8*
expenditures, public, 149–50
fined, 28
Pleistonax and, 60, 205*n21*
Plutarch's *Life of*, 56
re-elected, 125–26, 197*n14*
trial, first (438), **59–62**
Pericles, the younger, 9, 64, 65, 67, 195*n69*. See also Arginusae, Victors of
Perinthus, 114, 115, 162
Perlman, S., 86, 169, 171
Persia, 80, 144, 149
   accountability lacking in, 5
   Antalcidas supported by, 103, 104
   Athens seeks support of (397), 85, 213*n4*
   intervention threatened (367), 70
   Ionian Greeks and, 88, 91
   Leon's embassy to, 22, 165
   support given (Peloponnesian War), 39, 109, 121, 122, 163
   support given against Sparta (fourth century), 87, 88, 91, 96
Persian Wars, 9, 11, 19, 180
Phaeax, politician, 150, 151, 229*n38*
Phanias, admiral, 103, 104
Phanias, indicter of Cinesias, 154
Phanocritus, of Parium, 104
Phanomachus, general, 26, 28, **34–36**, 107, 126, 129, 134, 138, 161, 176, 194*n62*, 195*nn69, 73*. *See also* Potidaea, Athenian generals at
Phanosthenes, general, 224*n62*
Pharax, of Sparta, 85, 213*n4*
Pherae, 50, 73, 113
Phidias, sculptor, 31, 59, 60–61, 164
"Philaids", 57, 147
Philinus, 21, 22, 27, 28
Philip II, of Macedon, 11, 16, 156, 180
   at Chaeronea, 77–78
   Peace of Philocrates and, 30, 49–53 *passim*, 75, 107, 113, 160, 162

Philochorus, Atthidographer, 59, 88, 89, 91, 143
Philocles, of Anaphlystus, 88
Philocrates, trierarch, 96, 102, 106, 216*n59*
Philocrates, ambassador, 49, 50
   impeached by Hyperides, 160, 170
   indicted by Licinus, 156
   Peace of, 24, 30, 49, 52, 75, 165
Philon, of Acharnae, 20
Philon, of Aexone, 210*n97*
Philon, of Anaea, 194*n62*, 209*n87*
Philostratus, of Colonus, 69, 72
Philostratus, of Pallene, 108
Phlius, 69
Phocion, general and politician, 53, 171
Phocis, 50, 51, 52, 78, 87
Phoebidas, Spartan, 44, 81
Phormio, admiral, 24, 26, 195*n69*
Phrynichus, general, 108–11 *passim*, 135, 161
   correspondence with Astyochus, 38, 39, 40, 133
   deposed (412/11), 21, 27, **36–40**, 62, 129, 133–34, 166, 175, 194*n62*, 195*n69*, 198*n27*, 220*n35*
   opposed recall of Alcibiades, 36, 38, 39, 62, 133–34, 166, 175
Piraeus, 85, 109, 155, 157
   Iphicrates at, 41
   raided by Alexander of Pherae, 74
   raided by Sphodrias, 43
Plataea, 28
Plato, philosopher, 5–6, 8, 31, 182, 210*n97*, 211*n103*
Plato, comic poet, 152
Pleistoanax, Spartan king, 60, 205*n21*
Plutarch, 11, 59, 167, 168, 171, 224*n62*
   Aristides, bribery of, 135
   attack on Anaxagoras, 205*n25*
   Cimon's trial, 56, 57, 58, 204*n11*
   envy in political life, 181
   Hyperbolus, ostracism of, 150, 151, 152

Plutarch (*continued*)
 Lives. See Aristides, statesman,
  Nicias, general, etc.
 on Nicias, 10, 136–37, 178
 on ostracism, 227*n11*
 on Paches, 136–37, 139, 140
 party politics, 149
 Pericles, deposition of, 31, 32, 33,
  135–36, 196*n2*, 197*nn11, 14*
 Pericles, εὔθυναι of, 25, 60, 61
 rivalry of Pericles and Cimon, 57,
  164
 rivalry of Themistocles and Aristides, 24, 145, 146
 on Timotheus, 43, 202*n78*
Pollux, *Onomasticon* of, 13
Polyaenus, 49, 74, 202*nn65, 71*
Polycles, 76, 112
Polyeuctus, 159
Polystratus, 24
Potidaea
 enslavement expected, 198*n25*
 hard pressed by seige, 35, 126–27
Potidaea, Athenian generals at,
  34–36, 62, 107, 126–27, 132, 134,
  138, 161, 166, 175. *See also* Hestiodorus, general; Phanomachus,
  general; Xenophon, general
Pritchett, W. K., 34, 163, 174
proditio, 80. *See also* προδοσία;
  treason
prosecutors, in cases resulting from
  εὔθυναι, 56–57
Protomachus, general, 64, 65,
  195*n69. See also* Arginusae, Victors of
Proxenus, of Thebes, 78
Prytaneum, the, 50
Pseudo-Xenophon, 7
Pylos, 116, 124, 127, 135, 198*n26*,
  223*n60*
 Anytus sent to, 62, 63, 205*n27*
Pythian games, 51
Pythodorus, general, 139, 162,
  195*n69*, 220*n38*, 221*n44*

impeachment, 26, **115–17**, 120, 124,
  127–28, 134, 194*n62*
Thucydides on, 9, 120, 124, 129,
  132, 134, 135, 223*n60*

reforms of 462, 154
Reverdin, O., 13
Rhegium, 116
Rhodes, 46, 48, 147
 Thrasybulus' expedition to, 96–99
  passim
Rice, D., 43, 44
Robinson, C. A., 144, 171

Sacred War, 49
Salaminia, state trireme, 42
Salamis, 146, 147
Samos, 121
 Athenian withdrawal to, 36, 133
 besieged by Timotheus, 71
 democratic government, 109
 pillaged (Social War), 46
Samothrace, 97
Sardis, 88, 91, 214*n17*
Schmid, W., 128
Schömann, G. F., 189*n12*
Scironides, general, 21, 36, **38–40**, 62,
  129, 133, 134, 166, 175, 194*n62*,
  195*n69*, 198*n27*
Sciton, 154, 157
Scyros, 91
Sestos, 46, 71, 112
Seuthes, 97, 99
Sicily, 71, 154, 211*n97*, 229*n38*
 Aristophanes sent to, 95
 Athenian expedition to (426/25), 9,
  116–17, 127–28, 134, 150, 162
 generals' return from, mentioned,
  115, 124, 132
 Nicias in, 9, 178, 220*n43*
Sicyon, 70
Sidus, 90
Simmias, 32
Smicrus, 154, 157

Smith, G., 56, 143, 154
Smith, M., 10
Social War, 23, 25, 46, 48, 77, 165, 166, 172, 173, 176
Socrates, 9, 62, 68
Solon, 154, 171
Sophocles, general, 139, 195*n69*, 221*n44*
  impeachment, 26, **115–17**, 120, 124, 127–28, 134, 194*n62*
  responsible for delay, 116, 127, 162, 220*n38*
  Thucydides on, 9, 120, 124, 129, 132, 134, 135, 223*n60*
Sparta, 93, 144, 175, 180, 199*n50*
  Aegina protected by, 93
  Alcibiades' service with, 40
  Athenian fear of war with, 83, 212*n121*
  Athenian relations with, after 404, 84–85, 86, 101, 213*n4*
  bribery by Pericles alleged, 60, 61, 205*n21*
  Corcyra beseiged by, 41, 42
  Corinthian War against, 87–88, 93, 100
  defeat at Arginusae, 65
  Dionysius I ally of, 95
  Euboean revolt sparked by, 110
  Helot revolt against, 28, 58, 59, 148
  hostility towards, after 404, 86, 94
  Iasus taken by, 37, 133
  Megarian decree a test of, 44
  Messene free of, 70
  Mytilene supported by, 138
  peace embassies to (Corinthian War), 22, 88, **89**, 90, 91, 100, 214*n17*
  peace embassies to (Peloponnesian War), 22, 32–33, 107–8, 109, 125, 126, 197*n13*
  Pylos attacked by, 62
  Pythian games not attended by, 51
  Theban uprising against (379/78), 81–83, 107, 165

Themistocles and, 146, 147, 148, 151, 170
Timotheus and, 43, 44, 45, 166, 172, 175, 176
Speusippus, 154, 155, 157
Sphodrias, 43, 44
Stephanus, 156, 157
Stephen, of Byzantium, 79
Stesicles, 41
Stesimbrotus, biographer, 58
strategi, 131, 163, 169, 171. *See also* στρατηγός
Stratocles, general, 77
Struthas, satrap of Lydia, 91, 93, 96, 100
Strymon, river, 118, 130, 222*n52*
summary impeachment, 195*n70*
Susa, Greek embassy to, 70, 75
sycophancy, 10, 19, 37, 94
Syracuse, 9, 102
  supports Antalcidas, 95, 103
  triremes captured at Corcyra, 42

Teleutias, 93
Tenedos, 97, 155
Tenos, 74
Thalheim, T., 23
Thasos, 76, 97, 112, 212*n110*
  Cimon and, 55, 164
  Thucydides at, 118, 119, **130–31**, 132, 222*n52*
Thebes, 74, 93, 112, 175, 218*n17*
  Alexander of Pherae and, 73, 113
  alliance with Athens, 43, 45, 201*n55*, 214*n12*
  celebrates fall of Phocis, 51
  excluded from peace of 375/74, 201*n55*
  exiles, return of, 27, **81–83**, 161, 165, 171, 177
  hegemony recognized, 70, 72, 91
  Oropus lost to, 69–73 *passim*, 77
  Plataea attacked by, 28
  Sparta and, 85, 86, 87
  Timagoras and, 53

Themison, tyrant of Eretria, 69
Themistocles, 4, 10, 52, 139
  impeachment, 159, 170
  ostracism, 143, **146–48**, 149, 151
  Plutarch's *Life of*, 137
  rivalry with Aristides, 24, 135
    145–46, 151, 169
Theocrines, 154, 155
Theodorus, archon (438/37), 59
Theodorus, archon (347), 24
Theophemus, trierarch, 21, 22, 23.
  27, 28
Theophrastus, philosopher, 32, 60,
  150
Theotimus, general, 21, 112, 194*n62*,
  195*n69*, 209*n87*
Theozotides, 155
Theramenes, politician, 102, 218*n17*
  at Arginusae, 65
  δοκιμασία of, 20, 160
  prosecution of envoys, 108–11
  Victors of Arginusae attacked by,
    66, 67, 68, 75, 164, 165,
    207*nn50–51*
Thessaly, 41, 148
Thibron, harmost, 85
Thirty Tyrants, the, 68, 101, 104, 108
Thirty Years' Peace, 44
Thirwall, C., 128
Thrace, 78, 102, 121, 220*n44*
  Cimon in, 57
  Philip in, 50
  Thucydides in, 117, 118, 128, 130,
    131, 162, 222*nn52, 58*
  Timotheus in, 41, 111
Thrasybulus, of Collytus, 20, 28, 121,
  195*n69*
  acquittal, 26, 195*n72*
  democrat, 104, 105, 106
  impeachment, 23, **102–4**, 194*n62*
Thrasybulus, of Steiria, 9, 75, 104,
  171, 214*n12*, 216*n50*, 231*n82*
  aggressive Asian policy, 101, 106,
    166, 175, 176
  at Arginusae, 65, 66
  indicted for illegal proposal, 155

last expedition, **96–102**, 216*n59*
  moderates led by, 85, 86, 106
  rivalry with Agyrrhius, 105
Thrasyllus, general, 64, 65, 66, 122,
  162, 195*n69*. *See also* Arginusae,
  Victors of
Thucydides, son of Melesias, 61, 143,
  149, 150, 151, 169
Thucydides, historian, 11, 12, 139,
  178, 179, 182, 195*n69*
  on Alcibiades, 35
  Amphipolis, loss of, 117–20,
    128–32, 221*n52*, 222*n58*
  on Antiphon, 109–10, 208*n15*
  on Demosthenes (general), 100,
    216*n66*
  on Eucles, 221*nn44, 47*
  exiled, 10, 26, 27, **117–20**, 125,
    128–32, 194*n62*, 220*n44*, 222*n60*
  foresight lacking in Thrace, 162
  on Hyperbolus, 151
  influence of his ideas, 135, 167, 168
  Mytilenean debate, 7, 138 (*see also*
    Mytilene)
  on Nicias, 9, 220*n43*
  on Paches, 138–39, 140
  on Pericles, 31, 32, 33, 59, 125–26,
    129, 134, 175, 197*n13*
  on Phrynichus and Scironides,
    36–39, 129, 133–34, 135
  Potidaea, generals at, 34–35,
    126–27, 129, 134
  self-justification, 128–32, 225*n8*
  Sophocles, Pythadorus, and
    Eurymedon, 9, 116, 120, 124,
    127–28, 129, 134, 220*n39*
Thucydides, fourth-century Athe-
  nian, 154–55
Thyrea, 198*n26*
Timaeus, of Tauromenium, historian,
  117
Timagoras, envoy, 22, 23, 27, 53, 70,
  75, 165, 208*n67*
Timarchus, 22, 24, 49, 51, 210*n97*
Timocrates, 65
Timocreon, 147

Timomachus, general, 107, 172, 218*n24*
impeachment, 21, 27, 76, **111–12**, 165, 173, 194*n62*, 195*n69*, 209*n87*, 210*n97*
transport of Callistratus, 76, 111, 161, 165, 173
Timotheus, 9, 21, 113, 194*n62*, 195*n69*, 199*n44*
decree for, 155, 231*n71*
finances, 42, 200*nn52, 53*
fined, 28, 29
Iphicrates replaced by, 72, 208*n76*
Jason of Pharae and, 41, 43, 200*n54*
pro-Theban, 43, 93, 166, 201*n57*
replaced in Corcyrean command, 73
reputation for caution, 202*n78*
trial (373), 21, 23, 26, **40–45**, 71, 93, 166, 172, 173, 175, 199*n50*, 208*n76*
trial (ca. 355), 24, 25, 27, **45–49**, 77, 165, 166, 173, 176, 202*nn64, 73*
Zacynthian exiles returned by, 43, 44, 45, 166, 172, 176, 199*n50*
Tiribazus, satrap of Lydia, 90, 91, 93, 96, 100, 103
Tissaphernes, 36, 38, 39, 133
treason, 15, 17, 123, 195*n70*
alleged, 22, 40, 46, 55, 62, 63, 76, 77, 79, 80, 102, 104, 107, 108, 115, 134, 159, 176, 198*n27*
penalties for, 27
See also προδοσία
Treasurers of Athena (377/76), 26
trial *in absentia*, 27, 28, 75, 111, 120, 146, 159, 170
Triphylia, 70
tyranny, 5, 8, 80, 135

Vinogradoff, P., 7, 18

Wade-Gery, H. T., 57
Walcot, P., 181
Westlake, H. D., 129, 130, 137, 138, 163
Woodhead, A. G., 45
Wilamowitz-Möllendorff, U. von, 31, 57, 154

Xanthippus, 57, 79, 143, 145, 146, 147, 164
Xenophon, general, 26, 28, **34–36**, 62, 107, 126, 129, 134, 138, 161, 176, 194*n62*, 195*nn69, 73*. *See also* Potidaea, Athenian generals at
Xenophon, historian, 12, 24, 108, 112, 205*n25*, 224*n62*
Arginusae, Victors of, 65, 67, 68, 179, 206*n41*, 207*nn50–51*
on Aristarchus, 218*n17*
Callixeinus, starvation of, 68, 160, 170
Corinthian War, 87, 88, 214*n12*
events of 375–373, 199*n50*
on Pamphilus, 94
Thebes, liberation of (379/78), 81, 82
Theramenes, antipathy towards, 207*n50*
on Thrasybulus, 98, 100
Xenophon, Pseudo-, 7
Xerxes, 5

Zacynthus, 116, 127
exiles restored by Timotheus, 43, 44, 45, 166, 172, 176, 199*n50*
Zeus, 5
Herkeios, cult of, 14

INDEX
OF GREEK TERMS

ἀγὼν τιμητός, 16, 153, 230*n53*
ἄκριτος, 95, 195*n70*
ἀναγραφευς τῶν νόμων, 22
ἀπάτη, 79, 80
ἀποχειροτονεῖν, 224*n62*
ἀποχειροτονία, 6, **15**, 17, 19, 21,
 23–24, 26, 28, 31, 40, 56, 64, 97,
 113, 114, 120, 190*n5*, **191*n18***,
 220*n35*, 223*n62*, 224*n62*
ἀρετή, 110
ἀτιμία, 139. *See also* disfranchisement
ἄτιμος, 155
αὐτοκράτωρ, 89
ἀφιέναι, 218*n27*

βῆμα, 137
βουλευτής, 20, 85
βουλή, 14, 16, 17, 22, 23, 50, 65, 85,
 108, 142, 156, 157, 159, 170,
 190*n2*, 191*n11*, 211*n103*

γνώριμοι, 86, 213*n6*
γραφή, 19, 26
 ἀγραφίου, ἀδικίου, etc., 19
 ἀλογίου, 19, 26
 δωροδοκίας, 192*n28*
 νόμον μὴ ἐπιτήδειον θεῖναι,
 231*n81*

παρανόμων, 12, 142, **153–58**,
 160, 170, 173, 230*n52*, 231*n85*
 προδοσίας, 19, 192*n28*, 210*n94*

δεκασμός, 19
δῆμος, 33, 53, 83, 92, 110, 125, 132,
 135–40 *passim*, 142, 149, 151,
 160, 163, 167, 175–78 *passim*,
 198*n26*
δημοτικοί, 86
διαβολή, 36, 39, 133, 135
δικαστήριον, 22, 23, 137, 139,
 193*n50*. *See also* dicasteries
δίκη, 18
δοκιμασθῆναι, 190*n2*
δοκιμασία, 6, **14–15**, 19, 20–21, 26,
 160, 190*nn1–2*, 193*n33*
δραχμή, 28
δωροδοκία, 34, 55, 96, 116, 192*n28*
δώρων, 19

ἐγκτήματα, 156
εἰκοστή, 97
εἰσαγγελία, 6, 12, 13, **15–17**, 19, 20,
 21–24, 26, 40, 47, 56, 65, 73, 76,
 79, 111, 146, 157–60 *passim*, 170,
 173, 190*n9*, 191*nn11, 15, 18*,
 199*n50*, 202*n73*, 206*n41*, 209*n87*,
 210*nn94, 97*, 219*n33*, 232*n86*.
 See also eisangelia

εἰσαγγελτικὸς νόμος, 191n9
εἰς τὸ δέον, 60
εἰσφορά, 42, 94, 215n38
ἐκκλησία, 15, 16, 23, 24, 52, 65, 67,
    138, 142, 149, 160, 161, 177,
    211n103
    κυρία, 15, 16, 19, 60, 152
    See also Assembly, the Athenian;
    ekklesia
ἐκκλησιαστικός, 105
ἐπαιτιᾶσθαι, 34–35, 197n21
ἐπιεικεῖς, 86, 213n6
ἐπιστάτης, 19, 60, 194n66
ἐπιχειροτονία, 190n5
εὔθυναι, 6, 17–18, 19, 24–26, 45, 46,
    47, 49, 51, 56, 57, 60, 136, 137,
    139, 145, 167, 190n19,
    194nn61–62, 204n9, 227n20
εὔθυνοι, 18

θεσμοθέται, 15, 16, 17, 18, 21, 22, 27,
    28, 56, 108, 153
θεωρικά, 105, 156, 217n85

ἰδιώτης, 159
ἱεροσυλία, 60

καλοὶ κἀγαθοί, 149, 151
καταλύειν, 230n50
κλοπή, 19, 30, 31, 41, 65, 94, 96, 161,
    196n4, 215n34, 219n35. See also
    embezzlement
κρίνειν, 47

λαμβάνειν, 219n35
λογισταί, 18, 56, 192n20

μετακινεῖν, 203n1
μέταλλον, 19
μισθὸς ἐκκλησιαστικός, 105

νομοθέται, 156
νόμος, 22, 191n9, 231n81

ὀλίγοι, 149
ὅμιλος, 125
ὄστρακον, 142
ὀστρακοφορία. See ostrakophoria
οὐσία, 86, 213n6

παραπρεσβεία, 19, 52
πόλις, 148, 169, 180
πολιτεία, 203n1
πολλοί, 86
πορισταί, 22, 23, 26, 27
πράκτορες, 22, 23, 26, 27
πρέσβυς, 89
προβολή, 19, 68, 160, 170, 192n28
προβούλευμα, 16
προδοσία, 19, 34, 45, 55, 62, 69, 77,
    96, 117, 120, 161, 192n28,
    206n41, 210n94, 220n44. See also
    proditio; treason
πρόεδρος, 19
πωληταί, 22, 23, 26, 27

ῥήτωρ, 173

στάσις, 39, 68, 110
στρατηγία, 20, 25, 28, 30, 31, 32, 35,
    38, 56, 60, 65, 71, 97, 104, 105,
    111–14 passim, 122, 128, 129,
    131, 136, 138, 139, 169, 172, 173,
    174, 177, 178, 195n73, 205n30,
    208n65, 209n82
στρατηγός, ix, 6, 8, 12, 14, 20, 21,
    24–30 passim, 36, 42, 55, 56, 59,
    69, 70, 74, 75, 77, 78, 81, 82, 93,
    104–8 passim, 111, 118, 122, 124,
    125, 128, 132, 136–40 passim,
    154, 159, 161, 162, 165, 168,
    171–77 passim, 180, 192n30,
    202n64, 204n9, 209nn82, 87,
    216nn50, 59, 220n35, 221n47,
    200n50, 233n12. See also strategi
στρατιωτικά, 156
συνήγοροι, 18, 56, 108

ταμίας, 23, 210n97

ὑπογραμματεύς, 21, 22, 27, 28
ὑπωμοσία, 153

φεύγειν, 221n44

χαρίεντες, 86, 213n6
χορηγός, 147
χρήματα, 19

DESIGNED BY IRVING PERKINS ASSOCIATES
COMPOSED BY THE NORTH CENTRAL PUBLISHING CO.
ST. PAUL, MINNESOTA
MANUFACTURED BY CUSHING-MALLOY, INC.
ANN ARBOR, MICHIGAN
TEXT IS SET IN TIMES ROMAN, DISPLAY LINES IN
TIMES ROMAN AND TORINO ROMAN

Library of Congress Cataloging in Publication Data
Roberts, Jennifer Tolbert, 1947–
Accountability in Athenian government.
(Wisconsin studies in classics)
Bibliography: pp. 235–251.
Includes index.
1. Strategi, Greek—Legal status, laws, etc.
2. Impeachments (Greek law) I. Title.
II. Series. Law   342.38′506   81-69827
ISBN 0-299-08680-1   343.85026